Answers *to the* Health Questions People Ask *in* Libraries

A Medical Library Association Guide

Laura Townsend Kane

Rozalynd P. McConnaughy

Steven Patrick Wilson

with

David L. Townsend, MD, Medical Consultant

D1402315

Neal-Schuman Publishers, Inc.

New York   London

Published by Neal-Schuman Publishers, Inc.
100 William St., Suite 2004
New York, NY 10038

Printed and bound in the United States of America.

The paper used in this publication meets the minimum requirements of American National Standard for Information Sciences-Permanence of Paper for Printed Library Materials, ANSI Z39.48-1992.

Library of Congress Cataloging-in-Publication Data

Kane, Laura Townsend.
    Answers to the health questions people ask in libraries : a Medical Library Association guide / Laura Townsend Kane, Rozalynd P. McConnaughy, Steven Patrick Wilson ; with David L. Townsend.
        p. cm. — (Medical Library Association guides)
    Includes bibliographical references and index.
    ISBN 978-1-55570-642-5 (alk. paper)
    1. Medicine, Popular. 2. Medical libraries—Reference services. I. McConnaughy, Rozalynd P., 1976- II. Wilson, Steven Patrick 1973- III. Townsend, David L., MD IV. Title.

RC81.K2538 2008
610—dc22

                                                      2008037477

Table of Contents

List of Tables

Foreword

Dear Health Care Consumer:

As a physician, a large part of my practice consists of educating people and their families regarding various topics in medicine, including medical conditions, available treatments, and prevention of illness. These days, individuals are strongly encouraged to play an active role in their own health care in both educating themselves and participating with health care providers to make informed decisions regarding their care. I believe that this philosophy is extremely important. In my experience, patients who have the best understanding of their situation are typically the ones who fare the best—physically, emotionally, and psychologically.

The largest problem that health care consumers face is finding reliable sources of information. Consumers are bombarded with information, whether it be from the Internet, television advertisements, personal testimony, or a variety of other areas. Some of these sources can provide valuable information—however, many provide information that is misleading, inaccurate, or even dangerous. Therefore, it is important not only that a health care consumer be educated but also that the individual be *correctly* educated.

The goal of *Answers to the Health Questions People Ask in Libraries* is to provide an authoritative resource that answers some of the most common questions individuals have regarding health care. Not only will this resource provide direct answers to these questions, but it will also point readers to other reliable sources of information that will take a lot of the "guesswork" out of their research. While nothing can replace a good relationship with one's health care provider, having a convenient and comprehensive source of information, such as this book, will likely prove indispensable to the concerned or curious health care consumer.

We sincerely hope that you find this resource useful, informative, and interesting.

With warm regards,

David Townsend, MD
Internal Medicine
Wake Forest University Baptist Medical Center
Winston-Salem, North Carolina

Preface

*A**nswers to the Health Questions People Ask in Libraries* provides authoritative answers to the health questions most frequently asked in libraries, ranging from "How do I find a LASIK surgeon?" to "Does the flu vaccine cause the flu?" The quality of the information librarians provide people directly impacts their lives.

As librarians we typically direct people to credible sources of information in which answers can be found. But it is also our experience that there are frequently asked questions that could be answered in a "one-stop shop" book, saving time while putting reliable information into the hands of the people on both ends of the question–answer exchange. To ensure that all the answers are accurate, the authors have collaborated with a physician, Dr. David L. Townsend, a graduate of the Medical College of Georgia who is an internal medicine physician at Wake Forest University Baptist Medical Center in Winston-Salem, North Carolina. Dr. Townsend jumped at the chance to help with this project, explaining that there is a great need for a resource written for the general public that offers accurate information about health conditions. "People visit their doctors armed with all sorts of inaccurate health information they have gathered from the Web. We need more reliable health resources to help educate people about health concerns," he said.

With the team in place, and with the Medical Library Association's endorsement, the authors created a survey to collect information about common health questions asked in libraries. The survey was loaded onto a Web page, and a link to the online survey was sent to hundreds of libraries across the country using library-related electronic discussion lists (listservs). More than 270 librarians responded to the survey, many of them saying, "Please share the results!" The librarians who responded worked in public libraries, academic libraries, school libraries, hospital libraries, and special libraries. Nearly all 50 states in the United States were represented. We gathered and analyzed the survey data and include in this book the questions that came up most often.

Answers to the Health Questions People Ask in Libraries is intended for the general public and can be made available in doctor's offices, libraries, hospitals, and health clinics—in fact, anywhere health care consumers often visit. It is written in a simple and casual manner. The entries are easy to read, and important points are highlighted in text boxes that jump out from the page. URLs are included to point readers to important Web sites. The health concerns covered include cancer, AIDs, and diabetes; family health, from childhood to adulthood; nutrition and fitness; drug information; and alternative and complementary medicine.

Chapter 1, "Major Health Concerns," covers heart health, cancer, diabetes, and HIV/AIDs. The emphasis of this chapter is on prevention and early detection. Routine tests and screenings are described in detail.

Chapter 2, "Family Health," contains information that is important to family members of all ages. The questions and answers are divided into six categories: women's health and pregnancy, children's health, men's health, senior health, general family health, and vaccinations.

Chapter 3, "Nutrition and Fitness," provides questions and answers that fall into three categories: nutrition and exercise, vitamins and supplements, and alcohol and stimulants.

Chapter 4, "Complementary and Alternative Medicine," answers many common questions about medical products and practices that are not part of standard medical care. Topics fall within the following categories: healing systems (e.g., Ayurveda, naturopathy, and homeopathy); mind–body connections (e.g., yoga and meditation); herbal medicine (e.g., echinacea and gingko); manipulation and touch (e.g., chiropractic and massage therapy); and energy therapies (e.g., Reiki and acupuncture). The purpose of this chapter is to give readers factual information about these sometimes controversial topics.

Chapter 5, "Drug Information," discusses both prescription and over-the-counter medicines. Stressed throughout this chapter is the importance of learning as much as possible about a medicine before taking it.

Chapter 6 is called "Odds and Ends" because it provides information about unusual and misunderstood medical conditions. It also contains information about how technology (e.g., microwaves and cell phones) might affect a person's health.

Two additional features that will be helpful to readers are a "Glossary of Experts" and an annotated "Resources: Where to Go When You Want to Know about Health Care," both of which are located at the back of the book. The "Glossary of Experts" provides definitions of the various types of health care providers mentioned in the book. It also provides Web addresses for online directories to help readers locate doctors or other health care providers in their areas. The print and online resources will be helpful to those seeking additional health information.

The authors are confident that this book, which combines the authority of a physician with the clear, casual writing style that the layperson can easily understand, will help health care consumers learn more about health in general as well as about specific medical conditions. Of course, nothing can take the place of a visit to a doctor. But, as a supplement to regular visits to your health care provider, we hope this book proves valuable.

Acknowledgments

The authors are thankful for the support they have received from their families, friends, and co-workers throughout the duration of this project. As any author knows, writing is a lonely undertaking without encouragement and assistance from loved ones and co-workers.

Laura would like to thank her husband, Patrick, for always being there as a sounding board. She also thanks her parents, Millie and Dwight, for talking freely about their health care needs and questions. Finally, she would like to express her gratitude for having such great co-workers like Roz and Steve, and for having her "baby brother" involved in this book project. What a team!

Roz is grateful for the stick-to-it-iveness and linguistic skills of her co-authors. She would also like to thank her husband, Jeff, and her parents, Jack and Camille, for their encouragement and health information inquiries. She would also like to recognize her cat, Cosmo, for never giving her toxoplasmosis.

Steve would like to acknowledge his wife, Sarah, for anchoring him in life. He would like to thank his parents, Glenn and Carol Wilson, for bringing him to life. And he would like to re-echo Laura's sentiment above—he, too, feels lucky to work with such great people, even Laura Kane's "baby brother."

David would first like to thank God for His grace and sovereignty. He is also eternally grateful to his wife, Leah, for her tireless love, support, and patience—being the wife of a doctor is no easy task. He would furthermore like to thank his children, Ellison and Ethan, for being constant sources of joy, pride, and cuteness, and for being continual reminders of God's grace. Lastly, David would like to thank all of the mentors and friends he has made in the course of his career.

1

Major Health Concerns

Many of the health questions asked in libraries fall within four subject categories: heart health, cancer, diabetes, and HIV/AIDS (human immunodeficiency virus/acquired immunodeficiency syndrome). These four broad areas are considered major health concerns for all populations throughout the world. It is natural for people to want to explore these health concerns to gather enough ammunition to fight against them. Libraries have become the "go-to" place for this kind of exploration.

Our focus in this chapter is on prevention and early detection. The most effective way to fight health problems is to prevent them from happening in the first place. The second most effective way to fight health problems is to catch them early. This sounds simple, but many people are not aware that there are countless tests and screenings that can prevent a health problem or stop it in its tracks before it can get worse. Your doctor may recommend a certain test, yet you wonder if it's really necessary. You feel great. Why go through a stressful or potentially painful test? Because, simply put, it may save your life.

Before undergoing any screening test, you should try to find out as much about the test as you can. Ask your health care provider the following questions:

- Which tests do you recommend for me? Why?
- What are the different types of tests?
- How much do the tests cost? Will my health insurance plan pay for them?
- Are the tests painful?
- How soon will I learn the test results?

☞ For a more thorough list of questions, see "Questions to Ask if Your Doctor Recommends Tests" at www.stronghealth.com/questions/Tests.html.

HEART HEALTH

What is high blood pressure?

High blood pressure is also called *hypertension*. It damages your blood vessels. High blood pressure is a chronic illness that increases your chances of having a heart attack, heart failure, stroke, and kidney disease. Hypertension is often called a "silent killer" because it usually has no symptoms, so it is important to have your blood pressure checked regularly.

You should have your blood pressure checked at least every two years. It is a quick and easy procedure. An inflatable arm cuff and a pressure-measuring gauge are used to measure blood pressure. Your blood pressure reading will have two numbers: the systolic pressure (when your heart beats) over the diastolic pressure (when your heart relaxes). Your blood pressure is measured in millimeters of mercury (mm Hg.) An example of a blood pressure reading is 118 over 78 (or 118/78).

Following are some tips for getting accurate blood pressure measurements:

- Avoid coffee, alcohol, and cigarettes for at least a half hour before the reading.
- Wear short sleeves.
- Go to the bathroom before the reading.
- Before the reading, sit for a few minutes with your feet flat on the floor and your back supported.
- Get two readings with a few minutes between the readings, and then average the results.

The following are the National Heart, Lung, and Blood Institute's blood pressure categories:

- Normal = less than 120/80 mm Hg
- Prehypertension = 120/80 to 139/89 mm Hg
- Stage 1 high blood pressure = 140/90 to 159/99 mm Hg
- Stage 2 high blood pressure = over 160/100 mm Hg

One high reading does not mean you have high blood pressure. Your health care provider will take several blood pressure measurements on different days before diagnosing you with hypertension. You may be asked to check your blood pressure at home. Blood pressure measurements at home are usually lower and more accurate than readings in the office.

Monitoring your blood pressure at home can:

- help track your treatment by recording vital information between doctor visits;
- encourage better control by allowing you to gain a stronger sense of responsibility for your own health; and
- cut your health care costs by cutting down on the number of visits you need to make to your doctor or clinic.

There are different kinds of blood pressure monitors available. All monitors have the same basic parts: an inflatable cuff or strap, a gauge for readouts, and sometimes a stethoscope. They can be manual or digital. Each type has pros and cons. Talk over the choices with your health care provider. Also, keep in mind that certain health conditions prevent home monitors from working properly. Check with your doctor before purchasing one. Don't rely on the free blood pressure machines found in pharmacies, malls, and grocery stores. They aren't accurate, and many are not checked routinely.

African Americans, individuals with diabetes, people over 55, individuals with a family history of high blood pressure, and people who are overweight are more likely to have high blood pressure.

The following lifestyle changes can help prevent high blood pressure:

- Maintain a healthy weight.
- Eat a healthy diet low in fat, including fruits, vegetables, and low-fat dairy products.
- Reduce the amount of salt and sodium in your diet.
- Exercise for at least 30 minutes a day.
- Stop smoking.
- Follow instructions for taking medications.

- Drink little or no alcohol.
- Limit caffeine intake.
- Reduce the amount of stress in your life.
- Try relaxation techniques.

(See Chapter 3 for more information about healthy lifestyles.)

References

"Blood Pressure." *MD Consult Patient Education Handout.* USC School of Medicine Library, Columbia, SC. Accessed December 7, 2007. Keyword: blood pressure.

"High Blood Pressure." U.S. Food and Drug Administration Office of Women's Health. Accessed November 17, 2007. www.fda.gov/womens/getthefacts/hbp.html.

"High Blood Pressure: Getting the Most Out of Home Monitoring." Mayo Clinic. Accessed December 6, 2007. www.mayoclinic.com/print/high-blood-pressure/HI00016/METHOD=print.

"High Blood Pressure (Hypertension)." Mayo Clinic. Accessed December 1, 2007. www.mayoclinic.com/print/high-blood-pressure/DS00100/DSECTION=all&METHOD=print.

Verberk, W., A. Kroon, and P. DeLeeuw. "Home Blood Pressure Measurement: A Systematic Review." *Journal of the American College of Cardiology* 46, no. 5 (2005): 743–751.

"Your Guide to Lowering High Blood Pressure." National Heart, Blood, and Lung Institute. Accessed December 20, 2007. www.nhlbi.nih.gov/hbp/index.html.

How often should I have my cholesterol levels checked?

Knowing your cholesterol levels can help you and your health care provider evaluate your risk for developing heart disease, as well as your risk for having a heart attack or a stroke. A cholesterol test, also called a *lipid profile* or *lipoprotein profile*, measures the total cholesterol, HDL (high-density lipoprotein, the "good" cholesterol), LDL (low-density lipoprotein, the "bad" cholesterol), and triglycerides in your blood.

Before this blood test, you will need to fast for 9 to 12 hours. You can drink water before the test, but avoid other beverages and food. A blood sample is typically drawn from a vein in your arm, and your levels will be reported in milligrams per deciliter of blood (see Table 1-1). If you are 20 years old or older, you should have your cholesterol levels

Table 1-1. Understanding your test results

High-density lipoprotein (HDL) cholesterol	
Less than 40*	Poor
40 and above	Desirable
60 and above	Lowers your risk of heart disease
Low-density lipoprotein (LDL) cholesterol	
Less than 100	Optimal
100 to 129	Near optimal
130 to 159	Borderline high
160 to 189	High
190 and above	Very high
Triglycerides	
Less than 150	Desirable
150 to 199	Borderline high
200 and above	High
Total cholesterol	
Less than 200	Desirable
200 to 239	Borderline high
240 and above	High
*All levels are reported as milligrams per deciliter (mg/dL) of blood.	

checked at least once every five years. You should be healthy when you get tested. Wait at least six weeks after any illness, after stress from a surgery or an accident, or after having a baby to be tested.

Most doctors focus on your LDL total, not your total cholesterol. Not everyone's "goal LDL" will be the same. A person's goal LDL is determined by other medical conditions and cardiac risk factors that he or she may have. Your doctor will take all of these factors into consideration when determining what your ideal LDL should be.

If you are 20 years old or older, you should have your cholesterol levels checked at least once every five years or more often as directed by your doctor.

If you have high cholesterol, your health care provider will recommend lifestyle changes to help reduce your levels. One high reading does not necessarily mean you have high cholesterol, because cholesterol levels can vary over time. After another high reading from a cholesterol test, your doctor may prescribe cholesterol-lowering medications.

The following factors can cause high cholesterol levels:

- Heredity
- High-fat, high-cholesterol diet
- Being overweight
- Lack of exercise
- Smoking
- Hypothyroidism
- Some medicines, such as anabolic steroids, beta-blockers, epinephrine, birth control pills, and vitamin D

Try to consume less than 300 mg of cholesterol a day. The average man eats 337 mg of cholesterol a day, while the average woman consumes 217 mg.

Here are some lifestyle changes that can help you reduce your cholesterol levels:

- Maintain a healthy weight.
- Eat foods that are low in saturated fat, trans fat, and cholesterol.
- Exercise for at least 30 minutes a day.
- Stop smoking.

(See Chapter 3 for more information about healthy lifestyles.)

References

"Cholesterol." American Association for Clinical Chemistry. Accessed December 1, 2007. www.labtestsonline.org/understanding/analytes/cholesterol/multiprint.html.

"Cholesterol." American Heart Association. Accessed December 18, 2007. www.americanheart.org/presenter.jhtml;jsessionid=KKFQXHIJZST3QCQ FCXPSDSQ?identifier=4488.

"Cholesterol Test: Sorting Out the Lipids." Mayo Clinic. Accessed November 7, 2007. www.mayoclinic.com/health/cholesterol-test/CL00033.

"High Blood Cholesterol: What You Need to Know." National Heart, Lung, and Blood Institute. Accessed December 13, 2007. www.nhlbi.nih.gov/health/public/heart/chol/wyntk.htm.

"Total Cholesterol Test." *MD Consult Patient Education Handout.* USC School of Medicine Library, Columbia, SC. Accessed December 7, 2007. Keyword: cholesterol.

What is coronary heart disease, and can it be prevented?

Coronary heart disease (CHD) is sometimes called *coronary artery disease.* **It is the leading cause of death in the United States for both men and women.** A coronary artery is a blood vessel that carries blood to your heart muscle. With CHD, a fatty substance called *plaque* builds up and blocks the flow of blood and oxygen through these arteries. When this happens, your heart muscle doesn't get the blood and oxygen it needs to work properly. CHD can lead to serious health problems, including angina (pain or pressure in the chest) and heart attack.

Both men and women can get CHD, but it is not usually seen in men younger than 40 or in women of reproductive age. There are many different factors that affect the risk of CHD. Some can't be changed, like family history or advanced age. Other factors *can* be changed or controlled, like smoking, exercise, body weight, cholesterol, and blood sugar. There are many lifestyle factors and medications that can help reduce your risk of CHD and heart attack.

Ten ways to lower your risk of CHD

1. **Control your blood pressure.** High blood pressure (hypertension) increases your risk of CHD.
2. **Get tested for diabetes.** If you have diabetes, keep it under control. Because of risk factors such as high blood pressure, high cholesterol, obesity, and lack of exercise, people with diabetes are two to four times more likely to develop heart disease.

3. **Don't smoke.** Smoking raises your blood pressure. If you smoke, ask your doctor to help you make a plan to quit. After two or three years of not smoking, your risk of CHD will be as low as that of a person who never smoked.

4. **Reduce blood cholesterol and eat a healthy diet.** Eat foods that are low in cholesterol and saturated fats. "Bad" cholesterol (LDL) can build up on the inside of your arteries, causing them to narrow from plaque. Your body turns saturated fats into cholesterol. Fat lodged in your arteries is a disaster waiting to happen. It could trigger a heart attack or stroke. If diet and exercise don't get the numbers down, then medication may be needed.

5. **Exercise.** Regular exercise can make your heart stronger and reduce your risk of heart disease. Exercise can also help lower your blood pressure. Talk to your doctor about the right kind of exercise for you. Try to exercise almost daily for at least 30 minutes.

6. **Maintain a healthy weight.** Obesity places you at risk for high cholesterol, high blood pressure, and insulin resistance (a precursor of type 2 diabetes), the very factors that raise your risk of CHD. Your body mass index (BMI) will tell you if your weight is healthy *(see Chapter 3 for more information on BMI).*

7. **Reduce stress.** Studies have shown that there is a relationship between stress and CHD.

8. **Limit alcohol.** Drinking too much alcohol can raise blood pressure, cause heart failure, and lead to stroke. It can also contribute to other diseases.

9. **Ask your doctor about taking a low dose of aspirin each day.** Aspirin helps prevent CHD, but it also has some risks.

10. **Ask your doctor about taking vitamin supplements.** Studies show that some vitamins may lower a person's risk of CHD.

☞ Take the "Heart Disease Questionnaire" at www.yourdiseaserisk.harvard.edu to assess your risk of coronary heart disease and to get tips for prevention.

(See Chapter 3 for more information about healthy lifestyles.)

References

"ABCs of Preventing Heart Disease, Stroke and Heart Attack." American Heart Association. Accessed December 15, 2007. www.americanheart.org/presenter.jhtml?identifier=3035374.

"Coronary Artery Disease." U.S. National Library of Medicine. Accessed December 16, 2007. www.nlm.nih.gov/medlineplus/coronaryarterydisease.html.

"Coronary Heart Disease: Reducing Your Risk." American Academy of Family Physicians. Accessed December 19, 2007. http://familydoctor.org/online/famdocen/home/common/heartdisease/risk/239.html.

"Heart Disease Fact Sheet." Harvard Center for Cancer Prevention. Harvard School of Public Health. Accessed November 2, 2007. www.yourdisease risk.harvard.edu/hccpquiz.pl?lang=english&func=show&quiz=heart&page =fact_sheet.

Can heart disease be inherited?

Yes. Many studies have shown that people with family histories of heart disease are at a higher risk for developing coronary heart disease (CHD). This means that children of parents with heart and blood vessel diseases *may* be more likely to develop them. A family history of diabetes, gout, high blood pressure, or high blood cholesterol also increases the risk of heart disease.

You may have a "high risk" for heart disease if:

1. you have many relatives with heart disease OR
2. you have family members who had heart disease at a young age (before age 55 for a male or before age 65 for a female).

The risk increases the more closely related you are to the person or people in your family affected by the disease.

☞ Family history is an important tool to assess a person's risk for heart disease. Take a look at "Family Health History FAQs" at www.hhs.gov/faq/diseases/familyhealthhistory/index.html.

It is important to learn more about your family history. Ask questions, talk to relatives at family gatherings, and look at family medical records. Try to learn about the medical histories of your parents, grandparents, aunts and uncles, nieces and nephews, and siblings. Try to find out the following:

- Major medical conditions and causes of death
- Age of disease onset and age at death
- Ethnic background

Share your family medical history with your doctor. He or she will determine your risk for heart disease, make recommendations, and possibly order tests to detect disease early.

Even though you cannot change your genetic makeup, you can reduce your risk of heart disease by adopting a healthy lifestyle. This includes a healthy diet, exercise, and avoiding tobacco.

(For more information, see the previous section "What is coronary heart disease, and how can it be prevented?" Also, see Chapter 3 for more information about healthy lifestyles.)

References

"Am I At Risk?" Ferre Institute Cardiovascular Program. Accessed November 18, 2007. www.heartgenes.org/heartdiseaserisk.html.

"Heredity as a Risk Factor." American Heart Association. Accessed November 5, 2007. www.americanheart.org/presenter.jhtml?identifier=4610.

Can stroke be prevented?

A stroke is a medical emergency. Also called a *brain attack*, a stroke happens when blood flow to a certain portion of the brain stops. Within minutes, brain cells begin to die. Stroke affects millions of American men and women and can lead to disability or death. It is the third leading cause of death in the United States.

Nearly three-fourths of all strokes occur in people over the age of 65. The risk of stroke more than doubles each decade after the age of 55. Stroke is more common and more deadly for African Americans than for any other ethnic group in the United States.

Stroke is more common and more deadly for African Americans than for any other ethnic group in the United States.

There are two kinds of stroke:

1. **Ischemic stroke:** the most common kind; caused by a blood clot that blocks a blood vessel in the brain
2. **Hemorrhagic stroke:** caused by a blood vessel that breaks and bleeds into the brain

Stroke damage in the brain can affect the entire body, resulting in mild to severe disabilities. These include paralysis, numbness or weakness in part of the body, vision loss, memory loss, thinking problems, speech problems, and emotional problems.

The best treatment for stroke is prevention. Here are some things you can do to reduce your risk of stroke:

- Control your high blood pressure. Work with your doctor to get high blood pressure under control. This is the most important thing you can do to avoid a stroke.
- Don't smoke. If you do, quit.
- Manage your diabetes.
- Exercise and maintain a healthy weight.
- Eat right.

Controlling high blood pressure is the most important thing you can do to avoid stroke.

Every second counts during a stroke emergency. The longer blood flow is cut off to the brain, the greater the damage. Ischemic stroke can be treated with a drug that dissolves the clots that are blocking blood flow. **A person needs to be in the hospital within 60 minutes of having a stroke to be evaluated and treated.**

(See the following section "What are the warning signs of a heart attack or a stroke?" to learn how to spot the warning signs of stroke. Also, see Chapter 3 for more information about healthy lifestyles.)

References

"Understanding Stroke." Cleveland Clinic. Accessed October 31, 2007. www.clevelandclinic.org/health/health-info/docs/0900/0992.asp?index=5601.

"What You Need to Know About Stroke." National Institute of Neurological Disorders and Stroke. Accessed October 29, 2007. www.ninds.nih.gov/disorders/stroke/stroke_needtoknow.htm.

What are the warning signs of a heart attack or a stroke?

Heart attack and stroke are life-and-death emergencies. Every second counts. Make sure that you and the people you care about know the signs of stroke or heart attack—and know how to act fast.

Heart attack and stroke victims may benefit from new medications and treatments. For example, clot-busting drugs can stop some heart attacks and strokes in progress. But these drugs must be given quickly after heart attack or stroke symptoms first appear. This is why you must not delay. Get help right away.

Call 9-1-1 immediately if you suspect someone is having a stroke or a heart attack! Don't delay--get help right away!

Heart attack warning signs

- Chest discomfort—most often discomfort in the center of the chest that lasts for more than a few minutes or comes and goes and that can feel like pressure, squeezing, fullness, or pain
- Discomfort in other areas of the body—may include pain or discomfort in one or both arms, the back, the neck, jaw, or stomach
- Shortness of breath—may occur before chest discomfort
- Other symptoms, such as breaking out in a cold sweat, nausea, or lightheadedness

Sometimes people don't show all of these warning signs. This is especially true for women and diabetics, who may show *none* of the classic signs of heart attack. Many heart attacks start slowly as a mild pain or discomfort. Even if you're not sure it's a heart attack, get help right away. Don't wait more than five minutes to call 9-1-1.

Stroke warning signs

- Sudden numbness or weakness of the face, arm, or leg, especially on one side of the body
- Sudden confusion, trouble speaking or understanding

- Sudden trouble seeing in one or both eyes
- Sudden trouble walking, dizziness, loss of balance or coordination
- Sudden, severe headache with no known cause

Call 9-1-1 immediately if someone shows any of the warning signs of stroke. Every second counts.

References

"Act in Time to Heart Attack Signs: Heart Attack Warning Signs." National Heart, Lung, and Blood Institute. Accessed December 10, 2007. www.nhlbi .nih.gov/actintime/haws/haws.htm.
"Heart Attack, Stroke and Cardiac Arrest Warning Signs." American Heart Association. Accessed November 22, 2007. www.americanheart.org/presenter .jhtml?identifier=3053.
"Learn to Recognize a Stroke." American Stroke Association. Accessed December 6, 2007. www.strokeassociation.org/presenter.jhtml?identifier=1020.

CANCER

What are the risk factors for lung cancer?

Many lifestyle choices affect your chances of developing lung cancer. **Smoking is the main risk factor for lung cancer.** Cigarette smoking, as well as cigar smoking, pipe smoking, and hookah smoking, can all lead to lung cancer. Tobacco smoking causes 80 to 90 percent of all lung cancers. The more packs you smoke per day and the longer you have smoked, the greater your chances of developing lung cancer. Heavy alcohol drinking and smoking marijuana are other risk factors for lung cancer.

Secondhand tobacco smoke is also a risk factor. Inhaling second-hand smoke exposes you to the same cancer-causing agents that smokers inhale, but in smaller amounts. According to the American Cancer Society, a nonsmoker who is married to a smoker has a 30 percent greater risk of developing lung cancer than the spouse of a nonsmoker. In particular, **children should not be exposed to cigarette smoke.**

More people die from lung cancer than from any other kind of cancer.

Where you live and work can also play a role in your risk of lung cancer. If you live in areas with high levels of air pollution, such as cities or industrial areas, you are more likely to develop lung cancer. Arsenic in drinking water is another environmental factor that can cause lung cancer. Radon is estimated to cause 10 to 14 percent of all lung cancers. Radon is a gas that is created when uranium breaks down. It has no smell or taste. Individuals living in homes built over soil that contains natural uranium deposits may be exposed to high indoor levels of radon. If you are worried about radon in your home, you can purchase a test approved by the Environmental Protection Agency.

Cancer-causing agents (carcinogens) that can increase your lung cancer risk and may be found in the workplace include these:

- Asbestos
- Chromium
- Nickel
- Tar
- Soot
- Radioactive ores (uranium)
- Gasoline fuel
- Diesel exhaust
- Inhaled chemicals or minerals (beryllium, coal products, vinyl chloride, nickel chromates, mustard gas, and chloromethyl ethers)

Baby, body, and facial talcum powders do not cause lung cancer. Since 1973, all cosmetic talcum powders have been asbestos-free.

Your personal and family health histories influence your chance of developing lung cancer. If your parents or siblings have lung cancer, you are at an increased risk. You are also at an increased risk if:

- you have chronic obstructive pulmonary disease (COPD);
- your lungs are scarred from recurrent lung diseases, such as pneumonia or tuberculosis;
- you have had radiation therapy to the chest for cancer; and/or
- you are a smoker with asthma or emphysema.

Lifestyle changes can minimize your risk of lung cancer. These include eating a diet rich in fruits and vegetables and getting plenty of exercise. Smokers should avoid taking beta-carotene supplements, because they can further increase the risk of lung cancer. Some studies show an association between people who regularly use aspirin, ibuprofen (Advil), or naproxen (Aleve) and a reduced lung cancer risk. Smoking is by far the biggest risk factor. If you smoke, quit. Avoid secondhand smoke as much as possible.

If you are a smoker, the sooner you quit, the more you reduce your risk.

(See Chapter 3 for more information about healthy lifestyles.)

References

"Detailed Guide: Lung Cancer-Non-Small Cell: What Are the Risk Factors for Non-Small Lung Cancer?" American Cancer Society. Accessed December 5, 2007. www.cancer.org/docroot/CRI/content/CRI_2_4_2x_What_Are_the_Risk_Factors_for_Non-Small_Cell_Lung_Cancer.asp?rnav=cri.

"Lung Cancer (PDQ): Prevention." National Cancer Institute. Accessed December 17, 2007. www.cancer.gov/cancertopics/pdq/prevention/lung/patient.

"Non-Small Cell Lung Cancer." MD Consult Patient Education Handout. USC School of Medicine Library, Columbia, SC. Accessed December 17, 2007. Keyword: lung cancer.

Is there a screening test for lung cancer?

Many people die from lung cancer because it is usually found too late. While there are screening methods to detect breast, cervical, and colon cancers that help save lives, there is no widely accepted screening method for lung cancer. Researchers are trying to devise a cost-effective screening method for lung cancer.

A CT scan is a special kind of X-ray. CT stands for *computerized tomography*. These scans may also be referred to as CAT (*computed axial tomography*) scans. A spiral CT scan is one of the tests used to detect lung cancer. A sputum test (testing the bacteria in your spit) and a chest X-ray are two other tests frequently used to find lung cancer. A spiral (or helical) CT scan is more effective than X-rays and sputum tests for detecting lung cancer when it is suspected. The spiral CT scan can find smaller nodules that may be cancerous compared to the size of nodules identified with chest X-rays. More invasive tests are needed to collect samples of the questionable cells and tissues to determine whether they are cancerous. A CT scan can also be used to guide a needle to collect a biopsy sample.

During a spiral CT scan, you lie on a table and pass through an X-ray machine. The machine is shaped like a doughnut with a large hole. The machine will rotate around you and feed information to a computer, which will create images from the data. These images are three-dimensional models of the lungs. The spiral CT scan is a quick procedure; it scans the entire chest in 12 to 20 seconds while you hold your breath.

In the 1970s, CT scans of the lung took about an hour. Now, a CT scan takes 12 to 20 seconds.

While lung CT scans can detect cancer at early stages, the use of CT scans as a screening method remains controversial until further research is done. Right now there is not enough evidence to show that the benefits outweigh the risks. During a CT scan, you are exposed to radiation. (However, individuals are exposed to lower doses of radiation during a screening CT scan than a diagnostic CT scan.) Too much exposure to radiation can cause cancer. In addition to the radiation exposure, the scan may identify harmless growths that look like cancer. According to the National Cancer Institute, about 25 to 60 percent of CT scans of smokers and former smokers will show abnormalities that are not cancer. These "false positive" results can cause emotional stress and sometimes lead to needless additional testing.

During a computerized tomography (CT) scan, you are exposed to seven to eight times the amount of radiation than during a chest X-ray.

Some of the symptoms of lung cancer follow:

- Uncomfortable shortness of breath
- Coughing that lasts over two weeks
- Coughs that produce bloody phlegm
- Hoarseness that lasts two weeks or more
- Weakness

- Weight loss
- Loss of appetite
- Repeated bouts of pneumonia
- Wheezing
- Noisy breathing
- Pain in the back, chest, shoulders, or arms

If you think you have lung cancer or if you are at a high risk for developing lung cancer, you may want to ask your health care provider about having a lung CT scan.

References

Denoon, D. "Lung Cancer CT Scans No Help? CT Scans for Smokers Up Risks, Don't Cut Lung Cancer Deaths, Study Shows." WebMD. Accessed December 30, 2007. www.webmd.com/lung-cancer/news/20070306/lung-cancer-ct-scans-no-help.

"Detailed Guide: Lung Cancer-Non-Small Cell: How is Non-Small Cell Lung Cancer Diagnosed?" American Cancer Society. Accessed January 3, 2008. www.cancer.org/docroot/CRI/content/CRI_2_4_3x_How_Is_Non-Small_Cell_Lung_Cancer_Diagnosed.asp?rnav=cri.

Henschke, C., and P. McCarthy. *Lung Cancer: Myths, Facts, Choices-and Hope.* New York: W.W. Norton, 2002.

"Spiral CT Scans for Lung Cancer Screening: Fact Sheet." National Cancer Institute. Accessed January 3, 2008. www.cancer.gov/cancertopics/factsheet/lung-spiral-CTscan.

What tests are used to screen for colorectal cancer?

Cancer of the colon or rectum is also called *colorectal cancer.* It is the second leading cause of cancer death in the United States. If you are 50 years old or older, you should be screened for colorectal cancer. If you are at a high risk for developing colorectal cancer, talk to your health care provider; he or she may recommend that you begin screening sooner and more frequently.

Colorectal cancer is very treatable if detected early. After the first abnormal cells start to grow, it typically takes 10 to 15 years for them to develop into colorectal cancer. In many cases, regular screening prevents colorectal cancer. In 2005, only 50 percent of adults aged 50 and over had a colorectal endoscopy (sigmoidoscopy or colonoscopy).

The following are risk factors for colorectal cancer:

- Age (the older you are, the higher the risk)
- Family history of colorectal cancer
- Personal history of colorectal cancer or precancerous polyps
- Smoking
- Heavy alcohol use
- High-fat diet
- Obesity
- Sedentary lifestyle (lack of exercise)
- Inflammatory bowel disease, such as ulcerative colitis (Crohn's disease)
- An ethnicity associated with Jews of Eastern European descent
- Familial adenomatous polyposis
- Hereditary nonpolyposis colorectal cancer (Lynch syndrome)

(See Chapter 3 for more information about healthy lifestyles.)

African Americans are more likely than any other racial group to develop colorectal cancer and should start screening at age 45. Because they have a tendency to develop cancer in the upper areas of the colon, colonoscopy is the recommended screening method.

There are four tests used to screen for colorectal cancer. Your doctor may suggest a combination of the following screening methods.

Colonoscopy

A tool called a *colonoscope* is used to view the rectum and the entire colon. One to three days before the test, you maintain a clear liquid diet, and you take laxatives and possibly an enema to help clear the colon. Most patients are sedated for the procedure and receive pain medication. Because of the sedative, you will need to have someone come to the appointment with you in order to drive you home afterward. This procedure is similar to a sigmoidoscopy, but in a colonoscopy the entire colon can be examined. You lie on your left side, and the colonoscope is inserted into your rectum. Polyps and tissue samples can be collected for testing during this procedure. The procedures last from 20 to 60 minutes. You will need to stay at the clinic or hospital for about an hour after the colonoscopy for the sedative to wear off. Most individuals do not remember the procedure. After the procedure, you may experience mild cramps and gas. Walking may help you feel better. There is a small risk of bleeding or tears in the lining of the colon during this test. **A colonoscopy is by far the best screening method for colorectal cancer.** However, it may still miss small polyps. It is recommended every 10 years starting at age 50 for individuals with an average risk of colorectal cancer.

Fecal occult blood test (FOBT)

The FOBT detects microscopic amounts of blood in stool using a special solution that is added to a stool sample. It is recommended annually for individuals aged 50 and over. The test is inexpensive, and stool samples can be collected at home and then mailed to a laboratory. The FOBT is generally used to screen for early stages of cancer, although other methods of screening, such as colonoscopy (see the previous paragraph), are more sensitive and more highly recommended.

Sigmoidoscopy

A sigmoidoscope is used to view your rectum and the lower areas of your colon. The procedure is recommended every five years for individuals with an average risk of colorectal cancer. Twelve to 24 hours before the test, you maintain a diet of clear liquids, and you take laxatives or an enema to help clear out the bowel. For the procedure, you lie on your left side, and the sigmoidoscope is inserted into your rectum. The test takes about 15 minutes, and only one third of the colon is viewed. A sedative is usually not given for this procedure. You may feel pressure in your lower abdomen and experience some cramping during the procedure. Polyps and tissue samples can be collected for testing during the procedure. Polyps are small grape-like growths in the lining of the colon. Most polyps are not cancerous, but they can develop into cancer. Removing polyps reduces your risk of developing colon cancer. After the test, you may feel bloated and have gas pains. Walking may help you feel better. A sigmoidoscopy is less expensive than a colonoscopy and requires less preparation. There is a small risk of bleeding or tears in the lining of the colon during this test. The biggest disadvantage to this test is that polyps in the upper part of the colon will not be detected.

Barium enema

The barium enema test, which is sometimes called a *lower GI*, uses X-rays to view the entire colon. There are two kinds of barium enemas: single column and air contrast (double contrast). The double-contrast barium enema, which uses air in addition to liquid containing barium to view the colon, is more accurate. Before the test, you maintain a clear liquid diet, and you take laxatives and possibly an enema to help clear the colon. The test lasts 10 to 30 minutes. Sedation is not used, and you may feel mildly uncomfortable and experience some minor cramps. A barium enema is less expensive than a colonoscopy, but it may not find small polyps. If polyps are detected, a colonoscopy will be needed to remove them. Barium enemas are not typically recommended anymore, because sigmoidoscopies and colonoscopies are more accurate.

Virtual colonoscopy and DNA stool test are two screening tests currently under study.

References

"Cancer Trends Progress Report: 2007 Update." National Cancer Institute. Accessed February 2008. http://progressreport.cancer.gov.

"Colon Cancer Guide." Mayo Clinic. Accessed January 2, 2008. www.mayoclinic.com/print/colon-cancer/CO99999/PAGE=all&METHOD=print.

"Colorectal Cancer: The Importance of Prevention and Early Detection." Centers for Disease Control and Prevention. U.S. Department of Health & Human Services. Accessed January 2, 2008. www.cdc.gov/cancer/colorectal/pdf/about2004.pdf.

"Colorectal Cancer Screening: Questions and Answers." National Cancer Institute. Accessed January 4, 2008. www.cancer.gov/cancertopics/factsheet/Detection/colorectal-screening.

"Detailed Guide: Colon and Rectum Cancer." American Cancer Society. Accessed January 8, 2008. www.cancer.org/docroot/CRI/CRI_2_3 .asp?rnav=cridg&dt=10.

"Screening." National Cancer Institute. Accessed December 13, 2007. www.cancer.gov/cancertopics/wyntk/colon-and-rectal/page5.

What foods will keep my colon healthy?

You have probably seen ads for colon-cleansing products on TV or the Internet. They are frequently promoted as a method for removing toxins, boosting your immune system, and preventing constipation. While your doctor may ask you to do a colon cleansing before a colon cancer screening procedure, colon cleansing products do not prevent colon cancer and should not be used to "keep your colon healthy." These products lack medical evidence to support the claims. Many doctors deem the products unnecessary and potentially harmful. Colon-cleansing products can disrupt your body's fluid and electrolyte balance, which can lead to dehydration. If these products are used over a long period of time, they can cause malnutrition and anemia.

> Your colon, a curved tube that makes up most of your large digestive system, is about five feet long. A high-fiber diet helps keep your colon healthy.

To keep your colon and digestive system healthy, eat a high-fiber diet. A high-fiber diet prevents constipation and lowers your risk of heart disease, diabetes, and some cancers. Remember to drink plenty of liquids when eating fiber. Otherwise, fiber may slow down your digestive process. There are two types of fiber: soluble and insoluble. Both kinds of fiber are good for you. The average person eats 10 to 15 grams of fiber per day. Try to eat 20 to 35 grams of fiber a day from a variety of foods (see Table 1-2).

There is some evidence in the medical literature that suggests calcium, vitamin D, magnesium, or a multivitamin containing folic acid or folate may reduce your risk of colon cancer. However, while fiber is good for you, it may or may not prevent colon cancer. Some studies suggest that fiber may help prevent colon cancer, while other studies have shown that eating more fiber did not reduce the risk of colon cancer. More research on diet and colon cancer is being done. Diet studies are difficult to do, because it is hard to control what people eat. Also, a variety of methods are used in diet studies, so it is hard to compare the results of many studies.

The American Cancer Society recommends limiting your intake of high-fat foods, particularly foods from animal sources. Try to choose

Table 1-2. Examples of foods with fiber

Leafy vegetables	Wheat bran
Broccoli	Bran muffins
Pumpkin	Whole grain bread
Winter squash	Whole grain pasta
Artichokes	Barley
Dried peas and chick peas	Brown rice
Pears	Oatmeal
Berries	Oat bran
Dates	Wild rice
Figs and prunes	Cereals (bran flakes, shredded wheat)
Strawberries	Crackers (rye, whole wheat)
Apples	Beans
Coconut	Lentils
Citrus fruits	Nuts (almonds, Brazil, peanuts, pecans, walnuts)
Skins of potatoes	Pumpkin and sunflower seeds

most of your foods from plant sources. In addition to fruits and vegetables, food from plant sources also includes breads, cereals, grain products, rice, pasta, and beans. Eat at least five servings of fruit and vegetables every day, because they contain substances that help hinder cancer formation.

References

Asano, T., R. McLeod, and T. Asano. "Dietary Fibre for the Prevention of Colorectal Adenomas and Carcinomas (Cochrane Review)." *The Cochrane Library*, Issue 1, 2007. Chichester: Wiley.

"Colon Cleansing: Is It Helpful or Harmful?" Mayo Clinic. Accessed December 15, 2007. www.mayoclinic.com/print/colon-cleansing/AN00065/METHOD =print.

"Colon and Rectal Cancers." *MD Consult Patient Education Handout.* USC School of Medicine Library, Columbia, SC. Accessed December 14, 2007. Keyword: colon cancer.

"Detailed Guide: Colon and Rectum Cancer. Can Colorectal Cancer Be Prevented?" American Cancer Society. Accessed December 1, 2007. www .cancer.org/docroot/CRI/content/CRI_2_4_2X_Can_colon_and_rectum_ cancer_be_prevented.asp.

"Digestive Help Tips." The American College of Gastroenterology. Accessed December 17, 2007. www.acg.gi.org/patients/healthtips.asp.

Goldmann, D., and D. Horowitz. *American College of Physicians Complete Home Medical Guide.* New York: DK, 2003.

Margen, S. *Wellness Foods A to Z: An Indispensable Guide for Health-Conscious Food Lovers.* New York: Rebus, 2002.

When should I get my first mammogram?

A mammogram, or X-ray of the breast, is the most effective way to detect breast cancer or other breast problems. Once you reach age 40, you should have a mammogram every one to two years. After age 50, yearly mammograms are recommended. If you have a family history of breast cancer, or you have had breast cancer or other breast problems in the past, you may need to start getting mammograms before age 40. Talk to your doctor about when to start and how often you should have a mammogram.

Once you reach age 40, you should have a mammogram every one to two years. Women with a family history of breast cancer might need to have mammograms before age 40. After age 50, you should have a mammogram yearly.

Mammograms are important because they can detect some types of cancer before you or your health care provider can feel a lump. Finding breast cancer early means that a woman has a better chance of surviving the disease, and there are more treatment options.

During a mammogram, you will be asked to take off your shirt, bra, and jewelry. It takes just a few minutes for the radiologic technologist to take X-rays of each breast. Your breasts will be placed, one at a time, between two plastic plates. The plates press your breast to make it flat. This may be uncomfortable for a few seconds, but it allows the X-ray to show more of the tissue deep within your breast. Two or three different views of each breast will be taken.

Keep in mind that the mammogram is not a perfect procedure. Here are some limitations:

- "False negative" results can happen (everything may look normal, but cancer is actually present).
- "False positive" results can happen (it looks as if cancer is present, even though it is not). Mammograms only indicate possible cancerous areas. Only a biopsy (removing cells for further testing) can tell for sure.
- Mammograms do not detect all breast cancers.
- Finding cancer in the breast does not always mean a woman's life will be saved (if the cancer is fast-growing it may have already spread to other parts of the body).

All women should do a breast self-exam during the same phase of their menstrual cycle every month. If you feel a lump in your breast, report it right away even if you have had a recent mammogram that did not find any cancer. You should also have your health care provider do a clinical breast exam once a year.

☞ For information on how to do a breast self-exam, visit www.breastcancer.org /dia_detec_exam_5step.html.

Be sure to get a mammogram from a facility certified by the U.S. Food and Drug Administration (FDA). The X-ray machines and staff at these places must meet high standards.

☞ For a list of Food and Drug Administration–certified mammography facilities, visit www.fda.gov/cdrh/mammography/certified.html.

References

"Mammogram." *MD Consult Patient Education Handout.* USC School of Medicine Library, Columbia, SC. Accessed December 8, 2007. Keyword: mammogram.

"Mammograms." U.S. Department of Health & Human Services. Accessed December 8, 2007. http://womenshealth.gov/faq/mammography.htm.

"Screening Mammograms." *Our Bodies, Ourselves: The Boston Women's Health Book Collective.* New York: Touchstone, 2005.

"Screening Mammograms: Questions and Answers." National Cancer Institute Fact Sheet. National Cancer Institute. Accessed December 23, 2007. www.cancer.gov/cancertopics/factsheet/Detection/screening-mammograms.

Do I need to get tested for the breast cancer genes?

According to the National Cancer Society, over 192,000 women are diagnosed with breast cancer each year. Most women do not inherit breast cancer. Only 5 to 20 percent of women have a hereditary (inherited) form of the disease. Women with an abnormal (mutated) BRCA1 or BRCA2 gene have an increased risk of developing breast or ovarian cancer. Men who are BRCA2 carriers have an increased risk of breast cancer.

BRCA1 stands for BReast CAncer gene 1 because it was the first breast cancer–related gene identified. It was identified in 1994. BRCA2 (BReast CAncer gene 2) was the second breast cancer gene discovered. Researchers have found other breast cancer genes, and they are currently looking for more. BRCA testing will only look for BRCA1 and BRCA2 mutations.

Individuals with altered BRCA1 and/or BRCA2 genes have a 30 to 85 percent lifetime risk of breast cancer.

BRCA testing is not recommended as a screening test for the general public. The three screening tests commonly used for breast cancer are a mammogram, a clinical breast exam, and a breast self-exam.

BRCA testing should be considered only if:

- you have close relatives (male or female) who have breast cancer;
- you have close female relatives who have been diagnosed with ovarian cancer;
- your close relatives with breast or ovarian cancer were diagnosed before age 50;

- a BRCA mutation has been found in another family member; and/or
- you have an Ashkenazi (Eastern European) Jewish background.

People who have the BRCA test should meet with a genetic counselor before and after the test. A genetic counselor is a trained professional who can help you weigh the issues related to having a genetic test, such as the privacy and confidentiality of your medical records. Genetic counselors can also help you understand the test results. Although there is little medical risk with taking the BRCA test, the results can affect you emotionally and financially. The test results can have implications for you, and they may also affect other family members.

Even if you do not have a BRCA mutation, you can still develop breast cancer. On the other hand, although you have a higher risk for breast cancer if you test positive for a BRCA mutation, you may still never develop breast cancer.

If you do test positive for a BRCA mutation, you can consider some of the options for preventing cancer. The drug tamoxifen can help reduce the risk of breast cancer by almost 50 percent. More research is currently being conducted to determine the effectiveness of breast cancer prevention options.

Anyone considering BRCA testing should be well informed about the risks and benefits of undergoing the test and knowing the results.

References

Adams, S. "Breast Cancer." *5 Minute Clinical Consult Overview.* InfoRetriever. USC School of Medicine Library, Columbia, SC. Accessed December 18, 2007. Keyword: breast cancer.

"BRCA-1 and BRCA-2."American Association for Clinical Chemistry. Accessed December 5, 2007. www.labtestsonline.org/understanding/analytes/brca/test.html.

"Genetic Testing for BRCA1 and BRCA2: It's Your Choice." National Cancer Institute. Accessed November 17, 2007. www.cancer.gov/cancertopics/factsheet/Risk/BRCA.

"Learning About Breast Cancer." National Human Genome Research Institute. Accessed December 5, 2007. www.genome.gov/page.cfm?pageID=10000507.

DIABETES

What does a diabetes screening involve, and who should be tested?

Diabetes is a major health problem. It is one of the leading causes of death and disability in the United States. It involves the body's inability to make enough insulin (or to use the insulin already present) in order to move glucose, a sugar broken down from foods, from our blood into our cells. The glucose then builds up in the blood and passes out of the body through urine. This is a loss of an important energy source for the body.

While there are three types of diabetes—type 1, type 2, and gestational—type 2 is by far the most common. As many as 95 percent of diabetic patients probably have type 2, which often runs in families and is associated with being overweight, physically inactive, or a member of certain ethnicities. **The symptoms of type 2 diabetes may include some or all of the following:**

- Increased thirst and hunger
- Increased urination
- Blurred vision
- Sudden weight loss
- Wounds that heal slowly
- Fatigue
- Pain and burning in the hands and feet

If you experience any of these symptoms, or if diabetes runs in your family, you should ask your doctor about having a **blood glucose test.** In a blood glucose test, which is usually performed in the morning after fasting for at least eight hours, blood is drawn and then analyzed to see how much glucose is present. Those who score high (above 125 milligrams per deciliter [mg/dL]) on more than one test may be diagnosed as diabetic. Those with slightly elevated blood glucose levels (between 100 and 125 mg/dL) may be diagnosed as pre-diabetic. Data gathered by the U.S. Department of Health & Human Services for 2002 estimates that at least 54 million U.S. adults have pre-diabetes. This often leads to full-blown diabetes within ten years and can greatly increase their chances of developing cardiovascular disease.

Older people, overweight people, and certain ethnicities, including African Americans, Pacific Islander Americans, Native Hawaiians, Hispanics, and some Asian Americans, are at increased risk of developing type 2 diabetes.

Diabetes causes long-term complications that affect almost every part of the body. Diabetes can lead to the following:

- Blindness
- Heart and blood vessel disease
- Stroke
- Kidney failure
- Amputations
- Nerve damage
- Pregnancy complications and possibly birth defects
- An increased risk for certain infections

(See Chapter 3 for more information about healthy lifestyles.)

Diabetes causes long-term complications that affect almost every part of the body.

There are treatment options for diabetes. Your health care provider will monitor you carefully and help you learn to manage your diabetes.

References

"Diabetes Overview." National Diabetes Information Clearinghouse. Accessed December 14, 2007. http://diabetes.niddk.nih.gov/dm/pubs/overview.

"Preventive Services: Diabetes Screening, Supplies, and Self-Management." U.S. Department of Health & Human Services. Medicare. Accessed December 13, 2007. www.medicare.gov/health/diabetes.asp.

"What Diabetes Is." National Diabetes Information Clearinghouse. Accessed December 12, 2007. http://diabetes.niddk.nih.gov/dm/pubs/type1and2/what.htm.

Is diabetes hereditary?

There does appear to be a hereditary component to diabetes. This is true of both type 1 and type 2 diabetes and may eventually prove true for gestational diabetes as well. Hereditary risk factors differ for each type of diabetes. However, because not all people with hereditary risk factors develop diabetes, studies conclude that environmental triggers also play a role. A combination of hereditary and environmental factors can contribute to the onset of diabetes.

In type 1 diabetes, for example, it seems that risk factors need to be inherited from both parents. Certain environmental triggers are also needed. Researchers aren't yet positive what these triggers are, but some possibilities include these:

- Cold weather: Type 1 diabetes is more common in colder climates and occurs more often during winter than summer.
- Diet: Early diet may play a role, because it appears that those who were breast-fed and who didn't start eating solid foods until later ages are less likely to develop type 1 diabetes.
- Viruses: Certain viruses may trigger the onset of type 1 diabetes in those already at risk for developing the condition.

A combination of hereditary and environmental factors can contribute to the onset of diabetes.

On average, a woman with type 1 diabetes who is under 25 years of age will have a child with a 1 in 25 chance of developing type 1 diabetes. If the type 1 diabetic woman is over age 25 when the child is born, the child's risk actually goes down to 1 in a 100.

Type 2 diabetes, in comparison, shows even higher genetic and environmental bases than type 1. A family history of type 2 diabetes places you at much greater risk of developing the condition, especially if you live in a Western country. Moreover, being obese places you at increased risk of developing type 2 diabetes. This is especially true for obese children and those adults who have been obese for a long time. The children of women with type 2 diabetes have between a 1 in 7 and a 1 in 13 risk of developing type 2 diabetes themselves. This risk level goes up to 1 in 2 if both parents have type 2 diabetes.

Currently much less is known about whether gestational diabetes can be inherited. However, many women who experience gestational diabetes go on to develop type 2 diabetes later in life. Because both conditions involve risk factors for obesity and insulin resistance, it is possible that gestational and type 2 diabetes share certain genes in common.

☞ For more information about the hereditary factors of diabetes, read the National Institutes of Health's free online book, *The Genetic Landscape of Diabetes*, at www.ncbi.nlm.nih.gov/books/bv.fcgi?rid=diabetes.

References

The Genetic Landscape of Diabetes. National Institutes of Health, Online Books. Accessed December 19, 2007. www.ncbi.nlm.nih.gov/books/bv.fcgi?rid= diabetes.

"Genetics of Diabetes." American Diabetes Association. Accessed December 4, 2007. www.diabetes.org/genetics.jsp.

Will gestational diabetes hurt my baby?

Gestational diabetes, also called *gestational diabetes mellitus* (GDM), occurs in pregnant women who never had diabetes before. As with other forms of diabetes, gestational diabetes happens when your body either doesn't make enough insulin or can't completely use the insulin that it does make. The result is a buildup of glucose in your blood. **Glucose**, which is a type of sugar derived from broken down foods containing carbohydrates, can affect the health of your baby in the following ways:

- Your baby's body may become larger than normal, called *macrosomia*. This condition may make natural birth dangerous, requiring cesarean surgery instead. Moreover, macrosomic babies are at higher risk for becoming obese and developing type 2 diabetes later in life.
- Your baby may develop a low blood sugar level shortly after birth, a condition called *hypoglycemia*.
- Your baby can develop jaundice, in which her skin turns yellow.
- The baby's breathing function may be impaired, requiring oxygen or other treatment.
- The baby may have low mineral levels, leading to muscle cramping.

About 4 to 5 percent of all pregnancies in the United States involve gestational diabetes.

It is extremely important to have gestational diabetes treated immediately. Working closely with your health care provider, you can develop a specific plan. This may include such strategies as the following:

- Testing your blood sugar levels several times a day, which may help you adjust your diet to maintain more normal levels of sugar in your blood
- Eating healthy foods that help to control your blood sugar levels, which may require limiting the carbohydrates that you eat during your pregnancy
- Exercising regularly, which can help to use up the extra glucose in your blood
- Keeping a journal of your blood sugar levels, diet, and exercise activities throughout the day, which also will help you learn what kinds of diet and exercise activities work best for your body in maintaining normal sugar levels in your blood
- Taking insulin to control the diabetes when required by your doctor

After the baby is born, most women with gestational diabetes will regain normal blood sugar levels. However, it's a good idea to have your blood sugar levels tested about six weeks later, just to make sure. This follow-up test may also uncover your chances of developing type 2 diabetes in the future.

To test for gestational diabetes, an oral glucose tolerance test may be given. In this test, a woman's blood sugar levels are measured before and after drinking a sugar drink.

(See Chapter 3 for more information about healthy lifestyles.)

References

"Diabetes and Pregnancy Frequently Asked Questions." Centers for Disease Control and Prevention. U.S. Department of Health & Human Services. Accessed October 14, 2007. http://cdc.gov/ncbddd/bd/diabetespregnancy faqs.htm.

"Gestational Diabetes." American Diabetes Association. Accessed November 6, 2007. http://diabetes.org/gestational-diabetes.jsp.

"Gestational Diabetes." National Institutes of Child Health & Human Development. Accessed November 7, 2007. www.nichd.nih.gov/health/topics/Gestational_Diabetes.cfm.

HIV/AIDS

What are HIV and AIDS? How can I protect myself from them?

HIV (human immune deficiency virus) is a virus that destroys or damages the body's immune system. A healthy immune system keeps a person from getting sick. AIDS (acquired immunodeficiency syndrome) is a disease caused by the HIV virus. It is the most advanced stage of HIV infection.

When people have AIDS, their bodies can't fight disease. They get sick easily and have trouble getting well. They often die of an infection or cancer.

AIDS is a deadly disease, but it is preventable. Knowing how to protect yourself is important. HIV infection can be passed from person to person through body fluids (like blood, semen, and vaginal fluid). You can't tell if a person is infected with HIV by how they look. People who don't look or feel sick can still give you HIV.

To avoid getting infected with HIV:
- Don't have sex with a person who is infected or is having sex with others.
- Practice "safer" sex if you do have sex (see below).
- Don't share needles and syringes.

The "safest" sex is no sex. If you are having sex, "safer" sex is between two people who don't have HIV infection, who only have sex with each other, and who don't abuse injectable drugs. "Safer" sex also means using male latex condoms every time you have sex. *Never let someone else's blood, semen, urine, or vaginal fluid get into your anus, vagina, or mouth.*

You can't get HIV through casual contact, because HIV can't live for long outside the body. You can't get it by touching, shaking hands, hugging, swimming in a public pool, or giving blood. You can't get it through saliva, sweat, or tears. You can't get it by using hot tubs, public toilets, telephones, doorknobs, or water fountains. You also can't get it from food, mosquitoes, or other insects.

The risk of getting HIV through a **blood transfusion** in the United States is very low. In 1985, U.S. health care workers began testing all donated blood for HIV. Since then, each unit of donated blood is tested thoroughly for HIV and other diseases.

There is a risk of getting HIV from **tattooing, piercing, acupuncture, electrolysis**, or **shaving**. These procedures involve the possibility of getting infected blood on an instrument (needle or razor). However, if the instruments are properly sterilized, as required by the CDC (Centers for Disease Control and Prevention), the risk can be eliminated. Discuss infection control precautions with the provider before any procedure.

☞ For more information about HIV/AIDS treatment, prevention, and research, visit the AIDSinfo Web site at http://aidsinfo.nih.gov.

Should I be tested for HIV?

If you are infected with HIV, you can pass the virus to other people even when you have no signs of illness. You can pass HIV to another through your blood, vaginal fluid, or semen. A mother can also give HIV to her unborn child via the placenta or to a baby through breast milk.

You should be tested for HIV if you:

- have had unprotected sex with many sex partners;
- have a sexually transmitted infection;
- use illegal drugs;
- had blood transfusions or received blood products before 1985; and/or
- have a sex partner with any of the previous risk factors.

The following groups have the highest risk for HIV infection and AIDS:

- Sexually active homosexual men
- Bisexual men and their partners
- Intravenous (IV) drug users and their sexual partners

- People who share needles (for IV drug use, tattooing, or piercing)
- Heterosexual men and women with more than one sexual partner
- People given blood transfusions or blood products in countries where the blood is not rigorously tested
- Immigrants from areas with many cases of AIDS (like Haiti and sub-Saharan Africa)
- People who have sex with an HIV-infected partner or with anyone in the previous groups
- Babies born to HIV-infected mothers

Ask your doctor where you can get tested for HIV. Many community health centers, family planning clinics, hospitals, clinics that treat sexually transmitted diseases, and county health departments offer testing. *Do not use donating blood as a way of being tested!*

Is HIV treatable?

Testing positive for HIV is not an automatic death sentence. With proper treatment, the virus can be suppressed, and people can live normal lives. Getting tested and starting treatment early are very important.

> With early detection and proper treatment, the HIV virus can be suppressed, and people can live normal lives.

These are the keys to living a long life with HIV:

- Get good health care.
- Establish a solid relationship with your doctor, and follow his or her advice to the letter.
- Adhere to the appropriate therapies.
- Do all the things that are normally recommended for leading a healthy life:
  - Eat healthy foods.
  - Exercise.
  - Get enough rest.
  - Avoid alcohol, smoking, and drugs.
  - Avoid stress.

Maintaining good health won't prevent you from progressing to AIDS or cure it, but it will give you the best fighting chance you have. If you are HIV positive, your doctor will guide you on the road to proper treatment and a healthy lifestyle.

☞ For details on HIV treatment, read "Day One: After You've Tested Positive" at www.projectinform.org/fs/dayone.html.

(See Chapter 3 for more information about healthy lifestyles.)

References

Bartlett, J., and A. Finkbeiner. *The Guide to Living with HIV Infection*, 6th ed. Baltimore: The Johns Hopkins University Press, 2006.

"Day One: After You've Tested Positive. HIV Treatment Information." Project Inform. Accessed March 24, 2008. www.projectinform.org/info/dayone/index.shtml.

"HIV and AIDS: How to Reduce Your Risk." American Academy of Family Physicians. Accessed November 6, 2007. http://familydoctor.org/online/famdocen/home/common/sexinfections/hiv/005.html.

"HIV Infection and AIDS." *MD Consult Patient Education Handout.* USC School of Medicine Library, Columbia, SC. Accessed November 10, 2007. Keyword: HIV.

"HIV/AIDS: Risk Factors and Prevention of Transmission." MD Consult Patient Education Handout. USC School of Medicine Library, Columbia, SC. Accessed November 9, 2007. Keyword: HIV.

"How HIV is Spread." San Francisco AIDS Foundation. Accessed November 16, 2007. www.sfaf.org/aids101/transmission.html.

"How Safe is the Blood Supply in the United States?" Centers for Disease Control and Prevention. U.S. Department of Health & Human Services. Accessed November 2, 2007. www.cdc.gov/hiv/resources/qa/qa15.htm.

ASK THE EXPERTS

Following is a list of health care professionals who can help you answer more in-depth questions related to issues discussed in this chapter. A good starting point would be your primary care physician (your family physician, internist, pediatrician, or nurse practitioner). From there, he or she might recommend that you visit with other medical specialists or health care professionals. Each one has received specialized training in his or her area of expertise. *(See the Glossary of Experts for descriptions, online directories, and credentialing information.)*

- Cardiologists
- Endocrinologists
- Family physicians
- Gastroenterologists
- Genetic counselors
- Geneticists
- HIV specialists
- Internists
- Neurologists
- Nurse practitioners

- Nurses (RNs)
- Obstetricians and gynecologists (OB/GYNs)
- Oncologists
- Pediatricians
- Pulmonologists
- Radiologists
- Registered dieticians (RDs)
- Urologists

2
Family Health

Because most libraries offer services to families, it is natural that many family-related health questions are asked in libraries. After a visit to the doctor's office, you might find yourself going to a local library to research health conditions or to find answers to questions you were not able to ask at the clinic. Whether you are looking for more information about your child's immunizations or your elderly parent's arthritis, the library often serves as the place to find answers. In this chapter we will answer some of the most common questions related to family health.

WOMEN'S HEALTH

Why should I take folic acid before becoming pregnant?

Folic acid, also called *folate*, is a B vitamin that helps prevent birth defects. If a woman has enough folic acid in her body *before* she is pregnant and while she is pregnant, her baby is less likely to have a major birth defect of the brain or spine. In fact, studies show that folic acid could prevent up to 70 percent of some types of serious birth defects.

Folic acid taken **before and during pregnancy** could prevent up to 70 percent of some types of serious birth defects.

It is very important to get enough folic acid beginning one month before becoming pregnant and continuing for at least three months afterward. The birth defects linked to folic acid are formed in the first few weeks of pregnancy, often before a woman knows she is pregnant. Because half of all U.S. pregnancies are not planned, women who *could* get pregnant are urged to take folic acid daily *whether or not they are planning to become pregnant.*

Folic acid helps form a baby's brain and spine in early pregnancy. Not enough folic acid can cause defects called *neural tube defects.* The most common neural tube defects are spina bifida, anencephaly, and encephalocele. All of these defects occur during the first 28 days of pregnancy. This is why it is important to get enough folic acid every day if there's any chance a woman could get pregnant.

Neural tube defects occur very early in pregnancy, often before most women know they are pregnant. Taking folic acid DAILY can prevent these birth defects.

The U.S. Public Health Service recommends that all women of childbearing age get 400 micrograms (mcg; or 0.4 milligram [mg]) of folic acid daily. Folic acid is found in leafy green vegetables (like kale and spinach), orange juice, and enriched grains. For most women, though, it is difficult to get enough folic acid from foods. To reach the recommended daily level, you will need a vitamin supplement. Almost every multivitamin you can buy has all the folic acid you need. Check the label to be sure it says at least "400 mcg" of folic acid. You can also buy vitamin pills made only with folic acid.

How much folic acid is enough? **400 mcg** (or 0.4 mg) DAILY is recommended (in a supplement or a multivitamin).

References

American Medical Association, ed. "Neural Tube Defects." *Family Medical Guide.* New York: John Wiley & Sons, 2004.

"Folic Acid." Centers for Disease Control and Prevention. U.S. Department of Health & Human Services. Accessed January 4, 2008. www.cdc.gov/ncbddd/folicacid.

"Folic Acid and Pregnancy." Nemours Foundation. Accessed January 7, 2008. http://kidshealth.org/parent/pregnancy_newborn/pregnancy/folic_acid.html.

Somer, E. Nutrition for a Healthy Pregnancy: The Complete Guide to Eating Before, During, and After Your Pregnancy. New York: Henry Holt and Company, 2002.

I've heard that I shouldn't eat cheese or lunch meat during my pregnancy. Is this true?

Certain soft cheeses, unpasteurized milk products, processed meats, and some seafood products should be avoided during pregnancy. These foods can be a source of a bacterium called *Listeria monocytogenes*. In pregnant women this bacterium can cause listeriosis. This is a disease that can lead to miscarriage, fetal death, and severe illness or death of a newborn. This disease is very rare.

Listeria is often found in soil and water and on decaying plant material. Normally, it moves through your body without causing illness. However, in pregnant women and in people with weak immune systems, it can cause listeriosis.

Symptoms of listeriosis in pregnancy include the following:
- Chills
- Muscle aches
- Diarrhea or upset stomach

Contact your doctor if you have any flu-like symptoms. A blood or stool test can determine if you have listeriosis. Antibiotics are used to treat the disease in pregnant women and in infected newborns.

If you are pregnant, DO NOT EAT these foods:

- Soft cheeses such as feta, Brie, Camembert, blue-veined cheeses, and Mexican-style cheeses such as queso blanco or queso fresco (cheeses that are safe to eat include mozzarella, pasteurized cheese slices and spreads, cream cheese, and cottage cheese)
- Unpasteurized milk or milk products
- Hot dogs, lunch meats, or deli meats (unless they are heated until steaming)
- Refrigerated pates or meat spreads (unless they are canned)
- Refrigerated smoked seafood (unless it is an ingredient in a cooked casserole)
- Salads made in the store such as ham salad, chicken salad, egg salad, tuna salad, or seafood salad
- Unpasteurized ciders
- Unwashed raw vegetables

If you have recently eaten any of the above and *do not have any symptoms*, you do not need to be concerned.

Here are some tips to keep food safe to eat:

- Use precooked or ready-to-eat foods as soon as possible after purchase.
- Refrigerate or freeze uneaten portions promptly.
- Clean refrigerators often.
- Make sure your refrigerator is kept at or below 40°F.
- Wash hands and surfaces often.
- Keep raw and uncooked foods and liquids separate from other foods (be careful with fluid from hot dog packages or deli meats).
- Cook to proper temperatures (use a food thermometer): ground beef, 160°F; chicken, 170°F; turkey, 180°F; pork, 160°F.
- Wash raw vegetables well before peeling, cutting, or eating them.

References

Gelfand, M. "Clinical Manifestations and Treatment of Listeria Monocytogenes Infection in Adults." *UpToDate.* USC School of Medicine Library, Columbia, SC. Accessed January 6, 2008. Keyword: listeriosis.

"*Listeria monocytogenes* Risk Assessment Questions and Answers." FDA Center for Food Safety and Applied Nutrition. Accessed January 8, 2008. www.cfsan.fda.gov/~dms/lmr2qa.html.

Ogunmodede, F. "Listeriosis Prevention Knowledge Among Pregnant Women in the USA." *Infectious Diseases in Obstetrics and Gynecology* 13 (2005): 11–15.

"Protect Your Baby and Yourself from Listeriosis." USDA Food Safety and Inspection Service. Accessed January 7, 2008. www.fsis.usda.gov/Fact_Sheets/Protect_Your_Baby/index.asp.

Will morning sickness hurt my baby?

Morning sickness refers to the nausea and vomiting that some women experience when they are pregnant. The exact cause of morning sickness is unknown, but it is believed to be related to a rise in hormone levels. About 80 percent of all pregnant women experience some type of morning sickness. Many doctors believe that morning sickness is a good sign, because it means that the afterbirth (the placenta and fetal membranes) is developing well. In fact, studies have shown that women who have mild morning sickness are more likely to have a successful pregnancy.

About 80 percent of pregnant women have some form of morning sickness.

Morning sickness can become a problem for you and your baby only if it is very severe and you can't keep any foods or fluids down. This rare condition is called *hyperemesis gravidarum* and could result in hospitalization. Only a small percentage (about 1 percent) of women experience this extreme form of morning sickness. It usually occurs between weeks 4 and 10 of pregnancy.

Signs of severe morning sickness include the following:

- Severe nausea and vomiting
- Significant weight loss
- Decrease in urination
- Dehydration
- Headaches
- Confusion
- Fainting
- Jaundice

Talk to your doctor right away if you suspect you have severe morning sickness.

Only 1 percent of women experience the severe form of morning sickness called *hyperemesis gravidarum*. Most studies find that this condition has no effect on birth weight and is not related to an increased risk of birth defects.

Morning sickness is common in the morning, but for some women it can last all day. It usually begins in early pregnancy and tends to go away by the second trimester (the fourth month).

Here are some tips to relieve normal morning sickness:

- Eat small meals at least every two hours to keep something in your stomach. Eat *before* you feel queasy.
- Eat bland foods such as saltine crackers, vanilla wafers, or dry cereal when you feel nauseous. Keep a supply of these snacks by your bed, and eat a few before getting up in the morning.
- Avoid rich, fatty foods.
- Eat more carbohydrates, such as potatoes, rice, or toast.

- Avoid foods that smell bad to you (have someone else cook meals if cooking smells bother you).
- Drink beverages and soups between meals to avoid dehydration.
- Get plenty of rest, especially afternoon naps.
- Try wearing "acupressure" wrist bands. These are often used to prevent motion sickness and seem to be effective for morning sickness. They can be found in drugstores. *(See Chapter 4 for more information about acupressure.)*

There is no "right" food for everyone with morning sickness. Eat what "smells" good and appeals to you.

There is not a "perfect" food for everyone suffering from morning sickness. Basically, you should eat whatever food appeals to you (as long as it's not harmful to you or your baby). The sense of smell is heightened during pregnancy, so it is best to eat only foods that smell good to you.

If these tips don't give you relief, talk with your doctor. He or she may decide to try a prescription medication.

☞ For answers to many of your pregnancy questions, visit the American Pregnancy Association's Web site at www.americanpregnancy.org.

References

"Hyperemesis Gravidarum." American Pregnancy Association. Accessed January 15, 2008. www.americanpregnancy.org/pregnancycomplications/hyperemesis gravidarum.html.

"Morning Sickness." American Academy of Family Physicians. Accessed January17, 2008. http://familydoctor.org/online/famdocen/home/women/pregnancy/ basics/154.html.

Pirisi, A. "Meaning of Morning Sickness Still Unsettled." *Lancet* 357 (2001): 1272.

Somer, E. *Nutrition for a Healthy Pregnancy: The Complete Guide to Eating Before, During, and After Your Pregnancy.* New York: Henry Holt and Company, 2002.

Wilson, J., and D. Hill. "Nausea and Vomiting of Pregnancy." *American Family Physician* 68 (2003): 121–128.

What are the different kinds of birth control pills?

Traditional birth control pills have two female hormones, estrogen and progestin. If you take these pills, you will still have your period once a month. During the first 21 days of the month, you take active pills containing the hormones, and you take placebo pills for the last seven days. While taking the placebo pills, you will have your period. Some women may skip the placebo pills and start right away on a new pack to avoid their period during a vacation or other special occasion. This type of pill also comes in a chewable tablet form.

Seasonale and Seasonique are examples of **extended-cycle birth control pills.** With this type of birth control, you will take active pills containing the hormones for three months, and then you will take placebo pills for one week. Therefore, you will have your period only once every three months.

Lybrel is a new **continual birth control pill.** If you take Lybrel, you will not have a period at all, because it does not include a week of placebo pills. Some women experience unscheduled bleeding ("spotting") while taking Lybrel, but this side effect may go away during the first year. There has been some debate as to whether or not stopping a woman's period completely is unnatural or harmful. In response, the manufacturers claim that there are no medical reasons women need to have a monthly period. This debate will probably continue until there is concrete medical evidence supporting either argument.

Birth control pills do not protect against sexually transmitted diseases.

All birth control pills require a prescription, and they do not protect against sexually transmitted diseases (STDs). The pill is 99 percent effective at preventing pregnancy if you take it exactly as recommended and don't forget to take a pill. For the average user, the pill is 92 percent effective.

In 2002, the leading method of birth control was the pill. It was being used by 11.6 million women between ages 15 and 44. The birth control pill and female sterilization have been the two leading methods in the United States since 1982.

Few women experience side effects. Some possible side effects include headaches, spotting, nausea, vomiting, bloating, weight gain, decreased sex drive, breast tenderness, and depression. **Smokers should not take the pill, especially women over 35.** These women have an increased risk of blood clots. Women with a history of heart disease, high blood pressure, blood clots in the legs or lungs, breast cancer, uterine cancer, or liver cancer should also avoid the pill.

Women have reported positive side effects while taking the pill, including lighter periods, weaker cramps, and less acne. The pill may protect against anemia, ovarian cysts, and ovarian and endometrial cancers. Another benefit to the pill compared to other forms of birth control is the fact that after you stop taking it, you don't have to wait as long to get pregnant. Women generally start having their period again within three months after they stop taking the pill. Talk to your doctor if you don't get your period after six months.

There is also a **progestin-only pill**, which is sometimes called the "**minipill**." This type of birth control pill contains only the hormone progestin. It is very important to take this pill at the same time every day in order for it to be effective. Compared to traditional birth control pills, this type of pill may be less effective at preventing pregnancy.

The minipill is a safer choice for the following groups:

- Women over 35
- Women who smoke
- Women with high blood pressure
- Women who are overweight
- Women with a history of blood clots
- Women who are breast-feeding

The last type of pill is the **Plan B** pill, or the "**morning after**" pill. It is referred to as an emergency contraceptive because it is not for routine use. It can be used when a regular method of birth control fails or after unprotected sex.

References

"Birth Control Pill FAQ: Benefits, Risks and Choices." Mayo Clinic. Accessed January 3, 2008. www.mayoclinic.com/health/birth-control-pill/WO00098.

"Combination Pill." Mayo Clinic. Accessed January 7, 2008. www.mayoclinic
.com/health/birth-control/BI99999/PAGE=BI00015.

"Emergency Contraception." U.S. Department of Health & Human Services.
Accessed January 12, 2008. http://womenshealth.gov/faq/econtracep
.htm.

"FDA Approves Contraceptive for Continuous Use." U.S. Food and Drug
Administration. Accessed January 10, 2008. www.fda.gov/bbs/topics/
NEWS/2007/NEW01637.html.

Mosher, W. "Use of Contraception and Use of Family Planning Services in the
United States: 1982–2002." *Advance Data from Vital and Health Statistics, No.
350.* Centers for Disease Control and Prevention. Accessed June 2007.
www.cdc.gov/nchs/data/ad/ad350.pdf.

What can I do to relieve premenstrual syndrome symptoms?

Premenstrual syndrome (PMS) affects every woman differently. PMS has both physical and emotional symptoms. Some of the physical symptoms include bloating, headache, weight gain, tender or enlarged breasts, nausea, diarrhea, acne, hot flashes, joint or muscle pain, fatigue, and cramps. Some of the emotional symptoms are depression, anxiety, irritability, trouble concentrating, crying spells, and mood swings.

Conditions such as migraines, diabetes, asthma, epilepsy, multiple sclerosis, and irritable bowel syndrome may worsen during the premenstrual phase of the cycle.

Keep a diary of your symptoms, including their frequency and intensity. This information can help you discuss possible treatments with your doctor. **A variety of lifestyle and nutrition changes may help reduce PMS symptoms**. Here are some tips:

- Aerobic exercise and yoga help improve mood and relieve tension.
- Get at least eight hours of sleep at night.
- Limit alcohol and caffeine to decrease irritability.
- Drink lots of water or juice.
- Over-the-counter pain relievers, such as ibuprofen, aspirin, or naproxen, can reduce symptoms such as headache, cramps, and muscle pain.
- Vitamin E supplements may reduce breast tenderness.

- Limit salt and sugar consumption.
- Eat food rich in calcium. If you don't get enough calcium in your diet, take a supplement.
- Some research has found vitamin B6, magnesium, and calcium to be helpful in treating PMS symptoms.
- Birth control pills, which regulate hormones, may reduce symptoms.
- Your doctor may prescribe a mild diuretic (water pill) for bloating and swelling.
- Eat low-fat foods and include fish in your diet.
- Eat six small meals of complex carbohydrates (whole grains and vegetables) a day.
- Cope with stress by talking with friends or writing in a journal.

(See Chapter 3 for more information about healthy lifestyles.)

After adopting some of these lifestyle and nutrition changes, it may take two to three months to see results. If your symptoms are severe or disabling, you may have premenstrual dysphoric disorder (PMDD). About 3 to 10 percent of menstruating women have PMDD. Individuals with PMDD have five or more of these symptoms:

- Feelings of sadness or despair, or possibly suicidal thoughts
- Feelings of tension or anxiety
- Panic attacks
- Mood swings
- Lasting irritability or anger that affects other people
- Disinterest in daily activities and relationships
- Trouble thinking or focusing
- Tiredness or low energy
- Food cravings or binge eating
- Trouble sleeping
- Feeling out of control
- Physical symptoms, such as bloating, breast tenderness, headaches, and joint or muscle pain

If you have PMDD, your doctor may prescribe an antidepressant, such as a selective serotonin reuptake inhibitor (SSRI), or an antianxiety drug. Counseling may be recommended to help you cope with emotional problems.

References

Ferri, F. *Ferri's Clinical Advisor.* St. Louis: Mosby, 2007.

Hendrick, V. "Premenstrual Syndrome." U.S. Department of Health & Human Services. Accessed January 19, 2008. http://womenshealth.gov/faq/pms.htm.

"PMS: What You Can Do to Ease Your Symptoms." American Academy of Family Physicians. Accessed January 23, 2008. http://familydoctor.org/online/famdocen/home/women/reproductive/ menstrual/141.html.

"Premenstrual Syndrome." *Well-Connected In-Depth Reports, No. 79.* New York: Nidus Information Services, 2006.

"Premenstrual Syndrome (PMS) and Premenstrual Dysphoric Disorder (PMDD)." *MD Consult Patient Education Handout.* USC School of Medicine Library, Columbia, SC. Accessed January 19, 2008. Keyword: premenstrual syndrome.

What happens during a pelvic exam? What is a Pap test?

A pelvic exam is a checkup of your vagina (birth canal), cervix, uterus (womb), ovaries, and fallopian tubes. It is a way for your health care provider to examine your female organs and check for any problems. It is normal to be anxious or embarrassed about the exam, but rest assured that it is simple, takes only about five minutes, and usually isn't painful.

A **Pap test** (also called a *Pap smear* or *cervical smear*) is a test done during the pelvic exam to check for abnormal changes in the cells of the cervix (the lower part of the uterus that opens into the vagina). Abnormal cells can develop into cancer if not detected and treated.

Pap tests have reduced deaths from cancer of the cervix in the United States by 70 percent over the past 50 years.

Here is what happens during the pelvic exam:

- You will take off your clothing (including your underwear and bra) and put on a gown. A cloth will be draped over your lower body.
- You will lie on your back on the exam table with your knees bent and your feet in the "stirrups." You will be asked to slide your hips to the end of the table and let your legs fall to each side so that your legs are spread apart.

- Your health care provider will check the outside area of your vagina.
- A speculum (a thin instrument that can sometimes be lubricated) will be gently inserted into the vagina and then opened to hold the vaginal walls open. This allows the cervix to be seen. Try to relax and breathe slowly. You may feel a pulling sensation.
- Your health care provider will use a special tiny brush to collect cells from your cervix. This is the Pap test. The cells will be tested later in a lab. A sample of vaginal discharge may also be collected and tested.
- After the samples are taken, the speculum will be removed.
- The female organs will now be checked. Your provider will put one or two gloved fingers into your vagina and a hand on your lower belly to feel your fallopian tubes, ovaries, and uterus. This is done to make sure their size and shape are normal. It may cause a slight discomfort.
- Sometimes your provider will do a rectal exam by inserting one finger into the anus.

The steps may vary a bit, but generally this is what you can expect. You should feel free to ask the nurse or doctor any questions.

Often, your health care provider will also do a clinical breast exam during your visit. This is done to check for any lumps or other signs of breast problems. When your exam is over, your health care provider will answer any questions you have and tell you when to expect the results of the exam.

You should start having regular pelvic exams when you become sexually active or by the age of 21, whichever happens first.

The rule of thumb is to have your first pelvic exam after you become sexually active or when you turn 21, whichever comes first. However, you may need to have a pelvic exam before then if you have any of the following problems:

- Unexplained pain in the lower belly or around the vaginal area
- Vaginal discharge that causes itching, burns, or smells bad
- No menstrual periods by age 15 or 16
- Vaginal bleeding that lasts more than 10 days

- Missed periods, especially if you are having sex
- Severe menstrual cramps

Notify your doctor if you have any of the listed symptoms.
By having a pelvic exam and a Pap test, you are taking care of your reproductive health. Problems may be found that can be treated early. This exam is an important part of a woman's healthy lifestyle.

☞ To find out more about their first pelvic exams, teens can visit http://kid shealth.org/teen/sexual_health/girls/obgyn.html.

References

"Pap Test (Cervical Smear)." *MD Consult Patient Education Handout.* USC School of Medicine Library, Columbia, SC. Accessed January 12, 2008. Keyword: pap test.

"Pap Tests and Cervical Health: A Healthy Habit for You." National Cancer Institute. Accessed January 25, 2008. www.cancer.gov/cancerinfo/pap-tests-cervical-health.

"Pelvic Exam." *MD Consult Patient Education Handout.* USC School of Medicine Library, Columbia, SC. Accessed January 20, 2008. Keyword: pelvic exam.

"Your First Pelvic Exam: A Guide for Teens." Center for Young Women's Health. Children's Hospital, Boston. Accessed January 4, 2008. www.young womenshealth.org/pelvicinfo.html.

Do I need to take hormone therapy during menopause?

Not necessarily. Most women do not need any treatment for menopause symptoms. Symptoms may come and go, or they may remain persistent. Women with difficult menopause symptoms may choose to take hormone therapy (also referred to as *menopausal hormone therapy* [MHT]). Hormone therapy can help relieve hot flashes, night sweats, and vaginal dryness. It also may reduce the risk of colon cancer. Hormone therapy is not as popular as it used to be, because research has shown that it can increase serious health risks in some women.

Menopausal hormone therapy can increase the risk of stroke, blood clots, heart attack, gallbladder disease, and breast cancer.

Women using MHT are taking the hormones progesterone and estrogen. Women without a uterus (those who have had a hysterectomy) are given only estrogen. The U.S. Food and Drug Administration recommends taking the lowest effective dose for the shortest amount of time needed. MHT is available in a variety of forms: tablets, patches or lotion to be used on the skin, vaginal ring, vaginal cream, pellets placed under the skin, and shots. Possible side effects include breast tenderness, spotting, cramping, headaches, mood swings, and bloating.

MHT may increase a woman's risk of stroke, serious blood clots, heart attack, gallbladder disease, and breast cancer. Women over 65 may not want to begin MHT, because it could increase their risk of dementia. Discuss your health history and family history with your doctor to help decide if MHT is right for you. Women taking MHT should visit their doctor every six months to see if they should continue using it.

Spicy foods, hot beverages, caffeine, and alcohol may trigger hot flashes.

References

"Hormones and Menopause: Tips from the National Institute." National Institute on Aging. Accessed January 4, 2008. www.niapublications.org/tipsheets/hormones.asp.

"Menopausal Hormone Therapy." MD Consult Patient Education Handout. USC School of Medicine Library, Columbia, SC. Accessed January 2, 2008. Keyword: hormone therapy.

"Menopause." Well-Connected In-Depth Reports, No. 40. New York: Nidus Information Services, 2006.

"Menopause and Menopause Treatment." U.S. Department of Health & Human Services. Accessed January 7, 2008. http://womenshealth.gov/faq/menopaus.htm.

Is mental illness more common in women than in men?

Some forms of mental illness are more common in women than in men. Women are two to three times more likely than men to suffer from depression. Women are also twice as likely to experience post-traumatic stress disorder (PTSD). Alzheimer's disease, eating disorders, and anxiety disorders are all more common in women.

It is difficult to maintain a healthy balance between work and home life in today's fast-paced world. Women frequently experience stress or frustration as they juggle their multiple roles related to their career and private life. The good news is that women are more likely to seek help than men. Learning the warning signs and symptoms of mental illness will help you recognize a possible problem (see Table 2-1).

Table 2-1. Warning signs of mental illness

Mental illness	Possible symptoms
Alzheimer's disease	Anxiety, dementia, depression, recent memory loss, intellectual decline, personality change, delusions, social withdrawal
Anxiety disorders	Unrealistic or excessive anxiety or worry, sense of impending doom, hyperventilation, dizziness, nausea or abdominal distress, chest tightness
Depression	Depressed mood, fatigue, poor self-image, difficulty concentrating, thoughts of suicide
Eating disorders	Having unnatural concern about body weight, throwing up after eating, overexercising, not having periods, using medicines to keep from gaining weight, obsessing about calories and fat grams in food, lying about food intake, fainting
Post-traumatic stress disorder	Having flashbacks or nightmares about the event; avoiding places or people who remind you of it; having trouble sleeping; not being able to recall parts of the event; being irritable, angry, or jumpy

☞ To learn more about how differences between men and women affect the prevention, diagnosis, and treatment of disease, visit the Society for Women's Health Research's Web site at www.womenshealthresearch.org.

References

Celestino, F. "Alzheimer Disease." *5 Minute Clinical Consult Overview*. InfoRetriever. USC School of Medicine Library, Columbia, SC. Accessed January 9, 2008. Keyword: alzheimer.

"Eating Disorders: Facts for Teens." American Academy of Family Physicians. Accessed January 7, 2008. http://familydoctor.org/online/famdocen/home/children/teens/eating/277.html.

Katon, W. "Anxiety." *5 Minute Clinical Consult Overview.* InfoRetriever. USC School of Medicine Library, Columbia, SC. Accessed January 6, 2008. Keyword: anxiety.

Mannschreck, D. "Depression." *5 Minute Clinical Consult Overview.* InfoRetriever. USC School of Medicine Library, Columbia, SC. Accessed January 7, 2008. Keyword: depression.

"Mental Health." Society for Women's Health Research. Accessed January 5, 2008. http://swhr.convio.net/site/PageServer?pagename=hs_consumerfacts_mental.

"Post-Traumatic Stress Disorder, a Real Illness." National Institute of Mental Health. Accessed January 10, 2008. www.nimh.nih.gov/publicat/NIMH ptsd.cfm.

"Sex Differences in Mental Health." Society for Women's Health Research. Accessed January 11, 2008. http://swhr.convio.net/site/PageServer?page name=hs_facts_mental.

CHILDREN'S HEALTH

What are the benefits of breast-feeding my baby?

Doctors recommend that healthy women should try to give their babies breast milk for at least the first six months of life. Breast-feeding, sometimes called *nursing,* is a convenient and inexpensive way for a mother to feed her child. More important, breast-feeding offers many benefits to both baby and mother.

☞ The American Academy of Pediatrics recommends breast-feeding a child for at least six months after birth. For more information, visit www.aap.org/healthtopics/breastfeeding.cfm.

Benefits of breast-feeding for the baby

• Breast milk contains antibodies that protect your baby from infection.
• Breast milk is the "perfect" food for a newborn. It has just the right amount of fat, sugar, water, and protein that is needed for a baby's growth and development.

- Breast-fed babies have fewer ear infections, respiratory infections, rashes, and allergies than bottle-fed babies do.
- Breast-feeding reduces the risk of food allergies.
- Breast-feeding helps prevent diarrhea.
- Breast-fed infants tend to gain less unnecessary weight and to be leaner.
- Breast-fed babies have a lower risk of inflammatory bowel diseases, certain kinds of cancer, juvenile diabetes, asthma, eczema, and obesity.
- Studies show that breast-feeding boosts a child's physical and intellectual potential. Breast-fed babies, especially those who were born prematurely, tend to score higher on IQ tests than bottle-fed babies.
- Breast-feeding could help prevent sudden infant death syndrome (SIDS).
- The skin-to-skin contact provided during breast-feeding is valuable to infant development.
- Breast-feeding creates a unique bond between mother and baby.

Breast-feeding for six months or more is ideal. However, you and your baby will benefit even if you are able to breast-feed for only a short period of time.

Benefits of breast-feeding for the mother

- You will experience less bleeding after giving birth.
- Your uterus will return to its normal size more quickly.
- You will lose weight faster.
- Your risk of developing breast cancer later in life will be reduced (if you nurse for at least three months).
- Breast-feeding eliminates the need for preparing formula and sterilizing bottles.
- It saves time and money.
- It provides a much-needed chance to rest and relax.
- It is convenient.
- It helps you bond with your baby.
- It helps prevent pregnancy if you breast-feed exclusively for the first six months. However, breastfeeding is NOT a recommended

form of birth control; other methods should be used to prevent pregnancy, even by an actively breast-feeding mother.

In addition to the health benefits for mother and baby (see Table 2-2), breast-feeding provides social and economic benefits to the nation.

Social and economic benefits

- Reduced health care costs (because breast-fed infants are sick less often and need fewer prescriptions and hospitalizations)
- More productive workforce (breast-feeding mothers miss less work because their infants are sick less often)
- Less environmental waste from formula cans and bottle supplies
- Economic benefits to the family (because the cost of infant formula and bottle supplies is eliminated)

Table 2-2. Facts about breast milk

Breast milk is the "perfect" food for an infant. It cannot be duplicated artificially. It is unique because it:
- contains an ideal balance of nutrients that the baby can digest easily;
- changes over time to meet the changing needs of the growing baby;
- contains substances needed for brain development;
- provides immune factors that help the baby fight illnesses and allergies; and
- is sterile and is always the right temperature for feeding.

In certain situations, doctors will advise a woman not to breast-feed. If you have HIV or active tuberculosis, you should not breast-feed, because you could transmit the infection to your baby. Certain medicines, illegal drugs, and alcohol can pass through the breast milk and cause harm to your baby. Women with certain chronic illnesses may also be advised not to breast-feed.

Certain medicines, illegal drugs, and alcohol can pass through the breast milk and cause harm to your baby.

Even though breast-feeding is a natural process, it is not always easy. Working with a lactation consultant to learn how to breast-feed is highly recommended. Even with help, though, some women still have trouble breast-feeding. For these and other reasons, many women choose not to breast-feed.

Ultimately, whether or not to breast-feed is a woman's decision. Before your baby is born, talk with your doctor about breast-feeding and other infant feeding options.

References

American Academy of Pediatrics Work Group on Breastfeeding. "Breastfeeding and the Use of Human Milk." *Pediatrics* 100 (1997): 1035–1039.

"Benefits of Breastfeeding." National Women's Health Information Center. Accessed February 5, 2008. www.4woman.gov/Breastfeeding/index.cfm?page=227.

"Benefits of Breastfeeding [Issue Paper]." Raleigh, NC: United States Breastfeeding Committee, 2002.

The Children's Hospital Guide to Your Child's Health and Development. Boston: Children's Hospital Boston, 2001.

"Research on Breastfeeding." National Institutes of Child Health & Human Development. Accessed February 2, 2008. www.nichd.nih.gov/womenshealth/research/pregbirth/breastfeed.cfm.

Traisman, E., ed. *Guide to Your Children's Health.* New York: American Medical Association, 1999.

How much sleep does my child need?

Many parents wonder if their kids get enough sleep. A proper amount of rest helps children function better; their concentration increases, and they have longer attention spans. Sleep may help them recover from illness faster. A lack of rest can cause moodiness and may lead to behavior problems. Children with chronic illnesses and developmental disabilities are more likely to have sleep problems. Most sleep problems are related to poor sleep quality or quantity. If your child is not getting enough rest, he or she may show it by yawning or appearing drowsy. Other kids may react to a lack of sleep differently, becoming hyperactive and having poor impulse control.

Twenty-five percent of children will have a significant sleep problem some time during their childhood.

Table 2-3 lists the average amounts of sleep recommended by age group. Remember, every child is different. Some children may do well on less sleep, while others may need more sleep.

Table 2-3. Average amount of sleep recommended by age group

Age	Amount of sleep (per day)
Infant (up to 1 year)	14–20 hours (3- to 4-hour naps between feedings)
Toddler (ages 1–2)	11–13 hours (1 or 2 naps equaling 1.5–3.5 hours)
Preschooler (ages 3–5)	10–12 hours (1 nap)
Middle childhood (ages 6–12)	9–11 hours
Adolescent (ages 13–17)	9–10 hours

Source: "Sleep and Children: What's Normal?" *MD Consult Patient Education Handout.* USC School of Medicine Library, Columbia, SC. Accessed February 2, 2008. Keyword: sleep.

You can help your child become a good sleeper by establishing good bedtime routines and sleep habits. Here are some tips:

- Try to maintain a set bedtime and wake-up time every day, even on the weekends.
- Plan some quiet time at least a half hour before bed (reading, bathing, listening to soft music, etc.).
- If your child is hungry, it is okay to have a light snack before bedtime.
- Avoid caffeine several hours before bedtime.
- Spend time outside every day.
- Exercise daily.
- Don't let your kids fall asleep by watching TV.
- The bedroom environment should be consistently quiet, cool, and dark.
- Tucking your child into bed snugly will give them a sense of security.
- Create a kit for your kids to use when they have trouble sleeping. You could include a flashlight, a favorite book, and a CD.
- Help your teen maintain a bedtime that allows for the full hours of sleep needed at this age.

References

"All About Sleep." Nemours Foundation. Accessed February 1, 2008. www.kids
health.org/parent/general/sleep/sleep.html.

Behrman, R. *Nelson Textbook of Pediatrics.* Philadelphia: Saunders, 2004.

"Sleep and Children: What's Normal?" *MD Consult Patient Education Handout.*
USC School of Medicine Library, Columbia, SC. Accessed February 2,
2008. Keyword: sleep.

"Sleep and Preschoolers." Nemours Foundation. Accessed February 8, 2008.
www.kidshealth.org/parent/growth/sleep/sleep_preschool.html.

What is sudden infant death syndrome (SIDS), and how can I protect my baby from it?

Sudden infant death syndrome (SIDS) is the main cause of death in children between the ages of one month and one year. The majority of cases occur between two months and four months of age. In all cases, a diagnosis of SIDS implies an unexplained death.

Health care experts don't yet know what causes SIDS. However, they have pinpointed certain risk factors that may increase its likelihood.

SIDS Risk Factors

- Infant sleep position: Sleeping on the stomach seems to be highly related to SIDS rates.
- Smoke exposure: Research has found a connection between mothers who smoke during or after pregnancy and a higher rate of SIDS.
- Overheating: There may be a relationship between the type and amount of clothing and bedding covering the infant and the rate of SIDS.
- Infant bedding: Overly soft bedding may be connected to higher rates of SIDS.
- Various maternal risk factors: All of the following have been linked to a higher risk of SIDS: mothers who first get pregnant before age 20; anemia; late prenatal care; low weight gain during pregnancy; and maternal smoking during or after pregnancy.

What can you do to decrease the chances of SIDS? Following are the top ten steps recommended by the National Institute of Child Health and Human Development.

Ten Steps to Help Prevent SIDS

1. Always place your child on his or her back to sleep, never on the stomach.
2. Avoid loose bedding and/or soft objects in the sleep area.
3. Use a firm sleep surface, such as a crib mattress with a fitted sheet.
4. Don't let your infant sleep in bed with you. Place the infant in a separate sleep area, such as a crib.
5. Consider a dry pacifier when the infant is one month old (research shows that pacifiers significantly reduce a baby's risk for SIDS).
6. Dress your infant in comfortable sleep clothing, and keep the room at a comfortable temperature to avoid overheating.
7. Do not smoke or allow others to smoke around your infant.
8. Avoid products that claim to reduce SIDS, because most have not been adequately tested.
9. Talk to your health care provider before relying on a home monitor.
10. Finally, reduce flat spots on your infant's head by placing the baby on his stomach when awake and being watched. This will strengthen his neck and shoulder muscles. Also, avoid excessive time in car seats, and change the direction he sleeps in the crib, week to week.

- In the United States, most SIDS cases occur during the fall and winter compared to the spring and summer.
- SIDS occurs more often in boys than in girls.
- Some researchers believe that brain stem defects or slow maturation of the brain stem may make certain infants more susceptible to SIDS.

References

"Safe Sleep for Your Baby: Ten Ways to Reduce the Risk of Sudden Infant Death Syndrome (SIDS)." National Institutes of Child Health & Human Development. Accessed February 2, 2008. www.nichd.nih.gov/publications/pubs/safe_sleep_gen.cfm#risk.

"What Does a Safe Sleep Environment Look Like?" National Institutes of Child Health & Human Development. Accessed February 10, 2008. www.nichd.nih.gov/publications/pubs/upload/BTS_safe_environment.pdf.

"What is SIDS?" National SIDS/Infant Death Resource Center. Accessed February 13, 2008. www.sidscenter.org/WhatIsSIDS.pdf.

What is autism?

Autism, or autistic disorder, is a condition that affects the normal functioning of the brain. Autism often impairs a person's communication and social skills and causes him or her to display the same behaviors again and again. According to the National Institute of Mental Health, autism is one of five Pervasive Developmental Disorders and can usually be detected by the age of three. Because autism can range anywhere from mild to severe, it is often called a "spectrum disorder."

Your child may be autistic if he or she:

- doesn't respond in social interactions;
- avoids eye contact;
- focuses intently on one object for long periods of time;
- fails to respond to his or her name;
- is very sensitive to sound or touch;
- shows unusual behaviors and/or language; and/or
- does not respond well to changes in routine;

Check with your child's doctor if you suspect he or she may have autism.

Although there is currently no known cure for autism, early treatment and therapy can help. Some autistic children can grow up to lead near-normal lives. For this reason, you should talk to your pediatrician if you suspect that your child may have autism.

The MMR theory

In recent years researchers have been taking a close look at the theory that the measles-mumps-rubella (MMR) vaccine may cause autism. There appears to be no relation between the MMR vaccine and autism. However, a number of researchers believe more research is needed to see if the MMR vaccine may be a cause of autism in a small number of children. Because there is currently no evidence that the MMR vaccine causes autism, doctors recommend that children continue to receive the vaccine.

> The Centers for Disease Control and Prevention strongly suggests that parents continue using the MMR vaccine to protect their children from what are known to be potentially deadly illnesses.

References

"Autism Fact Sheet." National Institute of Neurological Disorders and Stroke. Accessed February 6, 2008. www.ninds.nih.gov/disorders/autism/detail_autism.htm.

"Autism Spectrum Disorders (Pervasive Developmental Disorders)." National Institute of Mental Health. Accessed February 7, 2008. www.nimh.nih.gov/publicat/autism.cfm.

"FAQs About MMR Vaccines & Autism." Centers for Disease Control and Prevention. U.S. Department of Health & Human Services. Accessed February 2, 2008. www.cdc.gov/nip/vacsafe/concerns/autism/autism-mmr.htm#3.

"What Is Autism?" Autism Society of America. Accessed February 10, 2008. www.autism-society.org.

MEN'S HEALTH

What does a prostate exam involve, and should I have one?

The prostate is a small gland in men, and it is about the size of a walnut. It helps to produce the fluid component of semen and is located just below the bladder and in front of the rectum. Because the prostate surrounds the urethra, which is the tube through which urine flows out of the body, some men with prostate problems may experience difficulties ejaculating and/or urinating. These include painful ejaculation, frequent trips to the bathroom, incomplete urination, and/or difficulty in beginning a urine stream.

> • Nearly 70 percent of prostate cancer cases occur in men who are 65 years or older.
> • African-American men have the highest rates of prostate cancer, while Native American and Asian men have the lowest rates.

If you are experiencing any problems ejaculating or urinating, it is important to share this information with your health care provider.

After a number of questions, your doctor may recommend one or more of the following common procedures:

- **Digital rectal exam (DRE):** Often done annually for men 50 years of age or older, the DRE is usually the first prostate exam performed. The patient may be asked to bend over or to lie on his side so the doctor can insert a gloved finger into the rectum. The doctor will then attempt to feel the prostate through the rectum wall, focusing on whether the prostate has any irregular surfaces.
- **Prostate-specific antigen (PSA) blood test:** Another common exam, the PSA blood test screens for the amount of PSA, a protein produced by the prostate, present in a sample of blood. While an elevated amount of PSA doesn't mean that you do have prostate cancer, it can help your doctor determine what may be happening with your prostate.
- **Transrectal ultrasound:** If prostate cancer is suspected, the doctor may use a probe inserted into the rectum to create an ultrasound image of the gland on a monitor. The doctor can then guide a needle to the suspected tumor location and collect a sample for screening.

Further procedures the doctor may recommend, depending on the results of the initial tests, include the following:

- Urinalysis (a diagnostic examination of a urine sample)
- Urodynamic test (a test that assesses the function of your bladder and urethra)
- Cystoscopy (a test that allows a doctor to see inside your bladder or urethra)
- Magnetic resonance imaging (MRI)
- Computerized tomography (CT)
- Surgery

Some of the test results will be available immediately. Others may require a few days' wait. Make sure to discuss the results with your health care provider. It's important to recognize that some men with prostate problems may experience no symptoms at all. For this reason, some health care providers recommend annual screenings for men over 50. For those with a family history of prostate cancer, some health care providers recommend annual screenings starting at age 40.

There are three main disorders of the prostate gland:
- Prostatitis: inflammation or infection of the gland
- Benign prostatic hyperplasia (BPH): normal growth of the prostate that occurs as a man ages
- Prostate cancer

References

"Medical Tests for Prostate Problems." National Kidney and Urologic Diseases Information Clearinghouse. Accessed February 8, 2008. http://kidney.niddk.nih.gov/kudiseases/pubs/medtestprostate/index.htm.

"Prostate Health: What Every Man Needs to Know." *FDA Consumer Magazine.* U.S. Food and Drug Administration. Accessed February 10, 2008. www.fda.gov/fdac/features/2006/306_prostate.html.

"The Prostate-Specific Antigen (PSA) Test: Questions and Answers." National Cancer Institute. Accessed February 7, 2008. www.cancer.gov/cancertopics/factsheet/Detection/PSA.

"What I Need to Know About Prostate Problems." National Kidney and Urologic Diseases Information Clearinghouse. Accessed February 9, 2008. http://kidney.niddk.nih.gov/kudiseases/pubs/prostate_ez/index.htm.

Is there a cure for erectile dysfunction?

Erectile dysfunction (ED), which may affect as many as 15 to 30 million men in America alone, is the inability to achieve or sustain an erection. The condition often interferes with or prevents sexual intercourse, often leaving the man too embarrassed to seek treatment. Yet there are a number of treatment options available to men of all ages.

Erectile dysfunction may affect as many as 15 to 30 million men in America.

The first step is to have a medical and sexual history completed by your family doctor or urologist. These histories may reveal whether or not the ED is a symptom of a larger condition or disease. Next, a physical exam can determine if the ED is a result of a nervous system problem or one caused by hormonal imbalances. There are also lab tests that can measure such things as your levels of free testosterone in the blood, which again may suggest endocrine system problems.

Once the doctor has uncovered a likely cause of the ED, the general practice is to start with the least invasive treatment options. Depending on how successful these treatments are, more invasive means may be required. Some of these treatments, from least invasive to most invasive, include the following:

- Lifestyle changes, such as quitting smoking, losing weight, and exercising
- Drug adjustments, such as trying different high blood pressure medicines if your current medicines are likely causing the ED
- Therapy for patients whose ED is likely the result of psychological issues
- Oral or locally injected medicines
- Vacuum devices
- In some cases, surgery

The most popular oral drugs for erectile dysfunction (such as Viagra, Cialis, and Levitra) work by causing muscles in the penis to relax, allowing more blood flow during stimulation. They do not cause immediate erections like locally injected drugs. They should not be used more than once a day. Men with certain medical conditions should not take these drugs. Check with your doctor.

Although it might not be possible to completely cure your ED, the large number of treatment options means that it is likely you can regain a healthy sexual lifestyle. The hardest part of the treatment may be getting over your embarrassment and seeking medical help.

References

"Erectile Dysfunction." Mayo Clinic Accessed February 13, 2008. www.mayo clinic.com/health/erectile-dysfunction/DS00162.
"Erectile Dysfunction." National Kidney and Urologic Diseases Information Clearinghouse. Accessed February 14, 2008. http://kidney.niddk.nih.gov/kudiseases/pubs/impotence.

Do men really deal differently with depression than women?

In the United States, up to 25 percent of people will experience a mental health issue each year. From anxiety disorders and panic attacks to schizophrenia, often there is a difference between men and women both in the likelihood of experiencing a mental illness and in how each gender deals with the condition (see Table 2-4). Depression tends to affect between two and three times more women than men. While both men and women exhibit similar core symptoms under depression, men tend to have much higher rates of suicide when depressed. There are many reasons for why this may be.

To begin, studies have found that men are more likely to use aggressive means to commit suicide. Unlike women, who prefer using prescription or nonprescription medicines in their suicide attempts, men are much more likely to resort to violent means. Moreover, men are less likely than women to seek help from their health care providers.

Table 2-4. Similarities and differences between men and women experiencing depression

Characteristics of depression often shared by men and women
- Upset sleep patterns
- Appetite changes
- Feelings of guilt
- Poor concentration
- Depressed mood
- Lack of interest or drive

Differences of depression between men and women
- More anger and irritability experienced by men
- More alcoholism and drug abuse in men
- Less doctor visits by men
- Men more likely to smoke

Some experts suggest that the following characteristics will help identify depressed men:

- Impulsivity and extreme behaviors
- Low stress tolerance
- History of substance and alcohol abuse
- Family history of suicide, alcohol abuse, and depression

Before puberty, depression is more likely to occur in boys than in girls. After puberty, it is more likely to occur in girls than in boys.

NOTE: It is important to realize that many forms of mental illness, especially depression, are treatable these days. Regardless if you are a man or a woman, if you suspect that you are suffering from depression, talk to your health care provider about getting screened and about your treatment options.

References

"Depression: Comprehensive Version." *MD Consult Patient Education Handout.* USC School of Medicine Library, Columbia, SC. Accessed February 14, 2008. Keyword: depression.
"Mental Health." Society for Women's Health Research. Accessed February 21, 2008. www.womenshealthresearch.org/site/PageServer?pagename= hs_consumerfacts_mental.
Winkler, D. "Gender-Specific Symptoms of Depression and Anger Attacks." *Journal of Men's Health & Gender* 3 (2006): 19–24.

Why do men usually live shorter lives than women?

Globally, men tend to die sooner than women. Moreover, for many of the leading causes of death, men tend to have higher death rates than women. In the United States, for example, women live, on average, a little more than five years longer than men. Researchers continue to explore the causes of this difference in life expectancy. The answer may lie in both biological and behavioral differences between men and women.

The leading cause of death in the United States and in many other countries is coronary heart disease (CHD). The fact that men tend to develop CHD up to 15 years earlier than women may explain, in part, why they tend to die sooner. Some of the possible explanations for this difference in CHD between men and women include the following:

- More men than women smoke.
- Up to a certain age, men tend to a have higher incidence of hypertension.
- Men tend to have lower levels of the good cholesterol (high-density lipoprotein, or HDL) and higher levels of the bad cholesterol (low-density lipoprotein, or LDL) relative to women.
- Men often have higher rates of abdominal obesity, which has been associated with higher CHD rates.

The second leading cause of death in the United States is cancer. Overall, men have a cancer death rate 1.5 times that of women. Because lung cancer is the leading cancer-related death, the difference in cancer death rate may in part be a product of men using tobacco products more often than women.

In terms of behavioral differences, men tend to have much higher death rates from violent causes, such as car injuries, firearm injuries, homicide, and suicide. Such differences may be caused by men's riskier behaviors related to alcohol consumption, illegal substance abuse, aggressive driving, etc. Finally, some studies have pointed out that men are less likely than women to see a doctor when symptoms arise. Delaying treatment until a condition worsens may in part explain the difference in death rates between the sexes.

Whether you are male or female, simple lifestyle changes may help prolong your life.

Overall, regardless of whether you are a man or a woman, simple lifestyle changes may help prolong your life. Talk to your family doctor about possibly having a CHD risk assessment performed and how changes in your diet and physical activity may help you increase the quality and length of your life.

(See Chapter 3 for more information about healthy lifestyles.)

References

Fodor, G., and R. Tzerovska. "Coronary Heart Disease: Is Gender Important?" *Journal of Men's Health & Gender* 1 (2004): 32–37.

Salzman, B., and R. Wender. "Male Sex: A Major Health Disparity." *Primary Care: Clinics in Office Practice* 33 (2006): 1–16.

SENIOR HEALTH

What can I do to prevent osteoporosis?

Osteoporosis is a disease that causes bones to weaken and break easily. Although women are more likely than men to develop the disease, men can also suffer from osteoporosis. This disease can be prevented. Prevention of osteoporosis is very important, because there is currently no cure.

Building strong bones, especially before the age of 30, can be the best defense against osteoporosis.

These steps can help build strong bones and prevent osteoporosis:

- Get your daily recommended amount of **calcium** (see the next paragraph).
- Get your daily recommended amount of **vitamin D**. You can get this with 10 to 15 minutes of exposure to the sun two to three times per week. Some people need to take vitamin D supplements. Check with your doctor.
- **Exercise** regularly. The best exercise for your bones is the weight-bearing kind, such as walking, hiking, jogging, weight training, tennis, and dancing.
- **Avoid smoking** and drinking alcohol in excess.
- Talk to your doctor about bone health, and ask if you should have a **bone density** scan to measure the density of your bones.

Calcium

Studies show that not enough calcium in your diet contributes to the development of osteoporosis. Getting enough calcium daily is essential to maintaining bone strength. The recommended daily calcium intakes are listed in Table 2-5.

Foods rich in calcium include low-fat dairy products (such as milk, cheese, and yogurt), dark green leafy vegetables (such as broccoli, collard greens, and spinach), sardines and salmon with bones, tofu, almonds, and foods fortified with calcium such as orange juice, cereals, and breads. If you are unable

Table 2-5. Recommended calcium intakes

Ages	Amount (mg/day)
Birth–6 months	210
6 months–1 year	270
1–3	500
4–8	800
9–18	1,300
19–50	1,000
51 or older	1,200
Pregnant and lactating women	
14–18	1,300
19–50	1,000

to get enough calcium through your diet, your doctor can recommend an appropriate calcium supplement.

Vitamin D

Vitamin D plays an important role in bone health, because it helps your body absorb calcium. Vitamin D is made in the skin after direct exposure to sunlight. From 400 to 800 international units (IU) daily is recommended. Usually 10 to 15 minutes of exposure to the sun two to three times a week is enough to satisfy the vitamin D requirement. The amount produced in the skin varies depending on time of day, season, latitude, and skin color. Use of sunscreen reduces the amount of vitamin D made in the skin. Also, studies show that vitamin D production decreases in the elderly, in people who are housebound, and in people in general during the winter. Depending on your situation, you may need to take vitamin D supplements. Check with your doctor.

Exercise

Regular exercise strengthens your bones and helps prevent bone loss. It also helps you to maintain muscle strength, coordination, and balance, which in turn help to prevent falls and related bone fractures. **The best exercise for your bones is the weight-bearing kind**, which forces you to work against gravity. Examples include walking, hiking, jogging, stair climbing, weight training, tennis, and dancing. The goal is at least 30 minutes of physical activity on most days, preferably daily. Check with your doctor before you begin a regular exercise program.

Avoid smoking and excess alcohol

Smoking and drinking too much alcohol is bad for your bones. Smoking may hinder calcium absorption, and drinking may be damaging to the skeleton.

Bone mineral density test

A bone mineral density (BMD) test is the only way to diagnose osteoporosis and determine your risk for future fractures. Because osteoporosis can develop undetected for decades until a fracture occurs, early diagnosis is important. BMD tests measure the density of your bones.

The test is painless and noninvasive. Talk to your doctor to see whether a BMD test is appropriate for you.

If you already have osteoporosis, you can live actively and comfortably by receiving proper medical care and making some lifestyle adjustments. Your doctor may prescribe certain medications and a diet rich in calcium and vitamin D, as well as a regular program of weight-bearing exercise.

☞ For more information about osteoporosis, visit the National Osteoporosis Foundation's Web site at www.nof.org. To read about specialists who treat osteoporosis, visit www.niams.nih.gov/bone/hi/osteoporosis_find_doc.htm.

(See Chapter 3 for more information about healthy lifestyles.)

References

Bennett, B. "The Low-Down on Osteoporosis: What We Know and What We Don't." *Word on Health.* National Institutes of Health. Accessed February 4, 2008. www.nih.gov/news/WordonHealth/dec2003/osteo.htm.

"Bone Loss and Osteoporosis." *Our Bodies, Ourselves: the Boston Women's Health Book Collective.* New York: Touchstone, 2005.

"Exercise for Your Bone Health." National Institute of Arthritis and Musculoskeletal and Skin Diseases. Accessed February 16, 2008. www.niams.nih.gov/bone/hi/bone_exercise.htm.

"For People with Osteoporosis: How to Find a Doctor." National Institute of Arthritis and Musculoskeletal and Skin Diseases. Accessed February 8, 2008. www.niams.nih.gov/bone/hi/osteoporosis_find_doc.htm.

"Osteoporosis Overview." National Institute of Arthritis and Musculoskeletal and Skin Diseases. Accessed February 16, 2008. www.niams.nih.gov/bone/hi/overview.htm.

"Osteoporosis Prevention." National Osteoporosis Foundation. Accessed February 7, 2008. www.nof.org/prevention/index.htm.

"Prevention: Calcium & Vitamin D." National Osteoporosis Foundation. Accessed February 15, 2008. www.nof.org/prevention/calcium.htm.

How can I relieve my osteoarthritis pain?

Currently, there is no cure for osteoarthritis, which is the most common type of arthritis. It typically affects the fingers, knees, and hips. There are a wide variety of possible treatments used to reduce pain and improve an individual's quality of life. Treatment plans should be customized for the individual, because the levels of pain and mobility vary from person to person. While one treatment may be helpful for one person, it may not work for another.

A variety of medicines are used to treat osteoarthritis. Acetaminophen, an over-the-counter drug, is commonly used to treat osteoarthritis pain. However, there are other options if acetaminophen is not helpful. Be sure to discuss any herbal supplements and vitamins you are taking with your doctor, because they can have negative interactions with medicines.

Arthritis is the leading cause of disability among adults 65 and over.

Following are some tips for managing your symptoms:

- Eat a nutritious diet, and exercise to maintain a healthy weight. Being overweight increases the amount of stress you put on your joints.
- Place an ice pack (or a pack of frozen vegetables wrapped in a towel) on the sore area for short periods of time.
- Take a warm bath or shower.
- Use heat packs on the sore area, taking care not to burn your skin.
- Rest the sore joint as needed, but don't become a couch potato.
- Do some stretching exercises or yoga.
- Use assistive devices, such as a walking cane, elastic knee support, grab bars, and tools to open jars and bottles, to help protect your joints from overuse.
- Wear supportive footwear/sculptured insoles.

Exercise is an important part of your osteoarthritis treatment plan.

Research studies have demonstrated that exercise reduces pain, improves mobility, and delays disability. Exercise is an important part of your osteoarthritis treatment plan. You should spend 30 minutes exercising each day (or, if you can't manage daily exercise, shoot for at least three times a week). Range of motion exercises, such as dancing and stretching, increase flexibility. Weight training and other strengthening exercises help build strong muscles and bones. To reduce swelling in your joints, try low-impact aerobic exercises such as swimming, walking, and riding a bike.

You may want to consider visiting a physical therapist or an occupational therapist. A physical therapist can develop a customized exercise program for you, as well as show you exercises that will help preserve the strength and use of your joints. An occupational therapist can show you techniques for daily activities, such as lifting things, that will help you take the stress off of your joints. Therapists can also give you tips on how to modify your home.

Osteoarthritis can be a progressive disease. If your pain becomes disabling or does not respond to treatments, your doctor may discuss surgery as an option. Individuals may have surgery to fix or replace joints with artificial ones. Hip and knee surgeries are the most common operations.

☞ Visit the Arthritis Foundation's Web site at www.arthritis.org/programs.php to learn about the variety of lifestyle improvement programs it offers, including an exercise program, an aquatic program, and a self-help program.

(See Chapter 3 for more information about healthy lifestyles.)

References

"Arthritis Advice." National Institute on Aging. Accessed February 1, 2008. www.niapublications.org/agepages/arthritis.asp.

"Arthritis Basics." National Center for Chronic Disease Prevention and Health Promotion. Accessed February 1, 2008. www.cdc.gov/arthritis/arthritis/key.htm.

Gilliland, B. "Arthritis, Osteo." *5 Minute Clinical Consult Overview.* InfoRetriever. USC School of Medicine Library, Columbia, SC. Accessed February 2, 2008. Keyword: osteoarthritis.

"Occupational and Physical Therapy for Arthritis." Cleveland Clinic. Accessed February 7, 2008. http://my.clevelandclinic.org/disorders/arthritis/hic_occupational_and_physical_therapy_for_arthritis.aspx.

Is there a cure for Alzheimer's disease?

Alzheimer's disease (AD) is a type of dementia that most often affects older people. It involves the build up of plaques and fiber bundles in the brain and the death of nerve cells in regions important to memory. For this reason, early symptoms usually involve mild forgetfulness. As with other forms of dementia, as the disease progresses, the symptoms will become more apparent. Eventually people with AD may be unable to perform even simple day-to-day activities such as brushing their teeth or dressing themselves. The average patient, once diagnosed, will usually live for 8 to 10 years. However, some have lived for 20 years or more after diagnosis. It depends on how progressive the disease is.

While there currently is no cure for AD, there are a number of treatments available, including drugs such as tacrine, donepezil, and galantamine. These drugs may temporarily control the symptoms of AD, making the patient more comfortable in the early to middle period of the disease. The drugs do not reverse damage that has already been done. They only serve to slow the progression of the disease.

Much research is currently being done to see what activities may help avoid or reduce the risk of developing AD. These activities include the following:

• Exercising regularly
• Lowering high blood pressure
• Lowering cholesterol level
• Controlling diabetes
• Maintaining high levels of mental stimulation

These activities won't prevent AD all of the time, but they may help to improve a person's overall health and possibly delay the disease's onset. Table 2-6 lists illnesses that are similar to AD.

Table 2-6. Illnesses that may look like Alzheimer's disease

Conditions that may cause symptoms similar to Alzheimer's disease (AD) include the following:

• Depression	• Poor diet
• Brain tumors	• Side effects of certain medicines
• Thyroid disease	• Certain infections such as HIV and syphilis

These conditions may be entirely treatable. Talk to your doctor if you are concerned that you may have AD or one of the other conditions.

(See Chapter 3 for more information about healthy lifestyles.)

References

"Alzheimer's Disease Fact Sheet." National Institute on Aging. Accessed February 23, 2008. www.nia.nih.gov/NR/rdonlyres/7DCA00DB-1362-4755-9E87-96DF669EAE20/4285/Alzheimers_Disease_Fact_Sheet706.pdf.

"Can Alzheimer's Disease Be Prevented?" National Institute on Aging. Accessed February 22, 2008. www.nia.nih.gov/NR/rdonlyres/63B5A29C-F943-4DB7-91B4-0296772973F3/0/CanADbePrevented.pdf.

"Understanding Alzheimer's Disease." National Institute on Aging. Accessed February 20, 2008. www.nia.nih.gov/NR/rdonlyres/F463CE6C-B0A7-47F4-882A-8EA143020193/0/understandingalzheimers.pdf.

What are the common signs of dementia?

Dementia is a problem in the brain that makes it hard for a person to think, remember, reason, learn, and communicate. As dementia gets worse, the person is no longer able to do everyday tasks and is unable to take care of himself or herself. Dementia also causes changes in behavior and personality. Alzheimer's disease is the most common form of dementia.

Mild memory loss is a normal part of aging. The extreme memory loss associated with dementia is NOT a normal part of aging. It is caused by the destruction of brain cells.

Dementia is not a normal part of aging. It is caused by the destruction of brain cells. A head injury, stroke, brain tumor, or disease (such as Alzheimer's disease) can damage brain cells.

Symptoms of dementia (see Table 2-7) may be mild at first but may get worse as time passes. Many of the problems are caused by memory loss.

Talk with your doctor if you have any of the signs of dementia. Tests can be done to determine if the signs are really caused by dementia. The sooner you know, the sooner you can talk to your doctor about treatment options.

If you suspect that a family member may have dementia, get him or her to see a doctor. It is a good idea for you to talk with the doctor before your relative's appointment. You can discuss the signs you have witnessed without embarrassing your relative.

Table 2-7. Common signs of dementia

- Experiencing memory loss (trouble remembering recent events or people, places, times, and dates; misplacing things)
- Having difficulty performing familiar tasks (such as getting dressed, fixing meals, shopping, taking medicines, balancing a checkbook)
- Asking the same questions repeatedly
- Undergoing personality changes (becoming moody, irritable, suspicious, or fearful)
- Becoming lost in familiar places
- Being unable to follow directions
- Neglecting personal safety, hygiene, and nutrition
- Having problems with language (forgetting simple words or using the wrong words)

☞ For more information about dementia, visit the National Institute of Neurological Disorders and Stroke's Web site at www.ninds.nih.gov/disorders/dementias/detail_dementia.htm.

References

American Medical Association, ed. "Degenerative Diseases of the Brain." *Family Medical Guide.* New York: John Wiley & Sons, 2004.

"Dementia." *MD Consult Patient Education Handout.* USC School of Medicine Library, Columbia, SC. Accessed January 31, 2008. Keyword: dementia.

"Dementia: Info and Advice for Caregivers." *MD Consult Patient Education Handout.* USC School of Medicine Library, Columbia, SC. Accessed February 8, 2008. Keyword: dementia.

"Dementia: What Are the Common Signs?" American Academy of Family Physicians. Accessed January 2, 2008. http://familydoctor.org/online/fam docen/home/seniors/mental-health/662.html.

GENERAL FAMILY HEALTH

Why should I worry about being overweight?

The Office of the Surgeon General states that over 300,000 deaths per year can be attributed to obesity. The risk of death rises with increasing weight. If you are overweight, you are more likely to develop the following health problems.

Type 2 diabetes

Type 2 diabetes is the most common type of diabetes in the United States. More than 80 percent of people with type 2 diabetes are overweight. By losing weight and increasing physical activity, you lower your risk for developing this disease.

Heart disease and stroke

People who are overweight are more likely to have high blood pressure, high levels of triglycerides (blood fats) and low-density lipoprotein (LDL) cholesterol (bad cholesterol), and low levels of high-density lipoprotein (HDL) cholesterol (good cholesterol). These are all risk factors for heart disease and stroke. Losing 5 to 15 percent of your weight can lower your chance for developing heart disease or having a stroke.

Losing as little as 10 to 20 pounds can reduce your risk of developing heart disease or having a stroke.

Cancer

Being overweight may increase the risk of developing several types of cancer, including cancers of the colon, esophagus, and kidney. Being overweight is also linked to uterine cancer and postmenopausal breast cancer in women. Weight loss, healthy eating, and sufficient physical activity may lower cancer risk.

Breathing problems

The risk for developing asthma and sleep apnea (a condition that causes a person to stop breathing for short periods during the night) is higher for overweight people. Weight loss can improve these conditions.

Osteoarthritis

Osteoarthritis is a common joint disorder and is made worse by extra weight. Weight loss can decrease stress on your knees, hips, and lower back and lessen inflammation in your body.

Gallbladder disease

The risk for gallstones and gallbladder disease is higher for those who are overweight. Slow weight loss of about one half to two pounds per week can reduce your risk for developing gallbladder disease. NOTE: *Fast weight loss of more than three pounds per week can actually increase your chance of developing gallstones.*

Fatty liver disease

Fatty liver disease can lead to severe liver damage or even liver failure. People who have diabetes are more likely to have fatty liver disease. People who are overweight are more likely to have diabetes. Losing weight can help you control your blood sugar levels and prevent the buildup of fat in your liver.

Reproductive problems

Obesity is associated with irregular menstrual cycles and infertility. Obesity during pregnancy increases the risk of death for both the baby and the mother and also increases the risk of maternal high blood pressure by ten times. Obese women are more likely to develop gestational diabetes and may have a higher chance of cesarean surgery. Obesity during pregnancy is also associated with an increased risk of birth defects such as spina bifida.

☞ To determine if you are overweight, use the online body mass index calculator at www.nhlbisupport.com/bmi. *See Chapter 3 for an explanation of body mass index.*

Tips for losing weight

If you are overweight, a slow and steady weight loss of one half to two pounds per week is safest. Try to make long-term changes in your eating and physical activity habits. Choose healthy foods, and exercise at least 30 minutes a day. Remember, maintaining a healthy weight goes a long way toward preventing many health problems!

(See Chapter 3 for more information about healthy lifestyles.)

References

"Do You Know the Health Risks of Being Overweight?" WIN: Weight-Control Information Network. National Institute of Diabetes and Digestive and Kidney Diseases. Accessed January 30, 2008. http://win.niddk.nih.gov/publications/health_risks.htm.

"Overweight and Obesity: Health Consequences." Office of the Surgeon General. U.S. Department of Health & Human Services. Accessed January 28, 2008. www.surgeongeneral.gov/topics/obesity/calltoaction/fact_consequences .htm.

What does a dental exam involve, and how often should I get my teeth examined by a dentist?

Several kinds of exams are performed at a dental office. One of the most common is known as a *dental checkup* and generally should be performed twice a year. During a dental checkup, you may be examined by two professionals: a dental hygienist, who cleans your teeth, and a dentist, who will perform a more thorough clinical examination.

You should have a dental checkup twice a year.

A typical checkup may include the following:

- **Cleaning:** Using professional instruments, the hygienist will remove as much tartar buildup, or calculus, as possible.
- **Polishing:** The parts of the teeth that show may next be polished with a mild abrasive, which helps to remove plaque and stains.
- **Prevention:** The hygienist may discuss with you proper tooth care, including how to brush and floss effectively.
- **X-rays:** Depending on your dentist's practice and knowledge of your particular dental health, X-rays, or radiographs, may be taken in order to look for decay and other oral health problems not readily visible.
- **Clinical examination:** Finally, the dentist will likely look at your teeth, gums, and X-rays in order to fully assess the state of your oral health. He or she might use tools to poke at your teeth, looking for soft, decayed spots that may be cavities.

When might you need more frequent X-rays?
If you are a child at high risk of tooth decay, if you are an adult with lots of fillings and crowns, if you have gum disease, if you are a smoker, or if you have xerostomia, called *dry mouth*, you may need X-rays more often so that your dentist can closely monitor your oral health.

Because everyone's teeth and oral health are different, from time to time a more elaborate exam, called a *comprehensive exam*, may be performed. In a comprehensive exam, the dentist looks for signs of tooth decay and/or gum disease. He or she will often exam your entire mouth, neck, and head area for signs of other medical conditions related to oral health.

People who have received an organ transplant, people with weakened immune systems, and people who are taking certain medicines (such as steroids) are at higher risk for certain types of oral health problems.

Try to keep your dentist informed about any medical changes or conditions that have occurred since your last checkup. Sometimes seemingly unrelated medical conditions can affect your oral health. Moreover, your dental health needs can change with age. It's important to see a dentist regularly and to let him or her decide how often you should have checkups or comprehensive exams to ensure the best care for your mouth and teeth.

☞ For more information about oral health care and dental exams, visit the American Dental Association's Web site at: www.ada.org.

References

"How Often Should Teeth by X-Rayed?" *Simple Steps to Better Dental Health.* Columbia University College of Dental Medicine. Accessed January 29, 2008. www.simplestepsdental.com.

"How Often Should You Go to the Dentist?" *Simple Steps to Better Dental Health.* Columbia University College of Dental Medicine. www.simplesteps dental.com.

"Oral Health for Adults." National Center for Chronic Disease Prevention and Health Promotion. Accessed January 28, 2008. www.cdc.gov/OralHealth/factsheets/adult.htm.

"Your Dental Visit: What to Expect." *Simple Steps to Better Dental Health.* Columbia University College of Dental Medicine. Accessed January 29, 2008. www.simplestepsdental.com.

When should I consider getting an eye exam?

As for most health problems, early detection of eye problems can increase the chance of successful treatment. That's why it is important to have your eyes examined regularly by an eye professional. Three types of professionals who perform eye exams are ophthalmologists, optometrists, and opticians. Ophthalmologists are licensed medical doctors who perform all types of eye care services, including prescribing lenses and sometimes performing surgery. Optometrists can diagnose many of the same disorders as ophthalmologists but may not be able to deal with more complex disorders, such as those that require surgery. Finally, opticians primarily fill corrective lens prescriptions and sometimes contact lens prescriptions. Which eye professional you go to will determine the extent of the eye exam you receive. A complete eye exam may include the following:

- A discussion of problems you are having and your medical history
- An exterior look at your eye health
- A measure of your vision and possible need for corrective lenses
- A careful examination of your eyes for possible diseases or conditions

According to the American Academy of Ophthalmology, a routine eye exam is an important preventive step to ensure that your eyes remain healthy. The Academy recommends the following schedule for eye exams based on age:

- Before age 3: Have your child screened during visits to his or her pediatrician. This is especially important if your child shows signs of crossed eyes, lazy eye (amblyopia), or drooping of the upper eyelid.
- Between ages 3 and 19: Children should have eye exams every year or every couple of years during routine pediatric or family doctor checkups.
- Between 20 and 39: Have your eyes examined at least once between 20 and 29 and twice between 30 and 39.
- Between 40 and 64: Have your eyes examined every two to four years, based on your eye doctor's recommendations.
- Over 65: Have your eyes examined every one or two years. This is the age when cataracts, glaucoma, and other eye conditions become more common.

This schedule is only a recommendation. People with certain medical conditions (such as diabetes) should have more frequent eye exams. If you are experiencing any eye pain or problems with your vision, you should visit an eye expert immediately. If eye disorders and/or conditions run in your family, you may want to schedule more frequent checkups.

> It is a myth that reading in dim light will permanently hurt your vision. It will lead to eye fatigue, but it won't damage your eyes forever!

> ☞ To see photos and images of different eye exams, visit the National Eye Institute's Web page at: www.nei.nih.gov/photo/eye%5Fexam.

References

"Common Eye Myths." Prevent Blindness America. Accessed January 29, 2008. www.preventblindness.org/eye_problems/eye_myths.html.

"Eye Examinations." National Eye Institute. Accessed January 30, 2008. www.nei.nih.gov/photo/eye%5Fexam.

"Eye Exams: What to Expect." The Foundation of the American Academy of Ophthalmology. Accessed January 29, 2008. www.eyecareamerica.org/eyecare/treatment/eye-exams.cfm.

"Eye Exams: What to Expect." Mayo Clinic. Accessed January 28, 2008. www.mayoclinic.com/print/eye-exams/MC00021/METHOD=print.

Why should I get routine blood tests?

Early detection of a problem can greatly increase your chance of getting effective treatment or decrease your chance of developing a disease altogether. For this reason, you should talk to your doctor about whether routine diagnostic examinations are a good idea. Some of the most routine procedures involve blood tests. Although there are different kinds of blood tests, most include the following steps:

- A needle is inserted into a vein by a doctor, nurse, or a special technician known as a *phlebotomist* (someone who has a lot of experience and/or training in gathering blood samples). This process is called a *venipuncture*.

- The blood is gathered into special tubes, which are labeled with your name and identification information.
- These tubes are then sent to a special lab for analysis.
- Sometimes the blood is processed—separated into its liquid and cellular components—before it is analyzed. It depends on what kinds of tests your doctor has ordered.
- A complex machine called a *blood analyzer* is often used to screen the blood.
- Finally, the results are sent back to your doctor for evaluation.

If you are worried about the pain of undergoing a venipuncture, ask your doctor about numbing creams, such as EMLA cream. Also, throughout the day, applying a moisturizer to the area you expect to have punctured may decrease the pain you experience.

What kinds of things are monitored by blood tests? **These are some of the most common substances:**

- **Electrolytes:** The amounts of minerals such as sodium, chloride, potassium, and bicarbonate are measured. These minerals control how different organs work and help keep your body's fluids balanced.
- **Blood urea nitrogen and creatinine:** Urea is a waste product that can build up in the blood if your kidneys are not working properly. Similarly, creatinine is filtered and excreted by the kidneys. Too much creatinine may suggest that there is a problem with your kidneys.
- **Glucose:** Glucose is a sugar that can cause problems if there is too much or too little in the blood. A high blood glucose level is often a symptom of diabetes.
- **Cells:** The complete blood count (CBC) is probably the most common and general blood test performed. In a CBC, the numbers and types of cells in your blood are counted and analyzed. This includes counts and descriptions of white blood cells (WBC), red blood cells (RBC), and platelets. By looking at the numbers and characteristics of each of the cell types, doctors can get a fairly good idea of your general health and whether you might have a disorder such as anemia or an infection.

Drinking eight to ten glasses of liquid a day may help with your blood flow and make it easier for a doctor or phlebotomist to locate a vein. But talk to your doctor first, because some tests require you to avoid certain foods and drinks prior to the test.

☞ For more information about various lab tests and their results, visit Lab Tests Online at www.labtestsonline.org.

References

"Basic Blood Tests." Nemours Foundation. Accessed January 16, 2008. http://kidshealth.org/parent/general/sick/labtest5.html.

"Complete Blood Count." American Association for Clinical Chemistry. Accessed January 16, 2008. www.labtestsonline.org/understanding/analytes/cbc/multiprint.html.

"Tips on Blood Testing." American Association for Clinical Chemistry. Accessed January 12, 2008. www.labtestsonline.org/understanding/testtips/bloodtips-2.html.

How can I reduce my risk of getting a sexually transmitted disease?

Sexually transmitted diseases (STDs) are infections that you get by having sexual contact with someone who is already infected. Sexual contact includes vaginal, oral, or anal intercourse; skin-to-skin contact in the genital area; kissing; and use of sex toys. The diseases usually affect the genital area (the penis or vagina).

The only sure way to prevent sexually transmitted diseases is to avoid sexual contact completely.

STDs affect men and women of all backgrounds and economic levels. The number of people affected by STDs rises each year. Some STDs may not cause symptoms, so a person who is infected may not know it and may pass the infection to a sex partner. In women, STDs can cause severe problems such as cancer of the cervix and tubal pregnancy. STDs can spread from a pregnant mother to her newborn baby and cause serious problems.

Sexually transmitted diseases (such as chlamydia, gonorrhea, and syphilis) caused by bacteria can be treated and often cured with antibiotics. Those (such as HIV/AIDS, genital herpes, genital warts, human papillomavirus, and hepatitis B) caused by viruses can be controlled *but not cured*.

These are symptoms of an STD:

- Unusual, strange-smelling discharge from the penis or vagina
- Sores, blisters, or warts around the vagina, penis, or rectum
- Burning or pain while urinating
- Itching, soreness, or redness around the vagina, penis, or rectum
- For women, sharp pains in the lower belly

If you have any of these symptoms or think you might have an STD, visit your doctor immediately.

Here are some tips for preventing STDs:

- The only sure way to prevent STDs is by not having sexual contact with anyone. This means avoiding vaginal, anal, and oral sex.
- Wait as long as possible before having sexual relations. The younger you are when you begin having sex, the more likely it is that you will develop an STD.
- Have just one sexual partner who is not infected and who is not sexually active with anyone else.
- Practice safe sex. Use a condom for vaginal, oral, and anal intercourse—every time.
- Have regular medical checkups, especially if you have more than one sexual partner.

☞ For more information, visit the Centers for Disease Control and Prevention's Division of STD Prevention Web site at www.cdc.gov/std/default.htm.

(See Chapter 1 for more information on HIV and AIDS.)

References

"Sexually Transmitted Disease Prevention." *MD Consult Patient Education Handout.* USC School of Medicine Library, Columbia, SC. Accessed January 6, 2008. Keyword: STD.

"Sexually Transmitted Diseases (STDs)." National Institute of Child Health & Human Development. Accessed January 15, 2008. www.nichd.nih.gov/ health/topics/sexually_transmitted_diseases.cfm.
"Sexually Transmitted Infections." *Our Bodies, Ourselves: the Boston Women's Health Book Collective.* New York: Touchstone, 2005.
"STIs: Common Symptoms & Tips on Prevention." American Academy of Family Physicians. Accessed January 13, 2008. http://familydoctor.org/ online/famdocen/home/common/sexinfections/sti/165.html.

VACCINATIONS

What are vaccines, and why does my child need them?

A vaccine is a medicine that helps prevent a disease. During the vaccination process (also called *immunization*), your child is given a shot or an oral dose that contains a dead, weakened, or partial germ that causes a particular disease. This stimulates your child's body to practice fighting the disease by making antibodies. These antibodies are then in place to fight the disease if your child is ever exposed to it. This process is called *immunity*. Immunizations have protected millions of children from potentially deadly diseases and have saved thousands of lives.

The best time to immunize children is when they're healthy. Vaccines work by protecting the body *before* a disease strikes. If you wait until your child gets sick, it will be too late for the vaccine to work. This is why healthy kids need to be immunized.

Many parents think a vaccine will give their child the actual disease that it's supposed to prevent. However, it's impossible to get a disease from a vaccine made with dead bacteria or viruses or with just part of the bacteria or virus. Only those vaccines made from weakened live viruses can possibly make a child develop a mild form of the disease, but it's almost always much less severe than the full-blown disease.

The risk of disease from a vaccine is extremely small.

Some parents wonder why a child should get a painful shot if vaccines aren't 100 percent effective. Vaccines aren't completely perfect, but they do work 85 to 99 percent of the time, and they are one of the most effective weapons against disease.

The short-term pain of a shot is nothing compared to suffering through a potentially deadly bout of diphtheria, pertussis, or measles. Not immunizing your children puts them and others at risk for illness.

Common reactions to vaccines are minor and include the following:

- Redness and swelling where the shot was given
- Fever
- Rash

In rare cases, immunizations can trigger seizures or severe allergic reactions. However, the risk of this happening is much lower than the risk of catching the disease if the child is *not* immunized.

☞ For a detailed list of possible side effects from vaccines, visit www.cdc.gov/vaccines/vac-gen/side-effects.htm.

Diseases that are rare or nonexistent in the United States (such as measles and polio) still exist in other parts of the world. Travel makes it easy to come into contact with these diseases. This is why it's important to continue to immunize children to protect them from potentially deadly diseases. Only when a disease is completely stamped out worldwide (like smallpox) can vaccinations be stopped.

Vaccines not only help keep your child healthy but also help all children by stamping out serious childhood diseases.

Most vaccinations are given from birth through six years of age, although a few vaccinations are given later in life. It's important to keep a record of your child's shots so you'll know when he or she is due for a booster (a periodic shot that offers continued protection). Talk to your pediatrician if you have any questions about vaccines.

☞ To find which immunizations your child will need, see the "Child & Adolescent Immunization Schedules" at www.cdc.gov/vaccines/recs/schedules/child-schedule.htm.

References

"Childhood Immunizations: First Line of Defense Against Illnesses." Mayo Clinic. Accessed January 9, 2008. www.mayoclinic.com/health/vaccines/ CC00014.

"Childhood Vaccines: What They Are and Why Your Child Needs Them." American Academy of Family Physicians. Accessed January 10, 2008. http:// familydoctor.org/online/famdocen/home/healthy/vaccines/ 028.html.

"Frequently Asked Questions About Immunizations." Nemours Foundation. Accessed January 31, 2008. http://kidshealth.org/parent/general/body/ fact_myth_immunizations.html.

"How Vaccines Work." Mayo Clinic. Accessed January 5, 2008. www.mayo clinic.com/health/vaccines/ID00023.

Can you get the flu from the flu vaccine?

The "flu"—an abbreviation of *influenza*—is a viral illness that often includes symptoms such as fever, muscle aches, general discomfort, headache, and sore throat. According to the Centers for Disease Control and Prevention (CDC), 5 to 20 percent of Americans get the flu every year, and approximately 36,000 of these die from the illness. Because the virus is spread through small droplets expelled when someone coughs or sneezes, it is fairly easy to catch and spread the illness from person to person. For this reason, yearly flu vaccines are recommended.

The flu shot will NOT give you the flu.

Currently there are two types of vaccinations: "the flu shot" and the "nasal-spray" flu vaccine. The **flu shot** is a needle-based vaccine usually given in the arm and containing an inactive, killed flu virus that will not cause flu symptoms but may cause minor side effects such as low-grade fever, aches, and/or soreness. The flu shot is approved for anyone older than 6 months, whether healthy or living with chronic illness.

The second vaccine type, the **nasal-spray vaccine**, actually contains a weakened version of the flu virus that may cause mild flu symptoms such as headache, coughing and/or sore throat, runny nose, and mild fever. For this reason, the nasal-spray vaccine—also called the *live attenuated influenza vaccine* (LAIV)—is intended for healthy people who are not pregnant and who are between 5 and 49 years of age.

Both types of vaccine work by causing your body to develop antibodies that provide some protection against influenza illness. Because these antibodies can take two or more weeks to develop after you get the vaccine, the CDC recommends getting vaccinated in October or November of each year, just ahead of the flu season (which can begin as early as October or as late as May).

Children between 6 and 23 months of age, adults over 65 years of age, and people living with chronic illness should get the flu vaccine every year.

Talk to a doctor before getting the flu vaccine if you or your child has had a serious reaction to a flu vaccine in the past or is:

- allergic to chicken eggs;
- sick with fever; and/or
- under 6 months of age.

The ingredients for the flu shot are usually grown inside of fertilized chicken eggs.

References

Hopkin, K. "Egg Beaters: Flu Vaccine Makers Look Beyond the Chicken Egg." *In Focus* Accessed January 16, 2008. www.sciam.com/article.cfm?articleID= 0005CA0F-B46F-101E-B40D83414B7F0000.

"Influenza Virus Vaccine." Center for Biologics Evaluation and Research. U.S. Food and Drug Administration. Accessed January 17, 2008. www.fda .gov/cber/flu/flu.htm.

"Key Facts About Influenza (Flu) Vaccine." Centers for Disease Control and Prevention. U.S. Department of Health & Human Services. Accessed January 18, 2008. www.cdc.gov/flu/protect/keyfacts.htm.

"Key Facts About Influenza and the Influenza Vaccine." Centers for Disease Control and Prevention. U.S. Department of Health & Human Services. Accessed January 9, 2008. www.cdc.gov/flu/keyfacts.htm.

What is the HPV vaccine, and who should get it?

The HPV (human papillomavirus) vaccine, named Gardasil, offers protection from the virus responsible for most cases of cervical cancer.

Cervical cancer is one of the leading causes of cancer death in women. Each year, cervical cancer strikes about 10,000 women and causes up to 4,000 deaths in the United States.

HPV is the most common sexually transmitted infection in the United States. It is responsible for most cases of cervical cancer as well as genital warts. A person who has HPV may not show any signs of the virus. Both men and women can get it and pass it along to their sexual partners without realizing it.

> The HPV vaccine is recommended for girls ages 11 to 12. It can stop cervical cancer before it even begins.

The HPV vaccine blocks two cancer-causing types of HPV. It is given as a series of three shots over the course of six months. Girls should be vaccinated well before they become sexually active. The vaccine is recommended for girls ages 11 to 12, but it can be given to girls as young as 9. It is also recommended for 13- to 26-year-old girls and women who have not yet received or completed the vaccine series.

> You should continue to have Pap tests to screen for cervical cancer regardless of whether you've gotten the HPV vaccine.

Women who are vaccinated could still develop cervical cancer for the following reasons:

- The vaccine protects against only two types of HPV that cause cervical cancer. There are about a dozen other types that also cause the disease.
- The vaccine doesn't protect women if they are already infected with one of the HPV types targeted by the vaccine.
- Some women may not get all three required doses of the vaccine (or they may not get them at the right time).

For these reasons, women should continue to have Pap tests to screen for cervical cancer regardless of whether they have gotten the HPV vaccine.

☞ For more information about HPV vaccines, visit the National Cancer Institute's "HPV Vaccines for Cervical Cancer" Web page at www.cancer.gov/cancertopics/hpv-vaccines.

References

"ACS Recommends HPV Vaccine but Cervical Cancer Screening Still Necessary." American Cancer Society. Accessed January 30, 2008. www.cancer.org/docroot/NWS/content/NWS_1_1x_ACS_Recommends_HPV_Vaccine.asp.
"Cervical Cancer Vaccine: Who Needs It, How It Works." Mayo Clinic. Accessed January 16, 2008. www.mayoclinic.com/print/cervical-cancer-vaccine/WO00120.
"HPV Vaccine Questions & Answers." Centers for Disease Control and Prevention. U.S. Department of Health & Human Services. Accessed January 13, 2008. www.cdc.gov/std/hpv/STDFact-HPV-vaccine.htm.
"Human Papillomavirus (HPV)." American Academy of Family Physicians. Accessed January 28, 2008. http://familydoctor.org/online/famdocen/home/common/sexinfections/sti/389.html.

Do I need shots before I travel?

When you travel to foreign countries, you may be exposed to certain illnesses that can be prevented with vaccines or medicine. **Before you travel, make sure you are up to date on all of the routine shots** (such as tetanus, polio, measles, and mumps). It's also a good idea to get the flu shot if you'll be traveling during flu season.

Visit your doctor at least two months before your trip. Your provider will let you know what shots or medicines you need. This decision is based on:

- the places you plan to visit;
- your age, medical history, and health; and
- your exposure risk.

You should also find out which countries require proof of vaccination before you can enter them.

☞ To find health information about specific countries (as well as which countries require proof of vaccination), visit wwwn.cdc.gov/travel/destinationList.aspx and click on the map.

Depending on where you travel, you might need vaccines against hepatitis A and hepatitis B, influenza, chickenpox, typhoid fever, yellow fever, meningitis, Japanese encephalitis, rabies, and other diseases. If you are going to a part of the world where malaria is common, such as Africa, Asia, and South America, you may need to take medicine to prevent malaria (a disease caused by a parasite that causes fever and flu-like illness).

After ensuring that you are up to date on your routine vaccinations, your doctor will tell you about the recommended vaccinations. These are not required, but you should get them to protect yourself and your family members from illnesses and to prevent infectious diseases from crossing borders. The only vaccine *required* by International Health Regulations is the yellow fever vaccination for travel to certain countries in sub-Saharan Africa and tropical South America.

☞ For up-to-date information about health and travel, visit the Centers for Disease Control and Prevention's Web site at http://wwwn.cdc.gov/travel/default.aspx or call the Traveler's Health Information Line at 1-877-FYI-TRIP.

If you are pregnant or breast-feeding, or if you will be traveling with infants or children, the Centers for Disease Control and Prevention's Web site (see the previous box) has detailed information for you.

Following are some tips for staying healthy while traveling:

- Eat steaming-hot, well-cooked food.
- Don't eat foods from street vendors.
- Don't eat unpasteurized dairy products or raw seafood.
- Peel fruits yourself.
- Drink bottled water or carbonated beverages.
- Avoid ice.
- Use bottled water to brush your teeth.
- Avoid swimming in freshwater lakes and streams.
- Use insect repellants that contain DEET.
- Use bed nets when you sleep in insect-infested areas.
- Avoid taking overcrowded transportation.
- Wear a safety belt and a helmet if you ride a motorcycle.
- Avoid driving at night or in unfamiliar areas.

Always take a first-aid kit when you travel. Table 2-8 lists items to include in your kit.

Table 2-8. Your travel first-aid kit
• Prescription medicines in their original containers • Medicine for diarrhea and upset stomach • Cough and cold medicines • Pain medicines • Decongestants and antihistamines for allergies • Antibiotic ointment, adhesive bandages, and hydrocortisone cream • Sunscreen and lip balm with an SPF of at least 15 • Motion sickness and antinausea medicine • Scissors, tweezers, nail clippers, pocket knife, thermometer, and mirror (remember, some of these items are not allowed in airplane carry-on bags)

References

"International Travel: Tips for Staying Healthy." American Academy of Family Physicians. Accessed January 10, 2008. http://familydoctor.org/online/famdocen/home/healthy/travel/311.html.

"Shots for Travel." *MD Consult Patient Education Handout.* USC School of Medicine Library, Columbia, SC. Accessed January 16, 2008. Keyword: travel immunization.

"What You Need to Know About Vaccinations and Travel: A Checklist." Centers for Disease Control and Prevention. U.S. Department of Health & Human Services. Accessed September 9, 2008. http://wwwn.cdc.gov/travel/contentVaccinations.aspx.

How often do I need to get a tetanus shot?

Three vaccines are given to prevent tetanus:

1. The Tdap vaccine is given to adolescents and adults.
2. The DTaP vaccine is given to children under seven.
3. The Td vaccine is given to adolescents and adults.

The Tdap and DTaP vaccines prevent tetanus (lockjaw), diphtheria, and pertussis (whooping cough). The Td vaccine prevents tetanus and diphtheria. Tetanus, diphtheria, and pertussis are serious diseases caused by bacteria.

Diphtheria

- Diphtheria is a throat infection that causes a thick covering in the back of the throat.
- Symptoms include fever, chills, hoarseness, and a barking cough.
- Diphtheria can lead to breathing problems, paralysis, heart failure, and death.

Tetanus

- Tetanus is a nervous system disease caused by bacteria found in the soil.
- Symptoms include painful muscle spasms all over the body and lockjaw (cannot open mouth or swallow).
- Tetanus can lead to heart failure, respiratory arrest, pneumonia, and death.

Pertussis

- Pertussis is a very contagious disease that causes violent, uncontrollable coughing.
- Symptoms include coughs that make breathing difficult, coughs with a high-pitched "whooping" sound, and diarrhea.
- Pertussis can lead to pneumonia, seizures, brain damage, and death.

☞ Keep track of how often you have vaccinations and booster shots. Use the form provided at this Web site to keep a record: www.1on1health.com/web/info/ vaccines/ english/d140002/Document.

Diphtheria and pertussis are spread from person to person. You can get tetanus from a rusty nail, dirty cuts, splinters, bug bites, and animal scratches. Your risk for developing tetanus increases if the wound involves soil or rusty metal.

☞ You should get a tetanus booster shot every ten years. To see the "Recommended Adult Immunization Schedule," visit www.cdc.gov/vaccines/recs/schedules/ adult-schedule.htm.

The DTaP vaccine is one of the recommended childhood immunizations, and most schools require children to have the vaccination.

Children typically start the series of five shots at age two months and finish the series when they are five years old. After receiving these first shots, everyone will need a booster shot for diphtheria and tetanus every ten years.

The Tdap and DTaP are relatively new vaccines. If you have never received a Tdap vaccine, your health care provider may recommend this shot to help prevent pertussis. You can get these shots from your health care provider or most local health departments.

If you did not have the tetanus shots as a child, you need to have a series of three shots. Afterward, you will need a Td booster shot every ten years.

Stiffness of the jaw and neck are the first symptoms of tetanus. Symptoms usually start to appear seven days after an injury, but symptoms may starts as early as three days or as late as three weeks. **If you suspect tetanus, seek help immediately.** It is best to receive treatment within three days of the injury.

References

"Diphtheria Tetanus & Pertussis Vaccines: What You Need to Know." Centers for Disease Control and Prevention. U.S. Department of Health & Human Services. Accessed January 12, 2008. www.cdc.gov/vaccines/pubs/vis/downloads/vis-dtap.pdf.

"Do I Need a Tetanus Shot?" American College of Emergency Physicians. Accessed January 16, 2008. www.acep.org/webportal/PatientsConsumers/HealthSubjectsByTopic/Immunization/Feat.

"Tetanus, Diphtheria Pertussis (Tdap) Vaccine: What You Need to Know." Centers for Disease Control and Prevention. U.S. Department of Health & Human Services. Accessed January 14, 2008. www.cdc.gov/vaccines/pubs/vis/downloads/vis-tdap.pdf.

Who should get a pneumonia vaccine?

Pneumonia is an infection in the lungs, and it is spread from person to person. It is caused by a variety of bacteria and viruses. Pneumonia affects around 500,000 people each year. The most common type of pneumonia is called *pneumococcal pneumonia.* Two kinds of vaccines are used to prevent pneumococcal disease: the pneumococcal conjugate vaccine and the pneumococcal polysaccharide vaccine. Bacteremia (blood infection) and meningitis (infection of the covering of the brain and spinal cord) are examples of other pneumococcal diseases that these vaccines help prevent. Side effects and severe reactions to these vaccines are rare. You can get these shots from your health care provider or most local health departments.

Pneumococcal conjugate vaccine

This vaccine is designed for young children. Children under two years of age should receive four doses of the vaccine spread out over time. This vaccine is part of the "Recommended Childhood Immunization Schedule" (available at www.cdc.gov/vaccines/recs/schedules/child-schedule.htm). It may also help prevent ear infections and is recommended for children under five who are at a higher risk for getting serious infections.

Pneumococcal polysaccharide vaccine

This vaccine is recommended for all adults 65 years of age and older. The protection from the vaccine lasts about six years. Six years after the first dose, individuals at a high risk for getting serious infections should get another shot. For example, elderly people may need to be revaccinated because the protective value of the shot may be lost at a faster rate in this age group. More than two shots is not recommended.

Another way to help prevent pneumonia is to get a flu shot each fall. The same viruses that cause the flu (influenza) can also lead to pneumonia.

Who is at a higher risk for pneumonia?

- Children under 2
- Adults 65 and over
- People in long-term care facilities
- Alaskan Natives
- Native Americans
- Individuals with certain medical conditions:
  - Chronic heart, lung, or liver diseases
  - Diabetes
  - Lymphoma

- Leukemia
- Cancer treated with X-rays or medicine
- Conditions requiring long-term steroid treatment
- Sickle cell anemia
- HIV infection or AIDS
- Bone marrow or organ transplantation
- Damaged spleen or no spleen
- Kidney failure
- Conditions requiring a medication that lowers resistance to infection

What is walking pneumonia? This is a weaker form of pneumonia that does not require hospitalization or bed rest.

References

"Pneumococcal Conjugate Vaccine: What You Need to Know." Centers for Disease Control and Prevention. U.S. Department of Health & Human Services. Accessed January 5, 2008. www.cdc.gov/vaccines/pubs/vis/downloads/vis-PneumoConjugate.pdf.

"Pneumococcal Pneumonia Shot." *MD Consult Patient Education Handout.* USC School of Medicine Library, Columbia, SC. Accessed January 5, 2008. Keyword: pneumonia.

"Pneumococcal Polysaccharide Vaccine: What You Need to Know." Centers for Disease Control and Prevention. U.S. Department of Health and Human Services. Accessed January 4, 2008. www.cdc.gov/vaccines/pubs/vis/downloads/vis-ppv.pdf.

"Pneumonia." *MD Consult Patient Education Handout.* USC School of Medicine Library, Columbia, SC. Accessed January 8, 2008. Keyword: pneumonia.

ASK THE EXPERTS

Following is a list of health care professionals who can help you answer more in-depth questions related to issues discussed in this chapter. A good starting point would be your primary care physician (your family physician, internist, pediatrician, or nurse practitioner). From there, he or she might recommend that you visit with other medical specialists or health care professionals. Each one has received specialized training in his or her area of expertise. *(See the Glossary of Experts for descriptions, online directories, and credentialing information.)*

- Cardiologists
- Dentists
- Dental hygienists
- Family physicians
- Fitness experts
- Geriatricians
- Infectious disease specialists
- Internists
- Lactation consultants
- Neurologists
- Nurse practitioners
- Nurses (RNs)
- Nutritionists
- Obstetricians and gynecologists (OB/GYNs)
- Occupational therapists
- Ophthalmologists
- Opticians
- Optometrists
- Pediatricians
- Periodontists
- Pharmacists
- Phlebotomists
- Physiatrists
- Physical therapists
- Psychiatrists
- Psychologists
- Rheumatologists
- Social workers
- Urologists

3

Nutrition and Fitness

Many people come to the library looking for information on how to maintain a healthy lifestyle. They are often frustrated by conflicting information they've gotten from the media. Our society is constantly being bombarded with advertisements about the best new diets, the most effective exercise plans, and the most recently developed miracle-inducing vitamin supplements. It's no wonder that people are confused. Everywhere you turn it seems that you're being told something different about health and fitness. What is truth, and what is fiction? In this chapter we will answer some of the most commonly asked questions about nutrition and fitness.

NUTRITION AND EXERCISE

I want to lose one pound per week. How should I do this?

When it comes to weight loss, cutting calories is the key. Calories are the energy in food that keeps your body functioning. Carbohydrates, fats, and proteins all contain calories and are the main energy sources for your body. The calories you eat are either converted to physical energy or stored within your body as fat. Unless you use these stored calories, this fat remains in your body.

If you eat more calories than you burn, you gain weight. If you burn more calories than you eat, you lose weight. One pound of body fat equals about 3,500 calories. To lose one pound per week, you'll need to reduce calories by 500 per day (500 calories × 7 days = 3,500 calories).

Following are some tips for cutting calories:

- **Combine eating less with exercise.** Eat 250 calories less per day AND exercise enough to burn 250 calories (for example, walking briskly for 45 minutes burns nearly 250 calories).
- **Choose lower calorie foods.** Drink skim milk instead of whole milk. Drink water or diet soda instead of regular soft drinks. Eat an extra serving of vegetables instead of an extra serving of meat.
- **Reduce portion sizes.** Take slightly less food than you think you'll eat. Be sure to put your food on a plate so you can see how much you're eating.
- **Check food labels.** The "Nutrition Facts" will tell you how many servings are in a package along with calories per serving. You might discover that you're eating more servings than you think.
- **Don't feel the need to clean your plate.** Eat slowly, and stop eating when you start to feel full.

Try cutting out one or two high-calorie items per day. Table 3-1 lists high-calorie foods and drinks you might skip.

Table 3-1. High-calorie foods and drinks

Foods/drinks	Calories
Cappuccino with regular milk and syrup (14 oz)	160
1 bottle (16 oz) of soft drink	202
1 large slice of thick-crust pepperoni pizza	301
1 large glazed doughnut	302
1 snack bag (3 oz) of nacho-flavored tortilla chips	424
Starbucks Caramel Frappuccino (16 oz) with whipped cream	430
Poppy seed muffin	495
French fries (large order)	500
2 cups chocolate ice cream	572

Remember that managing your calorie intake is only part of a successful weight management plan. Combining regular physical activity with healthy eating will help you achieve a healthy weight.

To lose one pound per week, you'll need to reduce calories by 500 per day.

References

"Counting Calories: Getting Back to Weight-Loss Basics." Mayo Clinic. Accessed November 17, 2007. www.mayoclinic.com/health/calories/WT00011.

Hensrud, D., ed. *Mayo Clinic Healthy Weight for Everybody*. Rochester, MN: Mayo Clinic, 2005.

I know I should exercise 30 minutes a day. Do I have to do it all at once?

Many people find it difficult to fit 30 minutes of exercise a day into their busy schedules. The good news is that you can exercise throughout the day to add up to 30 minutes (or more)! Any exercise, even in small amounts, can help you reach your fitness goals.

Try exercising for ten minutes, three times a day. Or try exercising for five minutes, six times a day. Turn your everyday activities into a fitness plan! It's easier to stick to a fitness program that includes things you have to do anyway. Here are some strategies:

- Walk for ten minutes during your lunch hour or during your break.
- Get up a little earlier in the mornings and go for a short walk.
- Take the stairs instead of the elevator.
- Park at the far end of a shopping center and walk to the store.
- While your child is at soccer practice, walk or jog around the field.
- Vacuum the house, rake the yard, or push a manual lawn mower.
- Swim laps in the community pool.
- Play football in the yard with your kids.
- Ride bikes with your kids.
- At work, get up often to stretch and walk around.
- Do squats while on the phone at work or at home.

To help you stick to your fitness plan, try to develop a schedule and stay with it. Keep an activity log so you can track how much exercise you're doing throughout the day. If you can get up to 30 minutes daily, you're well on your way to getting fit.

References

Hensrud, D., ed. *Mayo Clinic Healthy Weight for Everybody*. Rochester, MN: Mayo Clinic, 2005.
"Tips to Help You Get Active." WIN: Weight-Control Information Network. National Institute of Diabetes and Digestive and Kidney Diseases. Accessed November 10, 2007. http://win.niddk.nih.gov/publications/tips.htm.

What is the body mass index? How does it relate to chronic diseases?

Body mass index (BMI) is a value based on height and weight that is used to estimate whether a person is at a healthy weight. Values that indicate a healthy weight range from 18.5 to 24.9.

Excess weight strains the heart and can lead to serious health problems, such as heart disease, high blood pressure, kidney disease, type 2 diabetes, sleep apnea, varicose veins, and other chronic conditions. The BMI is a fairly simple way to evaluate a person's degree of excess weight.

It is important to remember that your BMI is not a perfect tool; it is only one of many factors used to predict your risk for certain diseases. Your doctor will conduct a complete medical evaluation before deciding whether you are at risk for certain chronic diseases related to being overweight. The medical evaluation should include a careful medical history, a physical exam (including calculation of your BMI and measurement of your waist circumference), and laboratory tests.

Here are the steps to calculate your BMI:

- Multiply your weight in pounds by 703.
- Divide that answer by your height in inches.
- Divide that answer again by your height in inches.
- Use Table 3-2 to see what category you fall into.

☞ To use an online BMI calculator, visit www.nhlbisupport.com/bmi.

Table 3-2. Body mass index (BMI) categories

BMI	Category
Below 18.5	Underweight
18.5–24.9	Healthy
25.0–29.9	Overweight
30.0–39.9	Obese
Over 40	Morbidly obese

BMI does not measure body fat. Instead, it *correlates* with body fat. The relation between body fat and BMI differs with age and gender. For example, women are more likely to have a higher percentage of body fat than men who have the same BMI.

BMI is not always an accurate way to determine whether you need to lose weight. For example, a body builder may have a high BMI because muscle weighs more than fat. It is also sometimes better for elderly people to have a BMI between 25 and 27 to protect against osteoporosis.

Do not use the BMI calculator for children. For children 2 to 20 years of age, a doctor will use BMI differently. If you suspect your child is overweight, talk to your child's doctor.

(For more information, see "Why should I worry about being overweight?" in Chapter 2.)

References

"AGA Guide: Obesity." American Gastroenterological Association. UpToDate. USC School of Medicine Library, Columbia, SC. Accessed November 9, 2007. Keyword: obesity.

"Body Mass Index." *MedlinePlus Medical Encyclopedia.* U.S. National Library of Medicine. Accessed November 10, 2007. www.nlm.nih.gov/medlineplus/ency/article/007196.htm.

Bray, G. "Clinical Evaluation of the Overweight Adult." UpToDate. USC School of Medicine Library, Columbia, SC. Accessed November 11, 2007. Keyword: obesity.

Hensrud, D., ed. *Mayo Clinic Healthy Weight for Everybody.* Rochester, MN: Mayo Clinic, 2005.

Is it better to work out in the morning or at night?

Experts disagree on when is the best time to exercise. Some believe that an early morning workout, before breakfast, can raise metabolism. This may help a person burn more fat during and after the exercise. Others point out that an evening workout can fight the stress of a work day. So which is the best time to exercise? Recent research suggests neither. In terms of performance and safety, the best time to work out may be in the late afternoon, between 2 p.m. and 4 p.m.

During the late afternoon the body's temperature is at its highest. Moreover, the muscles are more flexible. Working out at this time may allow for more powerful exercise sessions. It also decreases your chance of injury. Still, experts agree that some exercise, regardless of when it's done, is better than no exercise.

Exercise is beneficial at *any* time of day.

A better question may be *how to exercise*. Try to shoot for the following combination of activities, spread throughout the week:

- Two 20-minute sessions to build strength, such as weight lifting
- Three 30-minute sessions to build endurance, such as calisthenics
- Three 20-minute sessions involving aerobic activity, such as swimming, jogging, or brisk walking
- Daily flexibility sessions of between 10 and 12 minutes, which can be included after a warm-up or during a cool-down session
- Cool-down sessions of 5 to 10 minutes after a strenuous workout, which can be any low-level exercise, like slow walking or stretching

It may take a while to build up to these levels. And remember, you can always break up the sessions into small groups. Instead of doing 30 minutes of endurance activity, you can always do two 15-minute sessions. Whether you choose to exercise in the morning, the evening, or the late afternoon, the important thing is to increase your physical activity and make it a regular habit. For this reason, the best time of day to exercise is whenever you *will* exercise.

References

"Exercise: A Healthy Habit to Start and Keep." American Academy of Family Physicians. Accessed November 23, 2007. http://familydoctor.org/059.xml.

"Fit Facts: The Best Time to Exercise." American Council on Exercise. Accessed November 12, 2007. www.acefitness.org/fitfacts/fitfacts_display.aspx?itemid=53.

"Fitness Fundamentals: Guidelines for Personal Exercise Programs." The President's Council on Physical Fitness and Sports. Accessed November 13, 2007. www.fitness.gov/fitness.htm.

"Fitting in Fitness: Finding Time for Physical Activity." Mayo Clinic. Accessed November 8, 2007. http://mayoclinic.com/health/fitness/HQ01217_D.

Smith, S. "Experts Disagree on Ideal Time of Day to Exercise." CNN (Cable News Network). Accessed November 15, 2007. www.cnn.com/2003/HEALTH/diet.fitness/05/27/exercise.time/index.html.

I do aerobic exercise. Do I also need to do strength training?

Aerobic exercise is excellent for increasing endurance and strengthening the heart. However, it does not build upper body strength or tone muscles. By itself, aerobic exercise may not be the best solution for permanent weight loss. Aerobic exercise should be balanced with strength training for overall health and fitness.

Strength training exercises will help you:

- build muscle strength while burning fat—when your muscles are toned, your body burns fat more easily because your metabolism increases;
- develop strong bones—by stressing your bones, strength training increases bone density and reduces the risk of osteoporosis;
- reduce your risk of injury—building muscle helps protect your joints from injury;
- maintain flexibility and balance—building muscle helps maintain your flexibility;
- lower your risk for heart disease—strength training lowers the low-density lipoprotein (LDL, the so-called bad) cholesterol level;
- boost your stamina—as you grow stronger, you won't get tired as easily;
- improve your emotional well-being—strength training can improve your body image, boost your self-confidence, and reduce your risk of depression;

- get a better night's sleep—people who do strength training regularly are less likely to suffer from insomnia.

Muscle mass naturally diminishes with age. If you don't replace this muscle loss, you'll increase fat. Strength training is the only form of exercise that can slow down and even reverse the decline in muscle mass, bone density, and strength that comes with aging.

> If you are at risk for heart disease, check with your doctor before beginning strength exercises.

Equipment

The equipment you need to strengthen your muscles doesn't have to cost anything. You can, of course, join a gym or fitness center that offers various resistance machines and weights. But any heavy object—such as a plastic bottle filled with water or sand—that can be held in the hand can serve as a weight. Two 16-ounce cans duct-taped together makes a handy two-pound weight! Resistance bands are also inexpensive, portable, and effective.

Getting started

First, check with your doctor to be sure it's okay for you to start strength training. Once you have the go-ahead, remember to do the following:

- **Warm up and cool down.** Do five to ten minutes of stretching and gentle aerobic activity before and after your strength training session.
- **Start slowly.** Lifting weights, if done improperly, can cause serious injury. Choose a weight or resistance level heavy enough to tire your muscles after 12 repetitions. With proper weight or resistance, you can build muscle with just one set of 12 repetitions. When you can easily do 12 more repetitions, increase the weight or resistance.
- **Rest your muscles.** To give your muscles time to recover, wait 48 hours before working out the same muscle group.
- **Stop if you feel pain.** Mild muscle soreness is normal, but a sharp pain and swollen joints are signs that you have overdone it.

Seeing the results

If you work out 20 to 30 minutes two to three times per week, you will see improvement in your strength and stamina in just a few weeks.

With a regular strength training program, you can reduce your body fat, increase your lean muscle mass, and burn calories more efficiently.

References

"Exercise." *Well-Connected In-Depth Reports, No. 29.* New York: Nidus Information Services, 2006.

Mullen, D. "Strength Training for Weight Loss Success." Spine Universe. Accessed November 13, 2007. www.spineuniverse.com/displayarticle.php/article887.html.

"Strength Training: Get Stronger, Leaner and Healthier." Mayo Clinic. Accessed November 4, 2007. www.mayoclinic.com/health/strength-training/HQ01710.

"Weight-Training and Weight-Lifting Safety." American Academy of Family Physicians. Accessed November 18, 2007. http://familydoctor.org/198.xml.

Should I use heat or cold on my sore muscles and injuries?

It is sometimes confusing whether to use ice packs or warm compresses for pain. The following information can help you make this decision:

- Cold should be used in the first 48 hours after an acute injury, such as a newly sprained ankle or a pulled muscle. Cold reduces inflammation and helps prevent swelling. It also acts as a local anesthetic and thus relieves pain.
- Heat treatments are best for chronic pain such as from tight muscles or a sore back. Heat brings more blood to the area where it is applied and thus reduces joint stiffness and muscle spasms.
- You can alternate heat and cold for soft tissue damage or stretched ligaments (such as an ankle sprain). Apply cold for the first 48 hours. Then apply warmth to help restore range of motion.
- As always, speak with a health care professional for additional advice. Most clinics have nursing help lines you can call with questions about injuries.

Cold should be applied in the first 48 hours after an injury.

Types of cold packs

Ice towel:

1. Dampen a towel with cold water.
2. Fold the towel and place it in a plastic, sealable bag.
3. Place the bag in the freezer for 15 minutes.
4. Remove the bag from the freezer, and apply it to the injury.
5. Apply it for 15 minutes, three to four times daily.

Ice pack/cold compress:

1. Put ice in a plastic, sealable bag.
2. Fill the bag partially with water.
3. Seal the bag, squeezing the air out of it.
4. Wrap the bag in a damp towel, and apply it to the injury.
5. Apply it for 15 minutes, three to four times daily.

Types of warm packs

Warm towel:

1. Dampen a towel with warm water. Be sure the water is not scalding.
2. Apply it to the sore area for no longer than 15 to 20 minutes.

Heating pad:

1. Protect your skin from coming in contact with any type of heating pad.
2. Do not apply heat pads to broken skin.
3. Check your skin often during the treatment to avoid burns.
4. Do not apply pressure.
5. Do not apply for longer than recommended on the heating pad instructions.

Cautions

- It is risky to apply any of these treatments without first consulting your doctor.
- Cold treatments can cause skin damage, skin rash, and pain (*and sometimes even frostbite*). Be very careful with gel packs, which can

be excessively cold. Do not apply ice directly to the skin. Put a towel over the skin for protection. Do not apply ice for more than 20 minutes at a time.

- Heat treatments can cause burns.
- Do NOT use analgesic cream at the same time as the hot/cold treatment. This can cause rash or chemical burns. Wash the cream off before applying hot/cold packs.

References

Aiello, D. "The Hot and the Cold of It." Rehab Management. Accessed November 23, 2007. www.rehabpub.com/features/62004/2.asp.

Davis, M., P. Davis, and D. Ross, eds. *Expert Guide to Sports Medicine*. Philadelphia: American College of Physicians, 2005.

"Hot vs. Cold Treatment." The Gym Sports Resource Network. Accessed November 2, 2007. www.usgyms.net/hot_vs_cold.htm.

"Ice Packs vs. Warm Compresses for Pain." Oregon Health & Science University. Accessed November 1, 2007. www.ohsu.edu/health/health-topics/topic .cfm?id=10318&parent=11981.

Does eating before bedtime cause weight gain?

No, it does not matter what time you eat. The total number of calories you eat during the whole day and the amount of exercise you get will determine whether you gain weight. If you eat too many calories, your body will store the extra calories as fat.

Eating before bedtime does not cause weight gain. You gain weight when you eat more calories than you burn in an entire day.

Late-night snacking can be a problem for those who have already eaten their total number of calories before the end of the day. Consider how many calories you have eaten that day before you snack at night.

If you have a digestive disease, such as indigestion or gastro-esophageal reflux disease (GERD), you should avoid food near bedtime. To help your body digest food, you should stop eating three hours before bed and remain upright for a few hours after a meal.

Don't snack while watching TV or surfing the Internet at night. You can get distracted and may end up overeating.

Reference

"Tips to Help You Get Active." WIN: Weight-Control Information Network. National Institute of Diabetes and Digestive and Kidney Diseases. Accessed November 23, 2007. http://win.niddk.nih.gov/publications/tips.htm.

Is breakfast really the most important meal of the day?

Studies show that eating breakfast is good for your health. Not only does breakfast refuel your body and jump-start your day, it has a lot of other benefits. People who eat a healthy breakfast are more likely to:

- have better concentration in the morning;
- have more strength and endurance;
- consume more vitamins and minerals and less fat and cholesterol;
- control their weight; and
- have a lower cholesterol level, which reduces the risk of heart disease.

Breakfast is especially important for children and teenagers. If kids eat breakfast, they will learn better because they will be better able to concentrate on school work. They will also have the energy for the morning's activities.

Eating a healthy breakfast is a big key to weight loss.

If you think skipping breakfast will help you lose weight, think again. Studies show that people who skip breakfast actually tend to eat more throughout the rest of the day. Eating a healthy breakfast is a big key to weight loss because it boosts your metabolism, which helps burn fat for weight loss.

To eat a healthy breakfast each day, choose one item from at least three of the following food groups:

- Fruits and vegetables: apples, bananas, cantaloupe, grapes, raisins, carrots, green peppers, broccoli, salsa, 100 percent juice with no added sugar

- Grains: hot or cold whole-grain cereals, whole-grain muffins, bagels, crackers, whole-grain toast
- Dairy: skim milk, low-fat yogurt, low-fat cheese
- Protein: peanut butter, hard-boiled eggs, beans, lean slices of meat, water-packed tuna

Following are some tips for making breakfast successful:

- Start making breakfast the night before. Mix juice, slice fruit, or boil some eggs.
- Get up ten minutes earlier to give yourself time to eat breakfast. Kids need a little extra time to wake up before they are hungry for breakfast.
- Stock your kitchen with easy breakfast foods.

References

"Breakfast: Why Is It So Important?" Mayo Clinic. Accessed November 19, 2007. www.mayoclinic.com/print/food-and-nutrition/AN01119.

Davis, J. "Lose Weight: Eat Breakfast." WebMD. Accessed November 8, 2007. www.webmd.com/diet/features/lose-weight-eat-breakfast.

Duyff, R. *American Dietetic Association Complete Food and Nutrition Guide*, 3rd ed. New York: John Wiley & Sons, 2006.

"Healthy Breakfast: The Best Way to Begin Your Day." Mayo Clinic. Accessed November 23, 2007. www.mayoclinic.com/health/food-and-nutrition/NU00197.

"Why Breakfast?" *Nibbles for Health 6: Nutrition Newsletters for Parents of Young Children*. USDA, Food and Nutrition Service. Accessed November 11, 2007. www.fns.usda.gov/tn/Resources/Nibbles/why_breakfast.pdf.

What are the pros and cons of a low-carbohydrate diet?

There is a great deal of debate about whether or not "low-carb" diets are safe and effective. On the plus side, low-carb diets, which are usually higher in protein and fats, may:

- lower your saturated fat levels;
- help you lose more weight quickly;
- increase your good cholesterol (high-density lipoprotein) levels; and/or
- somewhat decrease your chance of developing coronary heart disease.

On the negative side, low-carb diets may:

- cause bad breath, diarrhea, constipation, and other digestive issues;
- make you dizzy, cause headaches, and/or affect your sleep;
- restrict your vitamin and mineral intake; and/or
- restrict your consumption of vegetables and fruit, which have been associated with decreases in certain kinds of cancer, diabetes, and other health conditions.

Keep a daily journal of what you eat. This will help you track your eating habits over a long period.

Overall, recent research has determined that low-carb, high-protein/high-fat diets may be safe in both the short and long term. In some cases, diets rich in fats and proteins may offer some health benefits as well. Still, many nutritionists believe that a diet rich in complex carbohydrates, such as whole-grain products, potatoes, and beans, may work just as well as low-carb diets in the long run. Moreover, diets rich in complex carbohydrates may provide more energy and nutrients than high-protein/low-carb fad diets. In the end it comes down to calories. A well-balanced diet combined with physical activity is the healthiest option for most people. To be sure, talk to your doctor.

☞ To learn more about healthy diet, visit the U.S. Department of Agriculture's Web site devoted to the food pyramid at www.mypyramid.gov.

References

"Change of Heart: No Link Between Low-Carb Diet and Heart Risk." Research Behind the News. *Journal of the American Dietetic Association*. USC School of Medicine Library, Columbia, SC. Accessed November 19, 2007.

"Is a Low-Carbohydrate Diet Right for Me?" *AAFP News & Publications*. American Academy of Family Physicians. Accessed November 12, 2007. www.aafp.org/afp/20060601/1951ph.html.

"Low-Carb Diet Better for Lipids than Low-Fat, High-Carb Diet." *This Week in Medicine*. USC School of Medicine Library, Columbia, SC. Accessed November 24, 2007.

Sharkey, B. and S. Gaskill. *Fitness and Health*, 6th ed. Champaign, IL: Human Kinetics, 2006.

"Weight Loss Diets." *MD Consult Patient Education Handout*. MD Consult. USC School of Medicine Library, Columbia, SC. Accessed on November 25, 2007. Keyword: diets.

VITAMINS AND SUPPLEMENTS

Which is better, getting your vitamins from food or from taking supplements?

The best way to get all of the vitamins you need is to eat a variety of healthy foods. A healthy diet includes fruits, vegetables, whole grains, and fiber.

Most people get all of the vitamins they need from food. Your doctor may suggest a multivitamin if you fall into one of these categories:

- Pregnant and breast-feeding women
- People with chewing or swallowing problems
- Menopausal women
- People with acute and chronic health problems
- Vegetarians
- People taking a medication that affects the way their body absorbs nutrients
- Alcoholics
- People who are lactose intolerant
- People who are unable or unwilling to consume a variety of foods

If you want to take a multivitamin or a specific supplement, talk to your doctor or to a registered dietician. A multivitamin can be used as a safety net or to complement your diet. Some people think that the more vitamins they get, the healthier they will be. This is not true. You should not try to get more than the recommended daily allowance of vitamins and minerals. When selecting a supplement, avoid products that are described as "megadoses" or "superpotency" on the labels. Some side effects of excessive amounts of vitamins are fatigue, diarrhea, and hair loss. More serious side effects include kidney stones, liver or nerve damage, birth defects, and even death.

References

Duyff, R. *American Dietetic Association Complete Food and Nutrition Guide*, 3rd ed. New York: John Wiley & Sons, 2006.

Moore, C. "Should Everyone over Age 75 Take a Multivitamin?" Cleveland Clinic. Accessed November 7, 2007. www.clevelandclinic.org/health /health-info/docs/3500/3523.asp?index=11776.

Do antioxidants prevent disease and slow the aging process?

Antioxidants do not magically reverse the aging process, but eating foods rich with antioxidants may reduce your risk of diseases related to aging. Antioxidants may help prevent macular degeneration, cataracts, cancer, cardiovascular disease, cognitive impairment, Alzheimer's disease, osteoporosis, cystic fibrosis, and immune dysfunction. Right now, there is not enough proof to support taking antioxidants in pill form to prevent diseases. Current scientific evidence suggests getting antioxidants from the foods you eat instead of by supplements. Talk to your doctor before you start taking antioxidant supplements. Your doctor may recommend supplements if you do not get enough of the nutrients you need from food.

Some supplemental antioxidants cause harm. Smokers taking beta-carotene may increase their risk of lung cancer.

Vitamins C, E, and A, beta-carotene, lycopene, and selenium are examples of antioxidants. Eating a variety of fruits and vegetables (see Table 3-3) is the best way to include antioxidants in your diet.

References

"Anti-Aging Therapies: Too Good to Be True?" Mayo Clinic. Accessed November 24, 2007. www.mayoclinic.com/health/anti-aging/HQ00233.

"Antioxidant Vitamins." American Heart Association. Accessed November 5, 2007. www.americanheart.org/presenter.jhtml?identifier=4452.

Duyff, R. American Dietetic Association Complete Food and Nutrition Guide, 3rd ed. New York: John Wiley & Sons, 2006.

"Lycopene: An Antioxidant for Good Health." American Dietetic Association. Accessed November 19, 2007. www.eatright.org/cps/rde/xchg/SID-5303FFEA-A120B9BE/ada/hs.xsl/nutrition_5328_ENU_HTML.htm.

"USDA National Nutrient Database for Standard Reference, Release 18." United States Department of Agriculture. Accessed November 13, 2007. www.ars.usda.gov/Services/docs.htm?docid=9673.

Table 3-3. Sources of antioxidant vitamins and minerals

Vitamins/minerals	Sources
Vitamin A	Beef liver, sweet potato, carrots, kale, mango, turnip greens, spinach
Beta-carotene	Broccoli, peas, pumpkin pie, cherries, mango, soy milk, asparagus
Vitamin C	Orange juice, peppers, grapefruit juice, strawberries, cantaloupe, cranberry juice, broccoli
Vitamin E	Sunflower seeds, almonds, wheat germ, peanut butter, vegetable oil, turnip greens, spinach
Lycopene	Tomato soup, spaghetti sauce, canned tomatoes, fresh tomatoes, watermelon, grapefruit, ketchup
Selenium	Brazil nuts, mixed nuts, fortified cereals, fish, turkey, bread stuffing, couscous

ALCOHOL AND STIMULANTS

How much coffee is too much?

Coffee is one of the most popular drinks in world. It also is one of the most debated. One recent study found that drinking filtered coffee does not increase your chance of heart disease. Another study found that two or more cups of coffee can increase some people's chances of heart disease. Other studies have reported coffee drinking as possibly offering protection against type 2 diabetes and colon cancer. So, is it healthy or dangerous? The answer may be both, and it may be the amount you are consuming that determines whether those cups of Java are good or bad for you.

Like red wine, coffee contains an ingredient called *phenol*, which may help maintain good cholesterol levels. On the other hand, unfiltered coffee can contain an ingredient called *cafestol*, which may raise your cholesterol levels. For this reason, it may be better to stick with filtered coffee or to at least limit your intake of unfiltered varieties, including espresso, Turkish coffee, and French pressed.

Too much caffeine can be unhealthy.

Another factor to consider is the amount of caffeine you consume. Because of its caffeine, coffee may affect your blood pressure. In moderate amounts this appears to pose no real danger for those with normal blood pressure. However, it may noticeably affect the health of those who consume excessive amounts of caffeine from coffee. Excessive caffeine can cause the following symptoms:

- Irritability
- Sleeplessness and anxiety
- Nausea and diarrhea

For this reason, a moderate amount of coffee a day—between two and three cups—is probably a safe bet. But experts warn that if you are sensitive to caffeine, under a great deal of stress, or suffer from hypertension, it may be best to avoid caffeine altogether.

Table 3-4 lists the amounts of caffeine contained in different types of coffee drinks.

Table 3-4. Caffeine content of different types of coffee drinks

Type of coffee drink	Caffeine (mg)
Plain brewed (8 oz)	135
Instant (8 oz)	95
Espresso (1 oz)	30–50
Decaffeinated, brewed (8 oz)	5
Decaffeinated, instant (8 oz)	3
Starbuck's Coffee Grande (16 oz)	259

Decaffeinated coffee still contains small amounts of caffeine.

References

"Caffeine Content of Common Beverages." Mayo Clinic. Accessed November 3, 2007. www.mayoclinic.com/health/caffeine/AN01211.
"Caffeine: How Much Is Too Much?" Mayo Clinic. Accessed on November 16, 2007. www.mayoclinic.com/health/caffeine/NU00600.
"Coffee: Does It Offer Health Benefits?" Mayo Clinic. Accessed November 18, 2007. www.mayoclinic.com/health/coffee-and-health/AN01354.
"Heart Healthy Diet: What Are the Components of a Heart Healthy Diet?" *MD Consult Patient Education Handout.* USC School of Medicine Library, Columbia, SC. Accessed November 14, 2007. Keyword: healthy diet.
"Prospective Cohort Study of Coffee Consumption and Coronary Heart Disease in Men and Women." Hurst's The Heart. AccessMedicine. USC School of Medicine Library, Columbia, SC. Accessed November 8, 2007. Path: coffee; heart disease.

Can alcohol be good for you?

Recent research has discovered that moderate alcohol use may be good for us after all. Drinking small amounts of alcohol a day may lower your risk for heart disease. Here are some theories as to why this may be:

- It may help with recovery after a heart attack.
- It may prevent the coronary arteries from constricting.
- It may help prevent clotting within already narrow arteries.
- It may raise the levels of good cholesterol.

In particular, red wine, which contains potential antioxidants, is being looked at closely to see if it may offer some protection from coronary heart disease.

(See Chapter 1 for more information about heart disease.)

Pregnant women should never consume alcohol due to the increased chance of birth defects.

Moderation is key. Too much alcohol has been shown to affect your health in the following ways:

- Raising the levels of stomach acid
- Preventing good sleep
- Causing gout, which is a buildup of uric acid in your joints
- Raising blood pressure
- Worsening diabetes by increasing your blood sugar levels
- Increasing your chances for different types of cancer
- Damaging your liver

Too much alcohol also, of course, impairs your judgment and slows your reaction time, which is why it is illegal to drive while intoxicated. For all of these reasons, limiting consumption to one to two drinks a day is probably safe for most people. This does not mean that you can save up your drinks until Friday night and binge all seven at one time. The benefits you may gain during the week will easily be negated by the excessive drinking. In fact, according to the American Heart Association, there are better ways to gain the same benefits without drinking, including becoming more physically active, eating a healthy diet, and lowering your blood pressure and cholesterol levels. For this reason, before adding alcohol into your diet, definitely talk to your doctor and consider other ways to get the same health benefits without the alcohol.

About how much is one drink?
One can of beer
One glass of wine
A 1.5-ounce shot of liquor

References

"Alcohol and Coronary Heart Disease." National Institute on Alcohol Abuse and Alcoholism. Accessed November 2, 2007. http://pubs.niaaa.nih.gov/publications/aa45.htm.

"Alcohol: Effects on Health." *MD Consult Patient Education Handout.* USC School of Medicine Library, Columbia, SC. Accessed November 13, 2007. Keyword: alcohol.

"Alcoholism." *MD Consult Patient Education Handout.* USC School of Medicine Library, Columbia, SC. Accessed November 13, 2007. Keyword: alcoholism.

"Alcohol, Wine and Cardiovascular Disease." American Heart Association. Accessed November 7, 2007. www.americanheart.org/presenter.jhtml? identifier=4422.

Duyff, R. *American Dietetic Association Complete Food and Nutrition Guide*, 3rd ed. New York: John Wiley & Sons, 2006.

Is it possible to be allergic to alcohol?

Before answering this question, it is necessary to distinguish an allergic reaction from a substance intolerance. In an allergic reaction, the body's immune system reacts to a substance that usually is not dangerous by itself. The allergic reaction can occur immediately, or even days later, as with poison ivy. An intolerance, however, may be caused by the side effects of a substance, as with some medicines. In these instances you may be able to continue exposure to the substance. With true allergens, however, avoiding the substance can be life-saving.

With all this in mind, alcohol allergies are rare. Most of the time when people have allergic reactions to alcohol it is actually the preservatives or other additives in the beer or wine that their immune systems are reacting to. Some of the most common additives that people react to are the following:

- Sulfites, commonly used to preserve wines
- Yeast in beer
- Histamines in wines
- The wheat or rye in beer

Between 47 and 85 percent of Asians have an intolerance to alcohol compared with non-Asians, who have intolerance rates of 3 to 29 percent.

When reactions to alcohol are not caused by true allergies to preservatives and additives, the drinker may in fact have an intolerance for alcohol. In such cases, the drinkers may experience a reddening of the face and neck called *flushing*. As opposed to a true allergic reaction, this reddening is caused by the inability to break down alcohol completely. People who have alcohol intolerance usually flush within minutes of drinking even a small amount of alcohol. Other symptoms of alcohol intolerance include the following:

- Nausea and dizziness
- Raised pulse
- Headaches
- Itchiness

Recent research has found that such people may have higher risks for cancers of the liver and esophagus. For this reason, people with alcohol intolerances should avoid alcohol altogether.

References

"Alcohol Allergy: Is There Such a Thing?" Mayo Clinic. Accessed November 8, 2007. www.mayoclinic.com/health/alcohol-allergy/AN00818.
"Differential Diagnosis of Anaphylaxis and Anaphylactoid Reactions." *MD Consult Patient Education Handout.* USC School of Medicine Library, Columbia, SC. Accessed November 5, 2007. Keyword: anaphylaxis.
"Diseases and Conditions: Allergy." Aetna Intelihealth. Accessed November 10, 2007. www.intelihealth.com/IH/ihtIH/WSIHW000/408/408.html.
"Wine, Beer and Alcohol Allergy." *Allergy New Zealand.* Accessed November 9, 2007. www.allergy.org.nz/allergies/aZAllergies/beerWine.php.

How do I select a substance abuse treatment program for a family member?

After someone accepts the fact that he or she has a substance abuse problem, the next step is to select a treatment program. There are a variety of substance abuse programs available, including inpatient programs, residential programs, methadone clinics, and outpatient treatment programs. The U.S. Department of Health & Human Services' Substance Abuse & Mental Health Services Administration (SAMHSA) maintains an online resource for locating alcohol and drug abuse treatment programs at http://dasis3.samhsa.gov. You can search the Substance Abuse Treatment Facility Locator by location, and it provides contact information, as well as details about the types of services provided.

SAMHSA's referral helplines:
1-800-662-HELP
1-800-662-9832 (Español)
1-800-228-0427 (TDD)

Here is a list of questions to ask when selecting a treatment program:

1. What type of accreditation or licensing does the program have?
2. What kind of service providers are involved in the treatment program? Do you have any Licensed Clinical Alcohol and Drug Counselors (LCADC) or medical doctors certified by the American Society of Addiction Medicine (ASAM) on staff?
3. Have there been studies that show the program works? Do you have any data on the program's effectiveness? Success rates?
4. What therapies does the program use? Detoxification? Individual and group counseling? A 12-step program? Other behavioral therapies? Medications? Life skills training?
5. How does the program keep track of the patient's progress? Is the patient's treatment plan altered to meet changing needs?
6. What will the program cost? What insurance plans do you accept? Are you willing to work with me on a payment plan?
7. How do you handle the issue of confidentiality?
8. Is the facility clean and well-kept?
9. How does the program handle relapse? Do they offer relapse prevention classes?
10. Is the treatment plan designed to meet the unique needs of an individual, such as age, gender, and ethnicity?
11. Can you meet the needs of an individual with a co-occurring mental illness? (Over half of the individuals with a drug abuse problem also have a mental illness, such as depression.)
12. Does the program offer aftercare? (Look for programs that offer at least a year of weekly or biweekly outpatient counseling. In addition, programs generally help patients find a self-help group.)

If you are looking for a program for your teenager, here are a few additional questions to consider:

1. How does the program meet the needs of teens?
2. How are parents involved in the program?
3. Can my child continue education during treatment?

☞ Use the following link to find contact information and advice about your state's alcohol and drug agency: http://findtreatment.samhsa.gov/ufds/abusedirectors.

References

"13 Questions to Ask When Choosing an Addiction Treatment Program." Partnership for a Drug-Free America. Accessed November 20, 2007. www.drugfree.org/Intervention/Treatment/13_Questions_to_Ask.

"Substance Abuse Treatment for Children and Adolescents: Questions to Ask." American Academy of Child & Adolescent Psychiatry. Accessed November 17, 2007. www.aacap.org/page.ww?section=Facts+for+Families&name=Substance+Abuse+Treatment+For+Children+And+Adolescents%3A+Questions+To+Ask.

ASK THE EXPERTS

Following is a list of health care professionals who can help you answer more in-depth questions related to issues discussed in this chapter. A good starting point would be your primary care physician (your family physician, internist, pediatrician, or nurse practitioner). From there, he or she might recommend that you visit with other medical specialists or health care professionals. Each one has received specialized training in his or her area of expertise. *(See the Glossary of Experts for descriptions, online directories, and credentialing information.)*

- Allergists
- American Society of Addiction Medicine (ASAM)–certified medical doctors
- Certified Chemical Dependency Counselors (CCDCs)
- Family physicians
- Gastroenterologists
- Licensed Clinical Alcohol and Drug Counselors (LCADCs)
- Nutritionists
- Dietetic technicians, registered (DTRs)
- Fitness experts
- Nurse practitioners
- Nurses
- Pediatricians
- Registered dieticians (RDs)

4

Complementary and Alternative Medicine

Is acupuncture effective? Can echinacea cure colds? Is massage therapy safe? Can meditation reduce stress? All of these methods fall within a category of medical practice called *complementary and alternative medicine*, or CAM for short. CAM is the term for medical products and practices that are not part of standard medical care. *Complementary* medicine means nonstandard treatments that you use *along with* standard ones. *Alternative* medicine means treatments you use *instead of* standard ones.

You see ads for CAM therapies everywhere. Are these practices and products really effective? Are they safe? Librarians hear these questions quite often when people visit their local libraries to find answers. In this chapter we will provide information to answer some of the most common CAM-related questions.

HEALING SYSTEMS

Is complementary and alternative medicine used to treat cancer?

Complementary and alternative (CAM) therapies for cancer are being researched. The National Cancer Institute and the National Center for Complementary and Alternative Medicine are co-sponsoring some of the studies.

Standard cancer treatments are studied for safety and effectiveness through a strict scientific process. This includes lab research and clinical trials with large numbers of patients. Little is known about whether CAM therapies are safe or effective in treating cancer.

A small number of CAM therapies are being used to help cancer patients feel better and recover faster. **They do not cure the cancer.** They are used together with standard cancer treatments to help relieve symptoms or side effects, to ease pain, and to enhance quality of life.

Some cancer patients use a small number of complementary and alternative therapies to relieve symptoms or ease pain. They are not cures.

The American Cancer Society has identified some therapies as helpful to some people when used along with medical treatment. As always, talk to your doctor about any method you are considering. Your health care provider will make sure that your medical treatments and your CAM treatments work well together.

The following are possible helpful complementary approaches:

- Acupuncture
- Aromatherapy
- Art therapy
- Biofeedback (using monitoring devices to help control physical processes, such as heart rate, blood pressure, and muscle tension)
- Massage therapy
- Meditation
- Music therapy
- Prayer and spirituality
- Tai chi (an ancient Chinese martial art)
- Yoga

If a treatment falls under any of the following categories, avoid it:

- It is claimed to cure cancer.
- You are told not to use it.
- It and/or a drug involved is a "secret" that only certain providers can give.
- It requires you to travel to another country.
- Its promoters attack the medical or scientific community.
- It is based on an unproven theory.

If you are unsure whether a treatment belongs in one of these categories, talk to your doctor.

☞ For more information, read the National Cancer Institute's fact sheet on CAM in cancer treatment at www.cancer.gov/cancertopics/factsheet/therapy/CAM.

(See Chapter 1 for more information about cancer.)

References

"Cancer and CAM." National Center for Complementary and Alternative Medicine. Accessed January 7, 2008. http://nccam.nih.gov/health/camcancer.

"Complementary and Alternative Medicine in Cancer Treatment: Questions and Answers." National Cancer Institute. Accessed January 5, 2008. www.cancer.gov/cancertopics/factsheet/therapy/CAM.

"Complementary and Alternative Methods for Cancer Management." American Cancer Society. Accessed January 7, 2008. www.cancer.org/docroot/ETO/content/ETO_5_1_Introduction.asp.

What is Ayurvedic medicine?

Ayurvedic medicine, or Ayurveda, is a type of complementary and alternative medicine (CAM) system that originated in India thousands of years ago. Ayurveda focuses on three things: preventing disease, healing disease, and increasing age longevity. An Ayurvedic belief is that when the body becomes out of balance with the universe, illness can result.

To diagnose an imbalance, an Ayurvedic practitioner may do the following:

- Interview you about your diet and lifestyle habits
- Look at the physical condition of your skin, eyes, teeth, weight, urine, stool, tongue, and overall appearance
- Carefully measure your pulse

Based on these examinations, the practitioner may prescribe any of the following:

- A special diet and/or enemas to cleanse the digestive tract
- Herbal medicines, such as amla, bacoba, and guggul
- Relaxation/exercise techniques, such as yoga, stretching, and meditation
- Massage of the "vital points" in the body where energy is believed to be focused

Nearly two-thirds of rural people in India still rely on Ayurveda as their primary health care system.

Some conditions that *may* benefit from Ayurveda:

- Arthritis
- Asthma
- Colitis
- Diabetes
- High cholesterol
- Insomnia
- Irritable bowel disorder
- Tension headaches
- Various mental disorders

Some Ayurvedic practices and medications may be toxic or dangerous, especially when combined with other herbs or prescriptions. If you are interested in seeing an Ayurvedic practitioner, make sure to ask him about his training and years of experience. Always talk to your regular health care provider about any alternative therapies and medicines that you are considering. According to the National Center for Complementary and Alternative Medicine, it is a bad idea to replace standard medical treatments with unproven CAM treatments. Talk to your doctor first.

References

Pelletier, K. *The Best Alternative Medicine: What Works? What Does Not?* New York: Simon & Schuster, 2000.

"What Is Ayurveda?" Ayurveda Holistic Community. Accessed January 12, 2008. www.ayurvedahc.com/articlelive/authors/1/Swami-Sadashiva-Tirtha.

"What Is Ayurvedic Medicine?" National Center for Complementary and Alternative Medicine. Accessed January 6, 2008. http://nccam.nih.gov/health/ayurveda.

What is the difference between naturopathy and homeopathy? Are there health benefits to either?

Naturopathy is an ancient form of medicine that focuses on treatments considered "natural" instead of on medicines or surgery. Naturopathy traces its roots to the healing techniques of ancient China, India, and Greece and to Native American cultures. People seek naturopathic care for various health purposes, such as overall wellness or treatment of chronic diseases or conditions.

Naturopathy focuses on "natural" treatments instead of medicines or surgery.

Modern naturopathy is based on six basic principles:

1. **Nature has the power to heal.** The naturopathic physician must remove obstacles to health.
2. **Treat the whole person.** Every aspect of the patient must be brought into harmonious balance.
3. **First, do no harm.** A physician should use methods and substances that are nontoxic and noninvasive if possible.
4. **Treat the cause.** Rather than suppress symptoms, the physician should treat the underlying cause of a disease.
5. **Prevention is the best cure.** A physician should focus on preventing disease as well as treating disease.
6. **Doctors should be teachers.** A doctor's task is to educate the patient and encourage him or her to be responsible for his or her own health.

Naturopathy seems to be fairly safe, especially if used together with standard medical care. However, it is not a substitute for standard medical care. In addition, some therapies can be harmful if not used properly. For example, herbs can cause side effects or interact with prescription or over-the-counter medicines.

Very few studies have been done to determine if naturopathic medicine as a whole is effective. Some studies indicate that it *could* be effective for specific conditions. As always, tell your doctor if you are considering naturopathic medicine.

Homeopathy is a system of medicine based on the principle of "like cures like." It was developed in Germany in the eighteenth century. People use homeopathic therapies for a wide range of health concerns, from prevention to treatment of injuries, diseases, and conditions.

"Like cures like" is a basic principle of homeopathy.

These are the key concepts of homeopathy:

• Every person has energy called a "vital force." When this energy is off balance, health problems develop. Homeopathy aims to stimulate the body's own healing ability.

- Treatment involves using small doses of "remedies" that would produce symptoms of illness in healthy people if given in larger doses. This is where the phrase "like cures like" comes from.
- Treatment is tailored to each person according to symptoms, lifestyle, emotional and mental states, and other factors.

Studies to determine whether homeopathy is effective have yielded contradictory results. In some clinical trials, the homeopathic remedy appeared to be no more helpful than a placebo (an inactive substance). In other studies, some positive effects were seen that were not readily explained in scientific terms.

Homeopathy takes a different approach from standard medicine. In fact, homeopathy has been the subject of much debate. A number of its key concepts do not follow the laws of science (such as chemistry and physics). Also, many users of homeopathic products do not also consult a professional. This is dangerous. It is important to consult your doctor if you use homeopathic products.

References

"Introduction to Naturopathy." National Center for Complementary and Alternative Medicine. Accessed January 10, 2008. http://nccam.nih.gov/health/naturopathy.

Pelletier, K. *The Best Alternative Medicine: What Works? What Does Not?* New York: Simon & Schuster, 2000.

"Questions and Answers About Homeopathy." National Center for Complementary and Alternative Medicine. Accessed January 9, 2008. http://nccam.nih.gov/health/homeopathy.

MIND–BODY CONNECTIONS

Can meditation reduce stress?

Meditation, a mind–body therapy, involves different methods or techniques to focus or control attention. Some of these methods are part of religious or spiritual traditions that are thousands of years old. Centering prayer, mindfulness meditation, Kabbalah, Zen Buddhism, Tibetan Buddhism, and transcendental meditation are all different types of meditation systems. Meditation is frequently part of yoga, tai chi, and qi gong sessions.

Prayer is the most widely used form of meditation.

Meditation practice usually involves sitting in a comfortable position in a quiet environment for several minutes. Some people may focus their attention on their breathing or on an image. The image may be a mental picture of a happy memory or a physical object like a burning candle. Others may repeat a mantra (a specially chosen word or set of words) to focus their attention. Beginners may find it difficult to meditate. It takes practice. For best results, try to find time each day for meditation.

As you practice meditating, you will learn how to let thoughts come and go. Meditation helps people become present in the here and now. Learning how to calm your mind can improve your emotional strength. This can help you cope with the difficulties you encounter throughout your life. You can also use meditation techniques to relax your body and relieve muscle tension. Meditation practice can also lead to inner peace.

People with the following conditions may consider practicing meditation to reduce stress and help them cope with daily life:

- Allergies
- Anxiety
- Arthritis
- Asthma
- Cancer
- Chronic pain
- Depression
- Eating disorders
- Fibromyalgia
- Heart disease
- High blood pressure
- HIV/AIDS (human immunodeficiency virus/acquired immune deficiency syndrome)
- Obesity
- Psoriasis
- Tension headaches

More research is needed to determine the positive effects of meditation on various conditions. Some studies have shown significant effects, while other studies have not. No adverse effects have been reported. If you have mental health issues, you may want to speak with your health care provider before you begin to practice meditation. During meditation, you may become aware of distressing events or thoughts that you have suppressed. This side effect has not been confirmed by research.

It is easy to incorporate meditation into your daily life. It is inexpensive, you can practice it by yourself, and it does not require any special equipment. **There is no wrong way to meditate.** Some fitness centers offer classes on guided meditation, or you can learn meditation techniques from books, videos, or audiotapes.

References

"Meditation." National Center for Complementary and Alternative Medicine. Accessed January 17, 2008. http://nccam.nih.gov/health/meditation.

"Meditation: Take a Stress-Reduction Break Wherever You Are." Mayo Clinic. Accessed January 17, 2008. www.mayoclinic.com/print/meditation/HQ01070/METHOD=print.

Rakel, D. *Integrative Medicine.* Philadelphia: Saunders, 2007.

What are the health benefits of yoga?

There are many different types of yoga. Most Americans practice a type of hatha yoga. Hatha yoga combines flowing postures, breathing, and meditation to enhance the connection between mind, body, and spirit. The traditional purpose of hatha yoga was to prepare people for meditation. Now it is frequently used as a form of exercise. Some people believe they lack the flexibility to try yoga. For them, yoga conjures images of people in pretzel-like shapes. This is not accurate. Yoga classes come in a variety of levels from beginner to advanced. There are also modifications a yoga teacher can show you to make poses easier.

☞ To find a yoga instructor in your area, search the Yoga Alliance's directory of registered yoga teachers at www.yogaalliance.com/teacher_search.cfm.

In addition to yoga studios, you can take yoga classes at gyms, community education centers, and senior citizen centers. There are individual and group classes, as well as classes designed for pregnant women or kids. Classes typically range from 20 minutes to 1 hour. You can also learn about yoga from books and videos. Yoga is practiced in bare feet on a soft, nonslip surface. Many people prefer to use an exercise mat or "sticky" mat.

Yoga can provide many health benefits. Yoga is most widely known to increase relaxation and lower stress. It also increases flexibility, strength, and stamina.

Yoga is also used to improve the following:

- Balance
- Circulation
- Coordination
- Digestion
- Fatigue
- Physical fitness
- Posture
- Range of motion
- Sleep

Some research suggests that yoga improves fatigue in people with multiple sclerosis, reduces low back pain, and improves a person's sense of well-being. The results of some yoga studies are disputed because they included only a small number of participants. More well-designed research is needed.

Research has also shown that yoga helps people control the following body functions:

- Blood pressure
- Body temperature
- Brain waves
- Breathing
- Heart rate
- Metabolism
- Skin resistance

Some people practice yoga to relieve symptoms of chronic diseases such as cancer, arthritis, asthma, and heart disease. Women practice yoga to reduce symptoms associated with menstruation, pregnancy, and menopause. People suffering from epilepsy, anxiety, headaches, depression, and memory problems may also find yoga to be helpful. Yoga may also reduce pain associated with carpal tunnel syndrome, osteoarthritis of the knee, and tennis elbow.

Talk to your doctor before starting a yoga program if you have any of the following conditions:

- Eye conditions such as glaucoma and retinal detachment
- Risk of blood clots
- High blood pressure that is difficult to control
- Osteoporosis or high risk of fractures
- High risk of muscle strain

(See Chapter 3 for more information on physical fitness.)

References

"Yoga." American Cancer Society. Accessed December 19, 2007. www.cancer .org/docroot/ETO/content/ETO_5_3X_Yoga.asp?sitearea=ETO.

"Yoga: Minimize Stress, Maximize Flexibility and Even More." Mayo Clinic. Accessed December 20, 2007. www.mayoclinic.com/print/yoga/CM00004/METHOD=print.

What is biofeedback?

Biofeedback is a type of mind–body therapy. People use biofeedback to improve their health by learning to control their body functions, such as blood pressure, skin temperature, muscle tension, and heart rate.

Biofeedback is used to treat at least 150 medical conditions.

During a biofeedback session, a biofeedback therapist will use monitoring equipment and interpret changes in body functions. Biofeedback therapists come from a variety of health-related backgrounds and are certified by the Biofeedback Certification Institute of America. They may work in a hospital, medical center, or physical therapy clinic.

Your therapist may use one of the methods listed in Table 4-1 to track your body functions.

Table 4-1. Biofeedback methods

Monitoring method	Used to measure or detect
Breathing rate	Breathing
Electroencephalogram (EEG)	Brain waves
Electromyogram (EMG)	Muscle tension
Electrodermal activity (EDA)	Perspiration rates
Finger pulse measurements	High blood pressure, anxiety, irregular heart beats
Thermal (temperature) biofeedback	Skin temperature

The type of measurement used depends on your health problem. If you have a problem with grinding your teeth, your therapist may use an electromyogram sensor to measure the muscle tension near your jaw. A monitor with electrodes will be applied to the skin near your jaw. With the help of your therapist, you will try to relax your jaw. Data from the sensor will create images or sounds on the monitor. This feedback will help you learn to reduce tension in the jaw muscle. A biofeedback session typically lasts 40 to 60 minutes.

It may take 6 to 30 therapy sessions to learn how to control involuntary responses without the use of the monitoring equipment. Caffeine, benzodiazepines, and opioids may lessen the effects of biofeedback training. Biofeedback is a safe procedure, but it should not be used as a replacement for conventional medical care. It can be used as a supplement to your current treatment.

Biofeedback promotes relaxation and may be helpful in treating the following health problems:

- Anxiety
- Asthma
- Attention-deficit/ hyperactivity disorder (ADHD)
- Bowel (fecal) incontinence
- Chronic constipation
- Chronic fatigue syndrome
- Chronic pain (neck or back)
- Depression
- Epilepsy
- High blood pressure
- Hot flashes
- Hyperventilation
- Irregular heartbeat
- Irritable bowel syndrome
- Migraines
- Raynaud's disease
- Side effects of chemotherapy (nausea and vomiting)
- Stroke rehabilitation
- Teeth grinding/jaw joint problems (including temporomandibular joint [TMJ] disorder)
- Tension headaches
- Urinary incontinence

☞ To find a biofeedback therapist near you, visit the Biofeedback Certification Institute of America's Web site at http://bcia.affiniscape.com.

References

"Biofeedback." *MD Consult Patient Education Handout.* MD Consult. USC School of Medicine Library, Columbia, SC. Accessed December 16, 2007. Keyword: biofeedback.

"Biofeedback: Using Your Mind to Improve Your Health." Mayo Clinic. Accessed December 15, 2007. www.mayoclinic.com/health/biofeedback/SA00083.

McPhee, S., M. Papadakis, and L. Tierney, eds. *Current Medical Diagnosis & Treatment.* Los Altos, CA: Lange Medical Publications, 2007.

HERBAL MEDICINE AND DIETARY SUPPLEMENTS

I've heard some herbal supplements can have adverse effects. Are herbal supplements safe to take?

Herbal supplements are dietary supplements that contain herbs. They come in tablets, capsules, powders, teas, and extracts. Although they may be advertised as a natural product, it does not mean they are safe. **These products can interact with prescription and over-the-counter drugs.** Herbal supplements can also have negative effects on your health if you do not follow the dosing instructions on the label, take too much of the product, or take the supplement for too long. Kava and comfrey are examples of herbs that have been linked to liver damage, and St. John's wort may reduce the effects of drugs used to treat depression, human immunodeficiency virus (HIV), cancer, or birth control.

Before you take an herbal supplement, find out about the possible side effects of the herb and talk to a trained health professional.

Like drugs, herbal supplements can also have side effects. Table 4-2 provides some examples of herbal supplements and their possible side effects.

Herbal supplements can also cause negative effects during surgery. If you are going to have surgery, it is important to let your health care team know what herbal supplements you are taking. You will probably need to stop taking the supplements at least two weeks before surgery. Garlic, ginseng, ginger, and ginkgo are examples of supplements that may cause bleeding. Other supplements such as kava and valerian can affect anesthesia.

Table 4-2. Herbal supplements and their possible side effects

Herb	Possible side effects
Echinacea	Upset stomach, dizziness, skin rash, diarrhea
Ephedra	High blood pressure, irregular heartbeat, seizures, stroke
Garlic	Bleeding, diarrhea, allergic reactions
Ginseng	Headache, skin rashes, high or low blood pressure
Goldenseal	High blood pressure, swelling
Licorice	High blood pressure, swelling

Children should not take herbal supplements, because most products are not tested on children. **Individuals with the following conditions should talk to their health care provider before taking herbal supplements:**

- Blood clotting problems
- Cancer
- Diabetes
- Enlarged prostate gland
- Epilepsy
- Glaucoma
- Heart disease
- High blood pressure

- Immune system problems
- Liver problems
- Mental health problems
- Parkinson's disease
- Pregnancy
- Stroke
- Thyroid problems
- Women who are nursing

☞ **To learn more about a particular herbal supplement, visit the following Web sites:**
- National Center for Complementary and Alternative Medicine: http://nccam.nih.gov
- National Institutes of Health Office of Dietary Supplements: http://ods.od.nih.gov/
- National Library of Medicine: www.nlm.nih.gov/medlineplus/druginformation.html
- U.S. Food and Drug Administration: www.fda.gov

Not only is it important to learn about the negative side effects of an herbal supplement, but you should also be aware of the quality of the product. Standardization is a quality control method used by manufacturers to ensure batch-to-batch consistency of their products. Unlike drugs, herbal supplements manufactured in the United States are not required to be standardized. Even if a product is labeled as standardized, the manufacturer is using its own definition.

Herbal supplements are sold in stores, online, and on TV. The Food and Drug Administration currently governs supplements as foods rather than as drugs. This means that herbal supplements meet laws that are less strict than the laws used for drug approval.

As a result, herbal supplements:

- may not contain the correct ingredients;
- may contain higher or lower amounts of the active ingredient;
- may be contaminated; and/or
- do not need research studies involving people to prove a supplement's safety or effectiveness.

If the supplement label contains a health claim, it will be followed by the disclaimer: "This statement has not been evaluated by the Food and Drug Administration. This product is not intended to diagnose, treat, cure, or prevent any disease."

When selecting an herbal supplement, look for the USP verification mark. USP stands for the United States Pharmacopeial Convention. The USP evaluates and tests dietary supplements for safety.

To receive the USP mark, the herbal supplement must:

- contain the ingredients listed on the label;
- contain the proper amounts of the ingredients listed on the label;
- meet acceptable limits for contaminants; and
- be manufactured using safe procedures.

Herbs have been used for thousands of years for a variety of health purposes, and research studies evaluating the benefits of herbal supplements are being conducted. However, these supplements can be harmful. Carefully weigh the evidence before taking any of these products.

References

"Dietary Supplements." U.S. Food and Drug Administration. Accessed January 20, 2008. www.fda.gov/womens/getthefacts/supplements.html.

"Frequently Asked Questions About USP Verification Program for Dietary Supplements." U.S. Pharmacopeia. Accessed January 21, 2008. www.usp .org/USPVerified/dietarySupplements/faq.html.

"Herbal Products and Supplements: What You Should Know." American Academy of Family Physicians. Accessed January 20, 2008. http://family doctor.org/online/famdocen/home/otc-center/otc-medicines/860 .html.

McPhee, S., M. Papadakis, and L. Tierney, eds. *Current Medical Diagnosis & Treatment.* Los Altos, CA: Lange Medical Publications, 2007.

"What's in a Bottle? An Introduction to Dietary Supplements." National Center for Complementary and Alternative Medicine. Accessed January 18, 2008. http://nccam.nih.gov/health/bottle.

Can echinacea help treat the common cold?

People often take echinacea (*Echinacea purpurea*) to prevent and treat the common cold. According to a Centers for Disease Control and Prevention study in 2002, echinacea is the most commonly used natural product. It is available in a variety of forms, including extracts, tinctures, tablets, ointments, and creams.

There is no strong proof that echinacea helps treat a cold.

Right now, there is not enough proof to claim that echinacea helps treat the common cold. Echinacea research is difficult to conduct because echinacea is prepared in many different ways, and this makes the results of different studies difficult to compare. The U.S. Food and Drug Administration does not regulate natural products in the same way as it does prescription drugs. Although a few studies suggest that echinacea may effectively treat a cold, no large, reliable studies have consistently proven this.

If you choose to use echinacea, keep in mind that other medicines might interact with it. You may have side effects or allergic reactions to echinacea, especially if you are allergic to plants such as ragweed. Be sure to check with your doctor before taking echinacea.

Doctors recommend that you avoid echinacea if you are pregnant or nursing. Little is known about the effects of echinacea on women who are pregnant or nursing.

Echinacea is native to Kansas, Nebraska, and Missouri. Some other names for echinacea are *hedgehog, black susans,* and *snakeroot.*

References

Barnes, P., E. Powell-Griner, K. McFann, and R. Nahin. "Complementary and Alternative Medicine Use Among Adults." *Advance Data Report, No. 343.* Atlanta: Centers for Disease Control and Prevention, 2002.

"Echinacea." *Review of Natural Products.* St. Louis, MO: Facts and Comparisons, 2005.

"Echinacea Natural Remedy." *MD Consult Patient Education Handout.* USC School of Medicine Library, Columbia, SC. Accessed November 19, 2007. Keyword: echinacea.

Linde, K., B. Barrett, K. Wolkart, R. Bauer, and D. Melchart. "Echinacea for Preventing and Treating the Common Cold." Cochrane Database of Systematic Reviews. USC School of Medicine Library, Columbia, SC. Accessed November 15, 2007. Path: echinacea; common cold.

Saper, R. "Clinical Use of Echinacea." UpToDate. USC School of Medicine Library, Columbia, SC. Accessed November 19, 2007. Keyword: echinacea.

Can taking ginkgo improve my memory?

Ginkgo (*Ginkgo biloba*) has been used for thousands of years to treat a variety of conditions. Ginkgo seeds are part of traditional Chinese medicine. **Gingko seeds are potentially toxic, so you should not eat them.**

Today ginkgo is one of the most popular herbal supplements. It comes in many forms: tincture, extract, tablets, capsules, or tea. Ginkgo is made from the leaves of the ginkgo tree, which is the world's oldest living tree species.

Ginkgo is also known as *ginkgo biloba, maidenhair tree, kew tree, fossil tree, yinhsing,* and *Japanese silver apricot.*

Early small studies showed that ginkgo helps improve memory in healthy adults. A large trial sponsored by the National Institute on Aging including more than 200 healthy adults over age 60 found that ginkgo taken for six weeks did not improve memory. Because the results of these memory studies are not consistent, more research is needed.

Researchers are also evaluating the use of ginkgo by individuals with Alzheimer's disease, dementia, and cerebral insufficiency (a syndrome related to coronary artery disease with symptoms such as difficulty concentrating, dizziness, headache, and confusion). Some studies show that ginkgo may be helpful in managing these conditions. The results of ginkgo studies have not been consistent, so larger, well-designed studies are needed.

Other research studies are looking at whether ginkgo is helpful in treating the following conditions:

- Altitude sickness
- Deafness
- Depression
- Gastric cancer
- Glaucoma
- Hemorrhoids (acute attacks)
- Macular degeneration
- Multiple sclerosis
- Painful legs from clogged arteries (claudication)
- Premenstrual syndrome (PMS)
- Ringing in the ears (tinnitus)
- Seasonal affective disorder
- Sexual dysfunction
- Side effects of chemotherapy
- Vertigo

It is important to talk to your health care provider about any herbs you are taking. **Ginkgo may interact with food or other medicines you may be taking.**

Ginkgo is relatively safe, and few people have had side effects. The following adverse effects have been reported:

- Allergy
- Anxiety
- Constipation
- Decreased muscle tone
- Diarrhea
- Dizziness
- Dry mouth
- Fast or irregular heartbeat
- Headache
- Insomnia
- Low blood pressure
- Nausea
- Upset stomach
- Vomiting
- Weakness

The following side effects were rare:

- Bleeding complications
- Rash
- Seizures
- Unusual bruising

Do not take ginkgo if you are pregnant or have diabetes, a bleeding disorder, or a seizure disorder (epilepsy). Children under 18 should not take ginkgo.

References

Birks, J. and J. Evans. "Ginkgo Biloba for Cognitive Impairment and Dementia." Cochrane Database of Systematic Reviews. USC School of Medicine Library, Columbia, SC. Accessed November 23, 2007. Keyword: ginkgo biloba.

"Ginkgo." National Center for Complementary and Alternative Medicine. Accessed November 18, 2007. http://nccam.nih.gov/health/ginkgo.

"Ginkgo Biloba." *MD Consult Patient Education Handout.* USC School of Medicine Library, Columbia, SC. Accessed November 24, 2007. Keyword: ginkgo biloba.

"Ginkgo (Ginkgo Biloba L.)." Natural Standard Research Collaboration. Accessed November 23, 2007. www.nlm.nih.gov/medlineplus/druginfo/natural/patient-ginkgo.html.

MANIPULATION AND TOUCH

Is chiropractic effective in treating back pain?

Chiropractic is a form of health care that focuses on the spine and the body's structure and on how they relate to overall health. Doctors of chiropractic, also called *chiropractors,* use a type of hands-on therapy called *manipulation* (or *adjustment*). Millions of Americans visit chiropractors each year.

Be sure to choose a chiropractor who has the Doctor of Chiropractic (DC) degree from a school certified by the Council on Chiropractic Education.

The following are basic concepts of chiropractic:

- Your body has a powerful self-healing ability.
- Your body's structure (mainly the spine) is related to how your body functions.
- The goal is to control the relationship between the body's function and the body's structure.

> Although no firm conclusions have been made, studies show that chiropractic treatment for low back pain is about as effective as standard medical treatment.

Chiropractic is most often used to treat problems with muscles, joints, bones, and connective tissue (cartilage, ligaments, and tendons). Many people visit chiropractors for treatment of low back pain, neck pain, and headaches.

Much research has been done on whether chiropractic is effective in treating low back pain. No firm conclusions have been made. However, the studies have suggested that for low back pain, chiropractic treatment is about as effective as conventional (standard) medical treatment.

The risk of complications from lower back chiropractic adjustment is very low. Still, it is important to talk to your health care provider when you are considering chiropractic treatment. This will help your doctor make sure that your regular health care and your chiropractic treatment work together.

☞ For more information about chiropractic, visit the American Chiropractic Association's Web site at www.acatoday.com/index.cfm. Click on "Patients."

Following are some tips to help avoid back pain:

- Maintain a healthy diet and weight.
- Remain active, and avoid prolonged bed rest.
- Warm up before exercising and other activities, such as gardening.
- Stretch after exercising.
- Maintain proper posture.
- Wear comfortable, low-heeled shoes.
- Sleep on a mattress of medium firmness to minimize any curve in your spine.
- Lift with your legs, keep the object close to your body, and do not twist when lifting.
- Make sure your computer workstation is ergonomically correct.

(See Chapter 3 for more information about a healthy lifestyle.)

References

"About Chiropractic and Its Use in Treating Low-Back Pain." National Center for Complementary and Alternative Medicine. Accessed January 13, 2008. http://nccam.nih.gov/health/chiropractic.

"Back Pain Facts & Statistics." American Chiropractic Association. Accessed January 15, 2008. www.amerchiro.org/level2_css.cfm?T1ID=13&T2ID=68.

"Chiropractic." U.S. National Library of Medicine. Accessed January 13, 2008. www.nlm.nih.gov/medlineplus/chiropractic.html.

Pelletier, K. *The Best Alternative Medicine: What Works? What Does Not?* New York: Simon & Schuster, 2000.

"What Is Chiropractic?" American Chiropractic Association. Accessed January 15, 2008. www.amerchiro.org/level2_css.cfm?T1ID=13&T2ID=61.

Can massage therapy reduce stress?

Massage therapy is the hands-on manipulation of the soft tissues and joints of the body. The practice dates back thousands of years in many cultures such as ancient Greece, ancient Rome, Japan, China, Egypt, and India. In the United States, massage therapy first became popular in the mid-1800s and was used for a variety of health purposes. Today, public interest in massage therapy continues to grow as the benefits become more widely known.

There are over 80 types of massage therapy. These are some popular examples:

- **Swedish massage:** Long strokes, kneading, and friction are used on the muscles, and the joints are moved to aid flexibility.
- **Deep tissue massage:** Patterns of strokes and deep finger pressure are used on tight or knotted muscles.
- **Trigger point massage:** Deeper, more focused pressure is placed on trigger points or "knots" that can form in the muscles.
- **Shiatsu massage:** Varying, rhythmic pressure from the fingers is applied to parts of the body that are believed to be important for the flow of vital energy.

In all types of massage, therapists press, rub, or manipulate the muscles and other soft tissues of the body. They most often use their hands and fingers but may also use their forearms, elbows, or feet.

The general purpose of massage therapy is to relax the soft tissues, to increase the flow of blood and oxygen to the massaged areas, and to decrease pain. Studies show that massage therapy can enhance relaxation and reduce stress. Stress makes some diseases and conditions worse. For this reason, massage therapy is sometimes recommended together with conventional medicine to treat certain conditions.

Massage therapy often enhances relaxation and reduces stress.

Scientists do not fully know what changes occur in the body during massage or how these changes may affect health. Studies are being done to answer these questions and to determine when massage therapy may be most helpful.

Massage therapy has few serious risks if the right cautions are followed and if the therapist is properly trained. Side effects may include temporary pain, bruising, swelling, or a sensitivity to massage oils.

Doctors recommend that you NOT have massage therapy if you have one or more of the following conditions:

- A bleeding disorder or you are taking blood-thinning drugs
- Damaged blood vessels
- Deep vein thrombosis (a blood clot in a deep vein, usually in the legs)
- Fever
- Open wounds, tumors, damaged nerves, infections, or inflammations in an area that may be massaged
- Weakened bones from osteoporosis, a recent fracture, or cancer

As always, check with your health care provider before having a massage. In particular, **check with your doctor if you have any of the following conditions:**

- Cancer
- Dermatomyositis (a disease of the connective tissue)
- Fragile skin
- Heart problems
- History of physical abuse
- Pregnancy

Before having massage therapy, ask about the following:
- The therapist's training, experience, and licenses or credentials
- Your medical conditions and whether the therapist has experience or specialized training with them
- The number of treatments you might need
- Cost
- Insurance coverage

References

"Benefits of Massage Therapy." MassageTherapy101. Accessed January 8, 2008. www.massagetherapy101.com/massage-therapy/benefits-of-massage-therapy.aspx.

"Massage and Stress." MassageTherapy101. Accessed January 7, 2008. www.massagetherapy101.com/massage-therapy/massage-therapy-and-stress-reduction.aspx.

"Massage Therapy as CAM." National Center for Complementary and Alternative Medicine. Accessed January 10, 2008. http://nccam.nih.gov/health/massage.

"Stress: Comprehensive Version." *MD Consult Patient Education Handout.* USC School of Medicine Library, Columbia, SC. Accessed January 8, 2008. Keyword: stress.

What are the benefits of infant massage?

Infant massage is a tradition within many ancient cultures and is now used worldwide. It promotes early bonding, which many studies have shown helps foster the emotional and physical growth of newborns. Children thrive from having a parent or other adult who provides physical closeness. Infant massage is a natural and pleasant way to bond with a baby. In particular, it can help premature babies grow and develop.

Infant massage is often used to foster the growth and development of premature babies.

Babies aren't as strong as adults, so you will need to be careful and massage your baby gently. Be sure to educate yourself with the many books and videos that are available on the subject. Some local hospitals have classes on infant massage.

The following procedures and tips are recommended to give your baby a massage:

1. Start after a bath or before sleep.
2. Use the pads of your fingers and apply pressure. Don't tickle.
3. Cradle your baby in your lap (face up) and start with gentle strokes to the face and head. Be careful to avoid the fontanel (soft spots on the top of the baby's head).
4. Move down the torso and rub the arms and legs.
5. You can also turn your baby on her stomach to give a gentle back massage.
6. Fifteen minutes, or two ten-minute sessions, a day is enough.

The benefits of infant massage include the following:

- It promotes bonding and attachment.
- It relaxes your child and decreases stress for you and your baby.
- It relieves your baby's discomfort from gas, colic, and constipation.
- It helps your baby sleep better and cry less.
- It stimulates brain development and sensory awareness.
- You will learn to understand and respond to your baby's cues.
- You will learn ways to soothe your baby.

References

"Bonding with Your Baby." Nemours Foundation. Accessed January 17, 2008. http://kidshealth.org/parent/pregnancy_newborn/communicating/bonding.html.

"Guide for First-Time Parents." Nemours Foundation. Accessed January 18, 2008. http://kidshealth.org/parent/pregnancy_newborn/pregnancy/guide_parents.html.

"Infant Massage." *MD Consult Patient Education Handout*. USC School of Medicine Library, Columbia, SC. Accessed January 19, 2008. Keyword: infant massage.

"Infant Massage: Communicating Parents' Love Through Touch." Infant Massage USA. Accessed January 17, 2008. www.infantmassageusa.org/imusa/aboutimusa.shtml.

Is acupressure effective in relieving nausea?

A number of studies have shown that acupressure *can* help relieve mild nausea associated with motion sickness or morning sickness. Acupressure may also relieve nausea associated with surgery and chemotherapy treatments.

Acupressure is the practice of applying finger pressure to specific points throughout the body. It has been part of traditional Chinese medicine (TCM) since 2000 BC. Acupressure is widely practiced throughout Asia for relaxation, for the promotion of wellness, and for the treatment of disease. Acupressure techniques are becoming more popular in North America and Europe.

Acupressure is a drug-free, easy way to help relieve nausea associated with motion sickness or morning sickness.

According to TCM, acupressure points are located along 14 bodily pathways. A single point (or a series of points) may be pressed with the fingers for relief of a particular symptom or to promote overall well-being of the body. The technique involves no drugs and can be done by someone trained in the technique, or it can be practiced at home. The risks are minimal (see "Warnings" in the next section).

The point on the body shown to be effective in treating nausea is called **the P6 (Inner Gate) point**. It is located in the groove between the two large tendons on the inside of your wrist that start at the base of your palm. Nausea may be relieved by pressing firmly on that spot with your middle and index fingers.

Acupressure bracelets, known on the market as Sea Bands, can be worn to ease motion sickness or morning sickness.

Warnings

Do not use acupressure to replace standard emergency procedures or licensed medical treatment. If you are seriously injured or have persistent symptoms, seek urgent medical treatment.

Acupressure should NOT be used:

- if you are pregnant, especially if more than 3 months (with the exception of the P6 point on the wrist, which can be pressed to relieve nausea);

- as the only treatment for illness (if you are sick, see a doctor);
- if you have a heart condition;
- just before or within 20 minutes after heavy exercise, a large meal, or bathing; and/or
- if the point in question is under a mole, wart, varicose vein, abrasion, bruise, cut, or any other break in the skin.

As always, it is best to speak with your primary health provider before starting any new therapeutic technique.

(See Chapter 2 for more information about morning sickness.)

References

"Acupressure, Shiatsu, Tuina." Natural Standard and Harvard Medical School. Accessed January 5, 2008. www.intelihealth.com/IH/ihtIH/WSIHW000/8513/34968/358869.html?d=dmtContent.

Boyd, K. "PointFinder: The Online Acupressure Guide." Accessed January 3, 2008. http://med.stanford.edu/personal/pointfinder/index.html.

"Nausea and Acupressure." *MedlinePlus Medical Encyclopedia.* U.S. National Library of Medicine. Accessed January 5, 2008. www.nlm.nih.gov/medlineplus/ency/article/002117.htm.

Somerville, R., ed. *The Medical Advisor: The Complete Guide to Alternative & Conventional Treatments,* 2nd ed. Alexandria, VA: Time Life, 2000.

Wong, C. "Natural Remedies for Morning Sickness." About.Com: Alternative Medicine. Accessed January 8, 2008. http://altmedicine.about.com/od/healthconditionsdisease/a/morningsickness.htm.

ENERGY THERAPIES

Is there any evidence that acupuncture is beneficial to your health?

Acupuncture involves small needles being inserted into specific parts of the body and then stimulated with heat or electricity. The practice originated in China over 2000 years ago. It is now regularly practiced by as many as one million Americans and continues to grow in popularity as a complementary and alternative medicine practice. Some studies have found evidence that acupuncture may offer relief from symptoms of these diseases and illnesses:

- Back pain
- Chemotherapy-induced nausea
- Dental pain
- Fibromyalgia

- Headaches
- Menstrual cramps
- Osteoarthritis
- Tennis elbow

According to the National Institutes of Health, there are three possible reasons why acupuncture may provide health benefits:

1. It may cause endorphins to be released into the central nervous system, which can reduce pain.
2. The nerves in the spinal cord may be stimulated to release certain chemicals, called neurotransmitters, that may reduce pain.
3. Blood flow may be increased around the insertion sites, promoting increased healing.

> When applied to the ear, acupuncture has been effective at managing some substance abuse problems. It may sometimes decrease a patient's need for prescription pain medicines.

For the most part, unless you have a bleeding disorder or you're taking blood thinners, acupuncture is very safe. The trick is to make sure that you are seeing an acupuncture practitioner who is licensed and certified. In the United States, there are two types of acupuncture practitioners: medical doctors who have taken hundreds of hours of additional training in acupuncture in order to supplement their clinical training, and "certified acupuncturists" who usually complete a master's degree program and pass a board exam administered by the National Certification Commission for Acupuncture and Oriental Medicine (NCCAOM).

> In the past, acupuncture needles were made of stone, bone, or even metals like gold and silver. Today they are usually sterile, stainless steel, and disposable.

References

"Acupuncture." American Cancer Society. Accessed January 23, 2008. www.cancer.org/docroot/ETO/content/ETO_5_3X_Acupuncture.asp.

"Acupuncture: An Alternative and Complementary Medicine Resource Guide." Alternative Medicine Foundation. Accessed January 20, 2008. www.amfoundation.org/acupuncture.htm.

"Acupuncture: Sharp Answers to Pointed Questions." Mayo Clinic. Accessed January 23, 2008. http://mayoclinic.com/health/acupuncture/SA00086.

"Get the Facts: Acupuncture." National Center for Complementary and Alternative Medicine. Accessed January 24, 2008. http://nccam.nih.gov/health/acupuncture.

Pelletier, K. *The Best Alternative Medicine: What Works? What Does Not?* New York: Simon & Schuster, 2000.

What does therapeutic touch therapy involve?

Therapeutic touch (TT) therapy, also called *energy field therapy*, is a complementary and alternative medicine practice in which a therapist uses her hands to manipulate energy in the patient's body. While the patient is sitting or lying down, the therapist performs four steps. A TT therapy session takes between 10 and 30 minutes and involves the following phases:

1. During the first phase, called *centering*, the therapist clears her mind to prepare herself for assessing the patient's energy field to find blockages causing pain and/or illness.
2. During the second phase, the therapist passes her hands over the patient's body. No actual touching occurs. Rather, with the palms down, the therapist moves over the patient's entire body, feeling for blockages in energy. These blockages may suggest illness.
3. During the third phase, the therapist releases the patient's bad energy. This is usually done by flicking the bad energy away while passing the hands over the body several times.
4. During the final phase, the therapist fills the patient with good, healthful energy.

Some people report a tingling and/or warm sensation when receiving therapeutic touch therapy.

Although many of the TT therapy claims are not supported by scientific evidence, there is some evidence that TT therapy may help reduce anxiety and some types of pain. Researchers believe this may be a placebo effect. TT therapy is generally considered safe, especially when used along with standard medical treatment under the supervision of a medical doctor or a professional nurse.

Therapeutic touch is popular among professional nurses, and it is taught in dozens of colleges and universities throughout the United States.

References

"Energy Medicine: An Overview." National Center for Complementary and Alternative Medicine. Accessed January 7, 2008. http://nccam.nih.gov/health/backgrounds/energymed.htm.
"Energy Therapies: Therapeutic Touch." The University of Texas MD Anderson Cancer Center. Accessed January 10, 2008. www.mdanderson.org.
Pelletier, K. *The Best Alternative Medicine: What Works? What Does Not?* New York: Simon & Schuster, 2000.
"Therapeutic Touch." American Cancer Society. Accessed January 8, 2008. www.cancer.org/docroot/ETO/content/ETO_5_3X_Therapeutic_Touch.asp?sitearea=ETO.

Can Reiki really increase relaxation and decrease pain?

Reiki is a complementary and alternative medicine (CAM) system developed in Japan. Reiki involves the manipulation of energy—called *ki*—using the hands and may involve direct contact. Placing his hands in 12 to 15 different positions for minutes at a time, the Reiki practitioner tries to correct improper energy flows in the patient. As in many of the other energy medicine systems, such as therapeutic touch, patients have sometimes reported increased relaxation and decreased pain. However, sometimes patients also report fatigue, tingling sensations, and general weakness.

Other benefits supposedly offered by Reiki therapy include the following:

• Increased natural healing of the body
• Boosted immune system
• Reduced stress and anxiety
• A calm mind

The word *Reiki* translates to "universal life spirit."

Some studies suggest that Reiki can affect nervous system functions such as heart rate and blood pressure and may reduce symptoms of depression and pain. However, experts warn that many larger studies are needed for serious conclusions to be made about Reiki's effectiveness. Such effects may be caused by psychological suggestibility, as in cases involving the placebo effect. Overall, like many of the other CAM practices, Reiki is generally considered safe as long as it is used together with standard medical practices. Always talk to your health provider before starting any CAM practice like Reiki.

Reiki is sometimes used by dying patients to achieve a sense of peace.

References

Carlson, J. *Complementary Therapies and Wellness: Practice Essentials for Holistic Health Care.* Upper Saddle River, NJ: Prentice Hall, 2003.

"Introduction to Reiki." National Center for Complementary and Alternative Medicine. Accessed January 13, 2008. http://nccam.nih.gov/health/reiki.

"Reiki." Aetna InteliHealth. Accessed January 14, 2008. www.intelihealth.com/ IH/ihtIH/WSIHW000/8513/34968/360056.html?d=dmtContent.

What are the differences and similarities between magnet therapy and polarity therapy?

While both magnet therapy and polarity therapy are considered complementary and alternative medicine (CAM) forms, and while it seems reasonable to associate the two together, they are quite different. The use of magnets to treat health conditions goes back at least to the early Egyptians. Polarity therapy, however, is a relatively recent CAM, appearing in the mid-twentieth century. Table 4-3 compares and contrasts the two CAM therapies.

As with other CAM practices, always talk to your primary health care provider before starting any magnet or polarity therapy.

Anyone with an implanted device, such as a defibrillator, an insulin pump, or a pacemaker, should not use magnet therapy, as this may affect the device's functioning. Pregnant women should also avoid magnet therapy.

Polarity draws much inspiration from traditional Indian medicine, or Ayurveda. It also is based on Hermetic philosophy.

Table 4-3. Magnetic therapy versus polarity therapy

Magnet therapy	Polarity therapy
Thousands of years old	Created in the mid-1900s
Therapy can be applied to the whole body or to just parts that are affected	Five or seven primary pathways in the body ("chakras") where energy flows are targeted
The magnetic fields and polarity of static magnets or electromagnetic magnets, which are measured in strength units called gauss (G), are the basis of therapy	A central belief is that all of the body's cells have a polarity—negative and positive poles
Some evidence suggests that pulsed electromagnets may help some types of fractures heal faster, but most magnet therapies are not supported by scientific evidence	There is no real evidence to support polarity therapy, and researchers have not yet closely examined its safety
Magnets marketed to consumers are often products that are worn, such as shoe insoles, belts, pillows, bandages, and bracelets. These are usually static (permanent) magnets. Electromagnets may include magnetic resonance imaging machines	Like Reiki and therapeutic touch, polarity therapy may involve passing hands over the body to manipulate energy fields. It may also incorporate yoga with gentle rocking and vocalizations all aimed at increasing relaxation
Experts agree that magnet therapy should not be used in place of more traditional medicine treatments	Experts agree that polarity therapy should not be used in place of more traditional medicine treatments

References

"Magnet Therapy." Aetna InteliHealth. Accessed January 12, 2008. www.inteli health.com.

"Polarity." Aetna InteliHealth. Accessed January 13, 2008. www.intelihealth .com.

"Questions and Answers About Using Magnets to Treat Pain." National Center for Complementary and Alternative Medicine. Accessed January 11, 2008. http://nccam.nih.gov/health/magnet/magnet.htm.

ASK THE EXPERTS

Following is a list of health care professionals who can help you answer more in-depth questions related to issues discussed in this chapter. A good starting point would be your primary care physician (your family physician, internist, pediatrician, or nurse practitioner). From there, he or she might recommend that you visit with other medical specialists or health care professionals. Each one has received specialized training in his or her area of expertise. *(See the Glossary of Experts for descriptions, online directories, and credentialing information.)*

- Acupuncturists
- Ayurvedic practitioners
- Biofeedback therapists
- Complementary and alternative medicine (CAM) practitioners
- Doctors of Chiropractic (DCs)
- Family physicians
- Herbalists (RHs)
- Homeopaths

- Massage therapists
- Naturopaths
- Nurses
- Nutritionists
- Pediatricians
- Pharmacists
- Registered dieticians (RDs)
- Yoga instructors

5

Drug Information

Walk down the aisles of a pharmacy and ask yourself, "How much do I really know about the medicines stacked on the shelves?" Likewise, how much do you know about the prescription medicines you or your family members take? If you can admit that you don't know much about the medicines, you are not alone. There are so many medicines available that it's impossible to know much about more than a few. However, many people realize that they can easily find out more about a medicine by using the drug information available in libraries as well as online.

The more you know about the medicines you take, the better. Using drugs safely is extremely important. The questions in this chapter cover many common concerns about both over-the-counter and prescription medicines.

OVER-THE-COUNTER MEDICINES

What is an over-the-counter medicine?

Over-the-counter (OTC) medicines are drugs you can buy without a doctor's prescription. These drugs are sold in pharmacies, grocery stores, and other common shopping areas. Chances are that you have used some of these products to relieve pain, nausea, or constipation or to treat flu or cold symptoms. Some OTC medicines prevent or cure diseases, such as tooth decay and athlete's foot. Others help manage chronic problems, such as headaches and migraines.

> When using an over-the-counter medicine, be sure to follow the directions on the package. Check with your doctor first if you take prescription medicines.

In the United States, the Food and Drug Administration decides whether a medicine is safe enough to sell over the counter. In most cases, OTC products are safe for healthy adults to use, as long as they follow the directions on the package. However, you should talk to your doctor before taking an OTC product if:

- you have health problems;
- you take any prescription medicines (combining OTC medicines with prescription medicines can lead to problems called "drug interactions" *(see "What are drug interactions?" later in this chapter)*; and/or
- you are trying to get pregnant, you are pregnant, or you are breast-feeding.

Talk to your pediatrician before giving your child an over-the-counter (OTC) medicine. Older adults should also check with their doctors before using OTC medicines.

OTC medicines are available in **generic** or **brand-name** forms. Generic drugs may be less expensive. Compare the lists of ingredients of the generic and the brand-name form. If the generic product has the same ingredients *and the same amounts of ingredients,* you may want to think about using it. Look for a product that will treat only the symptoms you have. If you have a runny nose, don't choose a product that also treats coughs and headaches. Ask your doctor or pharmacist if you have questions about which product to choose.

References

"OTC Drugs: Getting the Most from Your Medicine." American Academy of Family Physicians. Accessed October 31, 2007. http://familydoctor.org/online/famdocen/home/otc-center/basics/851.html.

"Over-the-Counter Medicines." U.S. National Library of Medicine. Accessed October 30, 2007. www.nlm.nih.gov/medlineplus/overthecountermedicines.html.

What are some safety tips for taking over-the-counter drugs?

Before you take an over-the-counter (OTC) medicine, read and understand the information on the drug label. Make sure you know and understand the following:

- Name of the drug (generic name and brand name)
- The ingredients
- What symptoms the active ingredients treat
- The dosage (amount of medicine to take)
- How many times a day it should be taken
- What time(s) of day it should be taken
- If it shouldn't be taken by people with certain health problems (such as asthma or high blood pressure)
- If you should avoid any activities while taking it
- The most common side effects and what to do if you have them
- The expiration date
- How to store the medicine properly
- Other special instructions

If you don't understand something about a medicine, ask your doctor or pharmacist.

Give all your doctors a written list of ALL the medicines you take, including prescription medicines, over-the-counter medicines, vitamins, and supplements.

Following are some safety tips for taking OTC products:

- Take only the recommended dose. Taking too much medicine can be harmful.
- Use OTC drugs only on a short-term basis. Don't take them for long periods of time unless your doctor tells you to.
- Before you take more than one medicine (OTC or prescription), talk to your doctor. Some drugs, taken together, can cause problems. *(See "What are drug interactions?" later in this chapter.)*
- Don't crush, break, or chew pills unless the label says to do this. Some medicines won't work right unless they're swallowed whole.
- When taking tablets or capsules, swallow them with plenty of water so that they don't become stuck in your esophagus.
- When taking a liquid medicine, shake the bottle before use to mix the ingredients.
- Read the label to see if you should avoid certain activities (such as drinking alcohol, driving a car, or operating machinery).

- Keep a written list of ALL the medicines you take. Include prescriptions, OTC medicines, herbal products, vitamins, and supplements. Make sure all your doctors have a copy of this list.
- Always give infants and children OTC medicines that are specially made for their age and weight. DO NOT give children adult products, not even in small doses.
- Don't use a medicine after it has expired.
- Keep the medicine in its original labeled container. Don't throw out the instructions and warnings (sometimes these are printed on the box). You may need this information at a later date.

When in doubt about a medicine, ask your doctor or pharmacist.

References

American College Of Physicians, ed. "Understanding Drugs." *Complete Home Medical Guide.* New York: DK, 2003.

"OTC Drugs: Getting the Most from Your Medicine." American Academy of Family Physicians. Accessed October 18, 2007. http://familydoctor.org/online/famdocen/home/otc-center/basics/851.html.

"Ten Ways to Be MedWise." National Council on Patient Information and Education. Accessed October 12, 2007. www.bemedwise.org/ten_ways/ten_ways.htm.

"Think It Through: A Guide to Managing the Benefits and Risks of Medicines." Center for Drug Evaluation and Research. U.S. Food and Drug Administration. Accessed October 11, 2007. www.fda.gov/cder/consumer info/think.htm.

What does it mean to have an adverse effect from an over-the-counter drug?

Even though you can buy certain drugs without a prescription, they can still be dangerous and cause you harm. Problems from over-the-counter (OTC) medicines are called *adverse effects* or *adverse reactions.* Side effects and drug interactions are two kinds of adverse effects you can experience from OTC drugs. Drug interactions include drug–drug interactions and food–drug interactions. *(See "What are drug interactions?" later in this chapter.)*

Most medications can cause some side effects. The side effects that occur vary dramatically among people. Everyone is unique and can react differently to medicines. Side effects are generally minor, but some people can experience life-threatening side effects.

The following are examples of side effects:

- Bleeding
- Bruising easily
- Confusion
- Constipation

- Diarrhea
- Difficulty breathing
- Indigestion
- Lack of appetite

- Nausea
- Rashes
- Vomiting

If you experience any of these symptoms, try to recall when they occurred and how long they lasted. Share as much information as possible with your doctor to help him or her determine if the symptoms are caused by the medicine, your illness, or something else.

Check what active ingredients are in the over-the-counter (OTC) medicines you are taking. Combining OTC drugs could result in taking too much of a common ingredient, and too much of any one ingredient might damage your liver or lead to other serious health problems.

Many factors can lead to adverse effects:

- If you have had a previous adverse reaction to a drug, you are more likely to have an adverse reaction to other drugs.
- Individuals who have food or other allergies are also more likely to develop allergies to medications.
- It is important to follow the dosing instructions. Taking too much of a medication can lead to adverse effects.
- Some medications have special instructions, such as avoiding the sun or certain activities. Ignoring these instructions can also cause adverse effects.
- Older adults are more likely to experience negative reactions to medicines.
- Individuals with chronic health problems, such as diabetes and asthma, are more likely to have adverse reactions to drugs.
- The more prescriptions and OTC drugs you take, the higher your chances are of having an adverse reaction.
- Poor communication with your health care providers and pharmacists can lead to adverse effects. You need to tell them about all the medicines you are taking, including herbal products.

References

"OTC Drugs: Reducing the Risk of Adverse Effects." American Academy of Family Physicians. Accessed November 6, 2007. http://familydoctor.org/online/famdocen/home/otc-center/basics/852.printerview.html.

Rybacki, J. *Essential Guide to Prescription Drugs.* New York: HarperCollins, 2006.

"Taking Medicines." National Institute on Aging. Accessed November 4, 2007. http://nihseniorhealth.gov/takingmedicines/toc.html.

What are the most common over-the-counter pain relievers?

Over-the-counter (OTC) pain relievers are medicines that help reduce or relieve many types of pain:

- Arthritis pain
- Back pain
- Earaches
- Headaches
- Menstrual cramps
- Pain after surgery
- Pain from inflammation
- Sinusitis
- Sore muscles
- Sore throat

There are two main types of oral OTC pain relievers: acetaminophen and nonsteroidal anti-inflammatory drugs (NSAIDs).

Acetaminophen (one brand name is Tylenol) relieves pain and reduces fever by working on the parts of the brain that receive pain messages and control the body's temperature. It can be used safely by *most* people on a long-term basis for arthritis and other chronic painful conditions. However, many medicines contain acetaminophen. If you are not careful, you could take more than is good for you. Taking too much could cause liver damage. Tell your doctor if you often have to take more than two acetaminophen pills a day. If you have kidney or liver disease, or if you have three or more alcoholic drinks a day, talk to your doctor before taking acetaminophen.

NSAIDs include aspirin, ibuprofen (brand names include Motrin and Advil), and naproxen (one brand name is Aleve). NSAIDs reduce fever and relieve pain by reducing the number of prostaglandins (hormone-like substances) that your body makes. Prostaglandins cause the feeling of pain by irritating your nerve endings. NSAIDs can also reduce inflammation (swelling and irritation).

Long-term use of NSAIDs can cause problems such as upset stomach, ulcers, and gastrointestinal bleeding. NSAIDs should be taken with food or milk, because the most common side effects are related to the stomach. Other side effects may include high blood pressure and kidney damage. If you are taking other pain medications, don't take NSAIDs without first talking with your doctor.

Never give aspirin to children, because it could cause a condition called Reye's syndrome.

You shouldn't take NSAIDs if you are allergic to aspirin or other pain relievers. Before taking NSAIDs (especially aspirin), talk to your doctor if you:

- take blood-thinning medicine or have a bleeding disorder;
- have bleeding in the stomach or intestines or have stomach ulcers;
- have liver or kidney disease; and/or
- have three or more drinks that contain alcohol every day.

For most people, OTC drugs are all they need to relieve pain or reduce fever. If an OTC drug doesn't help your pain or fever, call your doctor. Also, talk to your doctor if you have been taking the drug for more than ten days for pain or three days for fever. These can be signs that you have a more serious problem or need prescription medicine.

Call your doctor if you have been taking an over-the-counter drug for more than three days for fever or more than ten days for pain.

Topical pain relievers include creams, lotions, and sprays that are applied to the skin to relieve pain from sore muscles and arthritis. Some brand-name products include Aspercreme and BenGay. Some topical treatments contain a medicine like aspirin, while others "mask" the feelings of pain by making the skin feel warm or cold. In general, these topical medicines are safe, but be sure to follow all instructions carefully.

References

"Chronic Pain Medicines." American Academy of Family Physicians. Accessed November 12, 2007. http://familydoctor.org/online/famdocen/home/common/pain treatment/122.html.

"Pain Medicines." Cleveland Clinic. Accessed November 6, 2007. www.cleveland clinic.org/health/health-info/docs/3600/3663.asp?index= 12058.

"Pain Relievers: Understanding Your OTC Options." American Academy of Family Physicians. Accessed November 15, 2007. http://familydoctor.org/ online/famdocen/home/otc-center/otc-medicines/862.html.

What should I know when giving over-the-counter medicines to my child?

Children are more sensitive than adults to many drugs. Some drugs can cause serious illness or even death in children. **In general, children under two years shouldn't be given any over-the-counter (OTC) drug without the "OK" from a doctor.**

It is important to know how to give medicine to children. Following are some tips.

Read the label

Before giving an OTC medicine to your child, read all the labels and information on the package. If no dosage is given for children under 12 years old, do not give the medicine to your child. Check with your doctor or pharmacist first.

If a medicine's label does not list a dosage for children under 12 years of age, *do not* give it to your child. Check with your doctor or pharmacist first.

Be sure you know the *active ingredient* in the medicine. This is listed at the top of the "Drug Facts" label. The same active ingredient can be found in many medicines. If you are giving your child different medicines for different conditions, you may accidentally give him too much of the same active ingredient. This is dangerous. If you are confused about your child's medicines, check with your doctor or pharmacist.

The dosage for infants is usually different from the dosage for children. In general, check with your pediatrician before giving any medicine to an infant.

Give the correct amount

Make certain you understand how much medicine to give your child and when it is safe to give another dose. Not all medicines are right for an infant or a child. Medicines with the same brand name are sold in different strengths, such as infant, children, and adult formulas. The amount you give your child depends age and weight. For this reason, be sure you know your child's weight.

You will need to know your child's weight in order to give the right dose.

Use the dropper or cup that comes with the medicine

Liquid medicines usually come with a cup, spoon, or syringe to help measure the right dosage. Be sure to use it. A different tool (like a kitchen spoon) could hold the wrong amount of medicine. These are some common types of dosing tools:

- **Dosage cups** are for children who can drink from a cup. Look closely at the numbers on the side to get the right dose. Measure the liquid with the cup on a flat surface at eye level.
- **Dosing spoons** are for children who can drink from a cup but are likely to spill the contents. The spoon looks like a test tube with a spoon at the top end. Measure the liquid at eye level. Let your child sip the medicine from the spoon.
- **Droppers** are for children who can't drink from a cup. Measure the liquid at eye level. Give the medicine to your child quickly before it drips out.
- **Syringes** are for children who can't drink from a cup. Squirt the medicine into the back of the mouth or toward the inside cheek. If the syringe has a cap, be sure to remove the cap before giving the medicine to your child. It is a choking hazard.

Know the difference between a tablespoon (tbsp) and a teaspoon (tsp). Do not confuse them! A tablespoon holds three times as much medicine as a teaspoon.

Other precautions

- Give your child an OTC medicine only when it's truly necessary. For example, when your child has a cold, sometimes OTC medicines don't help or can cause unwanted side effects like excitability or drowsiness. Drugs are not always the answer when your child is sick.

- Watch your child closely for side effects or allergic reactions. Call your child's doctor if you see anything unusual.
- Avoid giving your child medicines that contain alcohol.
- Do not give aspirin to children, especially if they have chickenpox or flu symptoms. Such aspirin use has been linked to Reye's syndrome, a rare but serious condition that can cause death.
- Store medicines in a safe place and out of your child's reach. Use a child-resistant cap.
- Check the safety seal before opening a new medicine. If it is not intact, do not use the medicine.

Do not give aspirin to children or teenagers who have chickenpox or flu symptoms. This can cause the rare but serious Reye's syndrome.

References

"How to Give Medicine to Children." U.S. Food and Drug Administration. Accessed November 1, 2007. www.fda.gov/FDAC/features/196_kid.html.

"How to Give Medicine to Children: Do You Know How to Give Medicine to Children?" U.S. Food and Drug Administration. Accessed November 1, 2007. www.fda.gov/opacom/lowlit/medchld.html.

"Kids Aren't Just Small Adults: Medicines, Children and the Care Every Child Deserves." Center for Drug Evaluation and Research. U.S. Food and Drug Administration. Accessed November 4, 2007. www.fda.gov/cder/consumer info/kids.htm.

"Medicine and Your Child: How to Give Your Child Medicine." American Academy of Family Physicians. Accessed November 3, 2007. http://family doctor.org/online/famdocen/home/children/parents/safety/097.html.

Is it safe to take over-the-counter medicines while pregnant or nursing?

If you're trying to get pregnant, if you are pregnant, or if you are breast-feeding, check with your doctor before taking any medicines or herbal products. Even drugs you can buy without a prescription can cause birth defects or affect a nursing baby.

For women who plan to get pregnant

- If you're not pregnant yet, you can increase your chance of having a healthy baby by planning ahead. Talk to your doctor, nurse, or pharmacist to find out which medicines are safe to take before becoming pregnant.

- Your baby is most sensitive to harm 2 to 8 weeks after conception. This is the time when your baby's facial features and organs begin to form. During some of this time, many women do not know they are pregnant. This is why it's best to start acting as if you're pregnant *before you actually are.*

Take folic acid daily if you are trying to get pregnant. This simple step can prevent birth defects. Most prenatal vitamins contain the recommended amount of folic acid.

For women who are pregnant

- Avoid using medicines during your first trimester, if possible. The risk to your baby is highest at this time. Again, *check with your doctor* before using any medicine or herbal product.
- Acetaminophen (brand-name Tylenol) is usually safe for short-term pain relief during pregnancy.
- Don't take the following:
  - *Aspirin* (Bayer, St. Joseph). It can cause low birth rate and problems during delivery.
  - *Ibuprofen, naproxen,* or *ketoprofen* (Motrin, Advil, Aleve, Oruvail). These products, called *nonsteroidal anti-inflammatory drugs* (NSAIDs), can cause heart problems in your baby or problems during delivery.
  - Herbs, minerals ,and *amino acids.* No one is sure if these are safe for pregnant women, so it's best not to use them.
  - *Regular vitamins.* Some vitamins contain dosages that are too high for pregnant women. Ask instead about *prenatal vitamins.*
- Check the medicine's labels and package inserts. They will list any warnings about taking the drug while pregnant.

Not enough is known about the safety of many medications when taken by pregnant women. Pregnant women usually do not take part in clinical trials because there might be risks to the unborn baby. Testing on animals does not always predict how medicines will affect humans. This is why taking medicines while pregnant can be risky.

For women who are nursing

- Many medicines can pass from your breast milk to your baby *in very small amounts*. This is why it is very important to check with your doctor before taking any medications while nursing.
- Acetaminophen (Tylenol) and NSAIDs (such as ibuprofen) are usually safe for breast-feeding women to take for pain relief.
- Avoid aspirin. It comes out in your breast milk and can cause rashes and bleeding problems in nursing babies.
- Limit your use of antihistamines. They can cause side effects in your baby, such as drowsiness, crying, and sleep problems. Antihistamines may also decrease the amount of milk you produce.
- If your doctor prescribes an oral medicine, take it right after nursing or before your baby's longest sleep period. Watch your baby for signs of side effects, such as rash, sleepiness, diarrhea, colic, breathing trouble, or any other problem your baby did not have before you took the medicine.
- Always read the medicine's labels and package inserts. They will list any warnings about taking the drug while breast-feeding.

References

"Medication Exposures During Pregnancy and Breastfeeding: Frequently Asked Questions." Centers for Disease Control and Prevention. U.S. Department of Health & Human Services. Accessed October 18, 2007. www.cdc.gov/ncbddd/meds/faqs.htm.

"Medicine and Pregnancy." U.S. Food & Drug Administration Office of Women's Health. Accessed October 19, 2007. www.fda.gov/womens/getthefacts/pregnancy.html.

"OTC Drugs: Special Groups At Risk of Adverse Effects." American Academy of Family Physicians. Accessed October 15, 2007. http://familydoctor.org/online/famdocen/home/otc-center/basics/853.html.

"Over-the-Counter Medications and Breastfeeding." Cleveland Clinic. Accessed October 18, 2007. www.clevelandclinic.org/health/health-info/docs/3800/3882.asp?index=12353.

Can I drink alcohol when taking over-the-counter medicines?

Nonprescription or over-the-counter (OTC) medicines are often used to treat common illnesses. As with prescription medicines, it's important to follow your doctor's and the manufacturer's advice on how and when to take OTC medicines. Because certain OTC medicines can interact with alcohol, it is always a good idea to talk to your family doctor or pharmacist about whether or not alcohol should be limited or avoided when taking them. In particular, OTC medicines that treat coughs and colds, allergies, or sleep problems may contain ingredients known to interact with alcohol in some people. Mixing alcohol with some of these medications may cause excessive drowsiness, vomiting, breathing difficulties, internal bleeding, or other problems. Moreover, the alcohol may dilute or completely cancel out the OTC medicine's effects, making the medicine useless and sometimes toxic.

> Some over-the-counter medicines may contain as much as 10 percent alcohol by volume.

Always read the OTC labels, and, when in doubt, seek advice from a health care professional. **The National Council on Patient Information and Education recommends the following tips to use OTC medicines wisely:**

- Read the labels on the medicines, and make sure you follow the directions carefully.
- If you are not clear on the directions or have questions, talk to your pharmacist or another health care professional before taking the medicine.
- Take only the recommended dosage listed on the "Drug Facts" label.
- Talk to your doctor or pharmacist before you start combining OTC medicines.
- Keep a record of all of the OTC medicines and herbal supplements you take.

> Because aging slows down the body's ability to break down alcohol, older people are at increased risk of dangerous alcohol/over-the-counter interactions.

☞ To see a list of popular over-the-counter medicines that may interact with alcohol, check out the National Institute on Alcohol Abuse and Alcoholism's online guide "Harmful Interactions: Mixing Alcohol with Medicines" at http://pubs.niaaa.nih .gov/publications/Medicine/medicine.htm.

(See "What are drug interactions?" later in this chapter.)

References

"Be MedWise: Use Over-the-Counter Medicines Wisely." National Council on Patient Information and Education. Accessed October 30, 2007. www .bemedwise.org/brochure/bemedwise_english_brochure.pdf.

"Harmful Interactions: Mixing Alcohol with Medicines." National Institute on Alcohol Abuse and Alcoholism. Accessed October 27, 2007. http://pubs .niaaa.nih.gov/publications/Medicine/medicine.htm.

"Medicines: Use Them Safely." National Institute on Aging. Accessed October 22, 2007. www.niapublications.org/agepages/medicine.asp.

PRESCRIPTION MEDICINES

What is a prescription medication?

A prescription medication is a drug that requires a written statement, called a *prescription*, from your doctor in order for you to purchase the drug from a pharmacy. This prescription tells the pharmacist what you need and the name of the doctor who prescribed the medicine. Over-the-counter medications do not require a prescription.

Drugs have generic and brand names. You should be aware of both names for any medicine you are using. The generic name is shorthand for the chemical name for a drug. The brand name is a special name, or a trade name, given to a drug by a manufacturer. For example, methylphenidate is a generic drug name. Methylphenidate has many brand names, such as Concerta, Metadate, Ritalin, and Methylin.

All prescription drugs made in the United States are tested in clinical trials and approved by the Food and Drug Administration. New drugs are tested on animals first, and then the drugs go through three phases of human testing before they are approved. Some drugs may have an accelerated approval process if they are used to treat life-threatening illnesses that do not currently have effective treatments.

According to the California Board of Pharmacy, more than half the U.S. population receives at least one prescription drug each year. The average per year is 7.5 prescriptions per medicine user.

Prescription drugs have both risks and benefits. It is important to weigh these options with your doctor before you start taking any new drug. You may decide the cost and unwanted side effects outweigh the benefit you would receive.

To decrease the risk of side effects and drug interactions, be sure to tell your doctor:

- if you are taking any prescription or over-the-counter medicines;
- if you are taking any vitamins, dietary supplements, or herbal supplements;
- if you have a chronic illness or medical condition, such as high blood pressure;
- if you have any allergies, including foods;
- if you or a close family member have had any serious problems or allergic reactions to any drugs;
- if you are pregnant, nursing a baby, or planning to get pregnant;
- if you use alcohol or tobacco; and/or
- if you are on a special diet.

(See "What are drug interactions?" later in this chapter.)

To reduce the risk of side effects, read the printed information and instructions that come with your prescription medicine.

References

"Consumer Tips." California Board of Pharmacy. Accessed October 21, 2007. www.pharmacy.ca.gov/consumers/consumer_tips.

Griffith, H. *Complete Guide to Prescription & Nonprescription Drugs.* New York: Penguin Group, 2006.

"Taking Medicines." National Institute on Aging. Accessed October 23, 2007. http://nihseniorhealth.gov/takingmedicines/toc.html.

What health professionals are authorized to write prescriptions?

A straightforward answer to this question is, *any health professional licensed to write prescriptions.* Generally this means that licensed physicians are authorized to prescribe medications. Specialized health professionals, like nurse practitioners, podiatrists, dentists, veterinarians, and optometrists, may also be allowed certain prescription privileges. However, these specialized health professionals are sometimes limited by their state as to what classes of medications they can prescribe and for what purposes. An optometrist, for example, may be limited to prescribe only medications dealing with eye diseases or eye health.

In general, most prescriptions should not be given unless you have first been physically examined by a health professional. For this reason, it's a good idea to avoid online services that offer prescriptions without ever meeting with you for a physical exam. Getting prescriptions without first seeing your doctor can result in an incorrect diagnosis and, as a result, a prescription medicine that may not be right for you.

> The U.S. Food and Drug Administration allows each state to decide what it considers a valid prescription.

References

"Buying Prescription Medicine Online: A Consumer Safety Guide." U.S. Food and Drug Administration. Accessed October 19, 2007. www.fda.gov/buy onlineguide.

"Use Caution Buying Medical Products Online." U.S. Food and Drug Administration. Accessed October 18, 2007. www.fda.gov/fdac/2005/105_buy.html.

What do I need to know about getting a prescription filled?

After you receive a prescription from your health care provider, you need to choose how to get the prescription filled. You can buy prescription medications from pharmacies in-person, online, or by phone.

In-person pharmacies

Most people fill their prescriptions at local pharmacies, which are usually located within a drug or grocery store. To avoid waiting in line at the pharmacy, don't go there during the busiest hours, which are right after opening, during the lunch hour, and immediately after people get off of work.

When selecting a pharmacy, consider the following questions:

- What are the store hours?
- Is the pharmacy conveniently located?
- Does my health insurance limit where I can have the prescription filled?
- Does the pharmacy keep electronic patient records and check for drug interactions? *(See "What are drug interactions?" later in this chapter.)*
- Is the staff friendly and willing to answer questions?

If you use the same pharmacy for all of your prescriptions, your pharmacist can easily keep track of possible drug interactions. *(See "What are drug interactions?" later in this chapter.)*

Mail-order pharmacies

Some people use a mail-order pharmacy to fill their prescriptions, and some insurance companies require people to do so. Here's how it works. Your physician will phone or otherwise submit your prescription to the mail-order pharmacy. The prescription will be mailed to you, typically enough for three months. When you need a refill, you will call the mail-order pharmacy's automated phone system. It can take a week or longer to receive your medicine, so it is necessary to plan ahead. Mail-order pharmacies work best for drugs you will be taking over a long period of time. If you will only refill the medicine one time, a local pharmacy would be more appropriate.

Internet pharmacies

If you want to use an Internet pharmacy, you need first to take the time to carefully choose one that is reputable. Online stores may try to sell you fake drugs or medicines that are expired. While the cheap prices of drugs from outside of the United States may tempt you, keep in mind that they may not be safe. The U.S. Food and Drug Administration does not test drugs from foreign countries.

☞ The National Association of Boards of Pharmacy (NABP) maintains a database of safe online pharmacies. To search this database, visit www.nabp.net and click VIPPS (Verified Internet Pharmacy Practice Sites).

When you are evaluating an Internet pharmacy Web site, look for information about the company's privacy policies. Will it protect your health information? Make sure the Web site lists a physical address and phone numbers you can use for contact. Avoid sites that do not require a physical exam or a prescription from a doctor to buy a prescription medication.

References

"Buying Prescription Medicine Online: A Consumer Safety Guide." U.S. Food and Drug Administration. Accessed November 3, 2007. www.fda.gov/buy onlineguide.

Van Voirhees, B. "Getting a Prescription Filled." U.S. National Library of Medicine. Accessed November 2, 2007. www.nlm.nih.gov/medlineplus/ency/article/001956.htm.

Is it safe to buy prescription medicines online?

Although it is convenient to purchase medicines online, sometimes the risks can outweigh the benefits. According to the U.S. Food and Drug Administration (FDA), some of the medicines sold online are being distributed by unlicensed pharmacies, by people not qualified to determine the correct medicine for your condition, and by those who are not interested in protecting your private health information. Such distributors may even be dealing with medicines that are:

- counterfeit,
- dangerous,
- out of date,
- unapproved by the FDA for safety,
- mishandled, and/or
- mislabeled.

To avoid purchasing such dangerous products, first talk to your doctor about whether it is a good or a bad idea to fill your prescription online. There may be special steps needed to fill the prescription that would prevent you from considering online pharmacies. Next, make sure that the online pharmacy you are considering is a **state-licensed**

pharmacy in the United States. You also should look for a "Verified Internet Pharmacy Practice Sites Seal," which tells you that the online pharmacy meets state and federal rules for distributing medicines over the Internet.

> ☞ Before getting a prescription filled by an online pharmacy, check with your state board of pharmacy to see if it is state licensed and in good standing. You can find boards of pharmacy on the National Association of Boards of Pharmacy's Web site at www.nabp.info.

Other questions to consider when choosing a safe online pharmacy include the following:

- Does it require a prescription from a health professional licensed in the United States?
- Does it have valid contact information in the event you need to talk to a person?
- Does it list its policies for protecting your private health information?
- Does it have a licensed pharmacist available to answer any questions you may have?

> ☞ For the list of Verified Internet Pharmacy Practice Sites, go to www.vipps.info.

References

"Buying Prescription Medicine Online: A Consumer Safety Guide." U.S. Food and Drug Administration. Accessed November 10, 2007. www.fda.gov/buy onlineguide.

"Use Caution Buying Medical Products Online." U.S. Food and Drug Administration. Accessed November 6, 2007. www.fda.gov/fdac/2005/105_buy.html.

What is prescription drug abuse?

Using prescription drugs for nonmedical reasons is called *prescription drug abuse*. It is a form of substance abuse. People may abuse prescription drugs to get high, relieve stress, or lose weight. They may also combine the drugs with alcohol to increase the effects. Like illegal drugs, people can become addicted to prescription medicines.

According to the National Institute on Drug Abuse, 15 million people reported using a prescription drug for nonmedical reasons at least once during 2003.

These are three classes of commonly abused prescription drugs:

1. **Opioids:** Opioids (also called *narcotics*) are used to treat pain. Some examples of opioids include oxycodone (OxyContin), hydrocodone (Vicodin), and meperidine (Demerol).
2. **Central nervous system (CNS) depressants:** CNS depressants are sometimes called *sedatives* or *tranquilizers*. They can be prescribed for anxiety, panic attacks, and sleep problems. Pentobarbital sodium (Nembutal), diazepam (Valium), and alprazolam (Xanax) are examples of CNS depressants.
3. **Stimulants:** People with narcolepsy, attention deficit/hyperactivity disorder (ADHD), depression, obesity, and asthma may be prescribed stimulants. Some examples of stimulants are methylphenidate (Ritalin), amphetamine/dextroamphetamine (Adderall), and atomoxetine (Strattera).

Cough medicines that contain codeine are also commonly abused.

What to look for

People abusing prescription drugs may appear more forgetful and moody. They may have trouble paying attention and difficulty sleeping. They miss work or school, and they lose interest in things they used to enjoy.

Possible signs of prescription drug abuse

- Taking someone else's prescription drugs
- Visiting different doctors in order to get more prescriptions
- Lying about pain or discomfort to get pain medicine
- Writing fake prescriptions

"Pharmacy shopping" is another sign of prescription drug abuse. Pharmacists won't fill multiple narcotic prescriptions, and they take note if someone tries to get a refill too early. Hence, people use many different pharmacies, making it harder to track the prescriptions being filled.

Treatments are available to help people who are addicted to prescription drugs. If someone you know is abusing prescription drugs, convince him or her to see a doctor.

References

"Prescription Drug Abuse." *MD Consult Patient Education Handout.* USC School of Medicine Library, Columbia, SC. Accessed November 7, 2007. Keyword: prescription drug abuse.

"Prescription Drug Abuse Chart." National Institute on Drug Abuse. Accessed November 9, 2007. www.nida.nih.gov/DrugPages/PrescripDrugsChart.html.

What are some common prescription pain medicines?

Pain medicines, also called *analgesics,* usually fall into one of three categories: opioid medicines, nonopioid medicines, and adjuvant medicines.

Opioids, also called *narcotics,* are the most powerful class of prescription analgesics available. These are often used to treat severe pain, especially short-lived pain like the pain experienced after surgery. Probably the most well-known opioid is morphine, which can be taken by mouth or by injection. Some of the common side effects of taking opioids are drowsiness, nausea, constipation, and itching. Other common prescription opioids include codeine, fentanyl, hydrocodone, hydromorphone, levorphanol, meperidine, methadone, oxycodone, oxymorphone, pentazocine, and propoxyphene.

☞ For a chart of opioid pain medicines and their uses, see the *Merck Manual Home Edition* at www.merck.com/mmhe/sec06/ch078/ch078d.html.

Nonopioid pain medicines are usually effective in treating milder forms of pain. Depending on how high their dosage formulation is, some are available over-the-counter and some require a prescription. Ibuprofen, ketoprofen, and naproxen, for example, may be obtained over-the-counter or by prescription, depending on their dosages. Other common nonopioid analgesics that may be prescribed include acetaminophen, diflunisal, salsalate, celecoxib, diclofenac, etodolac, fenoprofen, flurbiprofen, indomethacin, ketorolac, meclofenamate, mefenamic. acid, meloxicam, nabumetone, oxaprozin, piroxicam, sulindac, and tolmetin.

The most common **adjuvant analgesics** prescribed for pain include antidepressants like amitriptyline, anticonvulsants like pregabalin, and local anesthetics like lidocaine. While these medicines are usually prescribed for other non-pain-related conditions, they sometimes are useful for certain patients who are experiencing less acute forms of pain such as that caused by nerve damage, migraines, or certain types of arthritis.

There are many possible treatments for pain other than over-the-counter or prescription medicines. Transcutaneous electrical nerve stimulation (TENS), for example, involves sending a small electrical current through the skin throughout the day or several times a day. This treatment option may be useful for chronic pain sufferers. Ask your doctor what other treatment options may be right for you.

References

"Pain Medicines." Cleveland Clinic. Accessed November 4, 2007. www.cleveland clinic.org/health/health-info/docs/3600/3663.asp?index=12058.

"Pain Relievers." *MedlinePlus Health Topics.* U.S. National Library of Medicine. Accessed November 13, 2007. www.nlm.nih.gov/medlineplus/painrelievers.html.

"Treatment: Pain." *Merck Manual Home Edition.* Accessed November 4, 2007. www.merck.com/mmhe/sec06/ch078/ch078d.html.

What is antibiotic resistance? Is it a serious problem?

Antibiotics are drugs used to treat infections that are caused by bacteria. Over time, bacteria can mutate to resist antibiotic treatment. This is called *antibiotic resistance.* Bacteria will become resistant faster when antibiotics are used too often or when they are not needed.

Antibiotic resistance is a serious public health problem. Antibiotic-resistant bacteria are tough to cure and costly to treat. Resistant bacteria need stronger, more toxic drugs to kill the infection. Some of these drugs are given intravenously in a hospital. People with antibiotic-resistant bacteria can be contagious for a longer period. This means that they can spread the infection to friends and family while doctors try new treatments to kill the bacteria. Resistant bacteria may even cause death.

Nearly 100,000 people die each year in the United States from infections they catch in the hospital, often because these bacteria are resistant to antibiotics.

Antibiotics are often used in hospitals because people in hospitals tend to have a weakened immune system. Thus, they can catch an infection more easily. About 190 million doses of antibiotics are dispensed each day in hospitals. This heavy use of antibiotics increases the speed with which the bacteria become resistant. More than 70 percent of the bacteria that cause infections in hospitals are resistant to at least one of the drugs commonly used to treat them.

Following are some tips to help prevent antibiotic resistance:

- **Don't ask your doctor to prescribe an antibiotic for a viral infection.** Many patients expect doctors to prescribe antibiotics for a cold or the flu. Colds, influenza, most sore throats, and most coughs are infections caused by viruses. Antibiotics do not cure these viral infections and will not help you feel better more quickly. Antibiotics are used to treat bacterial infections. Ear infections, strep throat, urinary tract infections, and some sinus infections are examples of bacterial infections. Doctors can use a test to find out if your infection is caused by bacteria. Many physicians give in to their patients' demands for antibiotics. It is estimated that every year in the United States, doctors write 50 million antibiotic prescriptions for illnesses for which antibiotics offer no benefit.

Antibiotics DO NOT cure a cold or the flu.

- **Use antibiotics exactly as directed by your doctor.** Many people using antibiotics start to feel better before they are finished taking all of their pills. Therefore, they stop taking them. Stopping treatment too soon may leave some of the bacteria alive and resistant to future antibiotic treatment. **When you are taking an antibiotic, it is important to finish the full dosage.**
- **Never save antibiotics to use for another time when you are feeling sick.** The antibiotic may not be suitable for your illness. You may not have enough pills to kill all of the harmful bacteria.

References

"Antibiotics: Too Much of a Good Thing." Mayo Clinic. Accessed January 3, 2008. www.mayoclinic.com/print/antibiotics/FL00075/METHOD=print.

"Antibiotics: When They Can and Can't Help." American Academy of Family Physicians. Accessed January 5, 2008. http://familydoctor.org/680.xml.

"General Information About Antibiotic Resistance." Centers for Disease Control and Prevention. U.S. Department of Health & Human Services. Accessed January 3, 2008. www.cdc.gov/drugresistance/community/faqs.htm.

"Health Care Topics: Antibiotic Resistance." American College of Physicians. Accessed January 5, 2008. www.doctorsforadults.com/topics/dfa_anti.htm.

"The Problem of Antibiotic Resistance." National Institute of Allergy and Infectious Diseases. Accessed January 5, 2008. www.niaid.nih.gov/fact sheets/antimicro.htm.

OTHER DRUG INFORMATION

What are drug interactions?

Drug interactions are problems that occur when a medicine you are taking reacts with some other substance. **There are three categories of drug interactions:**

- **Drug–drug interactions**, which occur when one drug reacts with another. An example of this would be taking both a sleep medication (sedative) and an allergy medication (antihistamine). The combination of a sedative with an antihistamine may cause you to become sluggish and unable to safely operate machinery or drive a car.
- **Drug–food interactions**, which occur when a drug you are taking has an unexpected reaction with a food or beverage that you consume. Alcohol, in particular, is known to have adverse reactions with some drugs, sometimes causing you to become too sleepy to safely operate a car, for example.
- **Drug–condition interactions**, which occur when a drug you are taking compounds a preexisting medical condition that you have. One example would be taking a nasal decongestant when you also have high blood pressure. The combination of the drug with the condition may lead to a dangerous interaction during which your already high blood pressure goes even higher.

There are a number of things you can do to prevent harmful drug interactions from happening:

- Discuss with your health professional all of the prescription and over-the-counter medicines, dietary/herbal supplements, vitamins, and minerals that you take and even foods that you eat. He or she may be able to point out potential drug interactions that may occur between any of the substances.
- Read the labels of everything that you take, especially over-the-counter medicines and prescription medicines, which list adverse drug interactions that may occur under certain circumstances.
- Make a list of any questions that you have about possible drug interactions, and talk to your doctor or pharmacist about them. You can even bring the medicines in with you so that the two of you can discuss the label instructions directly.

☞ For more information on common drug–drug interactions, visit http://familydoctor .org/online/etc/medialib/famdoc/docs/otc-drugdruginteractions.Par .0001.File.dat/otc_drugdruginteractionschart.pdf.

References

"Drug Interactions and Side Effects." American Heart Association. Accessed November 13, 2007. www.americanheart.org/presenter.jhtml?identifier=117.

"Drug Interactions: What You Should Know." U.S. Food and Drug Administration. Accessed November 14, 2007. www.fda.gov/cder/consumerinfo/drug interactions.htm.

"OTC Drugs: Reducing the Risk of Adverse Effects." American Academy of Family Physicians. Accessed November 14, 2007. http://familydoctor.org/ online/famdocen/home/otc-center/basics/852.printerview.html.

How do I know if a product is a drug?

Cosmetics containing color additives must be approved by the Food and Drug Administration.

There are many everyday items in your home that are considered drugs (see Table 5-1 for examples). According to the U.S. Food and Drug Administration, **a product is a medicine or drug if it changes the way your body works or if it treats or prevents a disease.** For example, antiperspirants are technically drugs because they prevent our sweat glands from making sweat. Regular mouthwash is not a medicine, but mouthwash that contains active ingredients that reduce plaque and gum disease is a medicine. Toothpaste that contains fluoride helps reduce cavities, so it is also considered a drug.

To find out if a product is a drug, check the label to see if it contains an active ingredient. An active ingredient is the chemical that makes the medicine work. Manufacturers may call products containing drugs *cosmeceuticals.*

Table 5-1. Examples of products that are drugs

Product	Why is it a medicine?
Sunscreen	Prevents skin damage from the sun
Moisturizer or makeup containing sunscreen	Prevents skin damage from the sun
Nicotine gum or patch	Treats nicotine (cigarette/tobacco) addiction
Dandruff shampoo	Treats dandruff
Hair growth products	Prevents hair loss
Acne and pimple products	Prevents/treats acne

References

"Frequently Asked Questions: Cosmetics and Your Health." U.S. Department of Health & Human Services. Accessed November 9, 2007. http://womens health.gov/faq/cosmetics.pdf.

"Medicines in My Home." U.S. Food and Drug Administration. Accessed November 15, 2007. www.fda.gov/medsinmyhome.

What are generic drugs?

Generic drugs are basically copies of brand-name drugs. They are nearly identical in all ways except perhaps the way they look. This is because while a patent on the drug's chemical formulation may have expired, the look of the drug may be trademarked. By law, generics must be the same as the brand-names in their strength, performance, safety, and use. Often the only difference between expensive brand-name drugs and their generic equivalents may be in their color, shape, or taste.

In all states, pharmacists are allowed to use a generic equivalent to a prescribed brand-name drug. The only requirement is that the pharmacist must ask your permission first.

Generic drugs are nearly always cheaper than brand-name drugs. This is because brand-name drugs cost more for a manufacturer to develop and produce. Talk to your doctor about whether a cheaper generic drug may be available to replace any brand-name prescriptions. Not all brand-name drugs have a generic counterpart, but many do.

☞ For more information about generic drugs, visit the Food and Drug Administration's "Office of Generic Drugs" Web page at www.fda.gov/cder/ogd/index.htm. There is even an online resource called the "Electronic Orange Book" for exploring whether a brand-name drug has a generic equivalent.

References

"Frequently Asked Questions About Generic Drugs." U.S. Food and Drug Administration. Accessed November 20, 2007. www.fda.gov/cder/consumer info/generics_q&a.htm.

"Generic Drugs." *Consumer Reports*. Accessed November 14, 2007. www.crbest buydrugs.org/PDFs/GenericDrugs-FINAL.pdf.

Why do elderly people have to be especially careful when taking medications?

Seniors are more likely to have multiple chronic health problems, and they may have to take multiple medications to treat these conditions. Fifty percent of people aged 60 and over take at least three prescription medicines regularly. Seniors may find it difficult to remember what medicines they are supposed to take and when they are supposed to take them. **Taking more than seven medicines dramatically increases the risk of experiencing side effects and drug interactions.** Therefore, seniors need to be extra careful with their medicines. *(See "What are drug interactions?" earlier in this chapter.)*

Seniors are three times more likely to experience adverse reactions to drugs.

Body functions decline as people age. Consequently, their bodies process drugs differently than the younger adult. Specifically, seniors may absorb medicines differently due to decreased liver and kidney functions. As metabolism slows down, drugs may stay in the system for longer periods of time; therefore, seniors may need longer intervals of time between dosages. Fluid levels decrease as people age, lean muscle mass decreases, and fat reserves increase. These body weight and composition changes therefore create the need for seniors to take smaller drug dosages. When they start taking a new drug, seniors may need to make extra trips to the doctor's office so that their health care provider can adjust the dosage.

As the number of drugs a person takes increases, so does the frequency of adverse reactions.

The following are tips for seniors who take medicine:

- If childproof caps are hard for you to open, ask your pharmacist to put regular caps on your prescription bottles.
- If you have trouble swallowing pills, ask if the drug is available in a liquid form. Do not crush or chew pills without first checking with a health care provider.
- Ask the pharmacist to print the drug label in a larger font size to help you read it.
- Buy a daily medicine reminder box at your pharmacy. Such boxes have a compartment for each day of the week to help you keep track. A clear box will make it even easier to see if you have taken your medicine for the day. Calendars and alarms can also be used as memory aids.
- To help keep track of why you are taking a drug, write "cough" or "blood pressure" (or whatever the drug is used to treat) on the drug label. This can also help your family members and caregivers.
- Ask your health care provider to review annually all of the medicines you are taking.
- Throw away expired medicines.
- If you have to take medicine at night, turn on the light and check the name of the medicine.

- Keep an updated list of all the prescription and over-the-counter drugs you are taking. Include any instructions for taking the medicine.
- You may have been prescribed medications from different specialists. It is your responsibility to let each doctor know all of the medicines you are taking.
- Let your doctor know about any side effects you are experiencing. Memory problems and dementia commonly occur as people age, but they can also be side effects of medicines. Changes in mood and energy are other signs that a medicine is not working properly. Do not stop taking a drug without first talking to your doctor.
- If you have trouble paying for your prescriptions, ask your doctor if there are cheaper versions or discounts available. You can also contact organizations like the American Diabetes Association for discounts.

References

"Consumer Tips." California Board of Pharmacy. Accessed November 5, 2007. www.pharmacy.ca.gov/consumers/consumer_tips.

"Information About Your Medicine." *MD Consult Patient Education Handout.* USC School of Medicine Library, Columbia, SC. Accessed November 7, 2007. Keyword: medicines.

"Multiple Medicines." *Consumer Reports.* Accessed November 12, 2007. www.crbestbuydrugs.org/PDFs/MultipleMedicines-FINAL.pdf.

Rybacki, J. *Essential Guide to Prescription Drugs.* New York: HarperCollins, 2006.

What should I worry about when taking multiple medications?

Following are a number of concerns about taking multiple medications at the same time:

- The chance of a drug interaction is increased. *(See "What are drug interactions?" earlier in this chapter.)*
- The chance of being prescribed an unnecessary medicine is increased.
- The cost of medical care is increased.

To avoid such problems, it's a good idea to regularly talk to your doctor and pharmacist about all of the medications that you are taking. Make sure to mention any over-the-counter medications in addition to the prescription medications. Also, share information about all vitamins, minerals, and supplements, because these can also interact with different medications in different ways.

These are some good questions to ask your doctor:

- Why exactly do I need this medication?
- Am I taking any duplicate medications that I don't need?
- Is this drug a permanent or a temporary treatment?
- Are there better, nonmedicine options for my condition, such as a lifestyle change?

☞ To check for interactions among multiple medications, visit www.drugdigest.org and click on the "Check Interactions" link. There are other interactive tools you might want to use on this Web site as well.

References

"Multiple Medicines." *Consumer Reports.* Accessed November 10, 2007. www .crbestbuydrugs.org/PDFs/MultipleMedicines-FINAL.pdf.
"Seven Steps to Safety." Drug Digest.Org. Accessed November 14, 2007. www.drugdigest.org/DD/Home/Safety/0,21909,,00.html.

ASK THE EXPERTS

Following is a list of health care professionals who can help you answer more in-depth questions related to issues discussed in this chapter. A good starting point would be your primary care physician (your family physician, internist, pediatrician, or nurse practitioner). From there, he or she might recommend that you visit with other medical specialists or health care professionals. Each one has received specialized training in his or her area of expertise. *(See the Glossary of Experts for descriptions, online directories, and credentialing information.)*

- Dentists
- Family physicians
- Internists
- Nurse practitioners
- Obstetricians and gynecologists (OB/GYNs)

- Pediatricians
- Pharmacists
- Psychiatrists
- Psychologists

6

Odds and Ends

The world is full of remarkable things. One of the most fascinating aspects of human health is that it is unpredictable. "Strange" things happen to you or to people you know all the time, yet it can be difficult to find information about unusual health conditions. As a result, these conditions are often misunderstood. This is where libraries come into play. Often you can find answers about a not-so-common condition in the stacks of a library that you can't find elsewhere. In this chapter, we will present facts about some uncommon or misunderstood health conditions. We will also cover some general questions about technology and how it affects your health.

UNUSUAL OR MISUNDERSTOOD HEALTH CONDITIONS

What determines if a disease is "rare," and what are some of the rarest medical conditions known?

According to the National Organization for Rare Disorders (NORD), a condition is considered rare in America if it affects fewer than 200,000 people in the United States. This criterion varies from country to country, however. In Japan, for example, the definition of "rare" requires that fewer than 50,000 people in Japan be afflicted with a given condition. Based on the American definition, there are over 6,000 rare diseases affecting approximately 25 million Americans. Unfortunately, because pharmaceutical companies stand to make less money on diagnostic tools and medications for rare conditions than for more common ones, they have historically ignored these conditions. For this reason, the U.S. Congress passed the Orphan Drug Act in 1983, which creates additional incentives for pharmaceutical companies to develop treatments for rare diseases.

These are some of the rarer conditions described in the *NORD Guide to Rare Disorders*:

- **Moebius, or Möbius, syndrome:** From the time they are born, individuals with Moebius syndrome show facial paralysis, which gives them a "mask-like" appearance most notable when they are laughing or crying.
- **Fibrodysplasia ossificans progessiva:** Occurring approximately once in every two million live births, this painful disorder of the muscles, tendons, and ligaments can result in the formation of permanent bone growths that limit mobility. Children born with this rare disorder have characteristic short big toes.
- **Proteus syndrome:** This is an extremely rare condition in which the body experiences overgrowth of skin, bone, and fatty tissue in a patchy way across the body.
- **Hutchinson-Guilford progeria syndrome (HGPS):** HGPS, or simply *progeria*, occurs in approximately one out of every eight million births and involves premature aging in children, resulting in characteristic aging features and premature death from atherosclerosis.
- **Congenital hypertrichosis lanuginose (CHL):** CHL, or *Ambras syndrome*, or *werewolf syndrome*, occurs in approximately one out of every one billion births (some believe one out of every ten billion births) and involves excessive lanugo hair (fine body hair) growth over the entire body with perhaps the exception of the soles of the feet and the palms of the hands.

☞ According to the Proteus Syndrome Foundation (www.proteus-syndrome .org/index.htm), the syndrome became more widely known when it was discovered that Joseph Merrick, popularly known as "the Elephant Man," suffered from an extreme form of Proteus syndrome rather than neurofibromatosis, which is a nervous system disorder involving tumor growth on nerves.

References

"About NORD." National Organization of Rare Disorders. Accessed January 31, 2008. www.rarediseases.org/info/about.html.

National Organization of Rare Disorders. *NORD Guide to Rare Disorders*. Philadelphia: Lippincott Williams & Wilkins, 2003.

What are phobias, and what are some of the wildest phobias that people have developed?

Phobias are a fairly common type of anxiety disorder in which a person develops an overwhelming fear of an object (like a spider) or situation (like public speaking). It is estimated that nearly 8 percent of American adults have phobias at any given time. **These fears usually fall within one of three categories:**

1. **Agoraphobia**—the fear of being in a place or situation where something bad may happen and you may become trapped, with rescue being impossible. Women are most likely to develop agoraphobia. Often the fear develops after one or multiple panic attacks, which involve a sudden terror with symptoms such as sweating and faintness.
2. **Social phobia**—the fear of being embarrassed in public, often while performing some action in front of others. Speaking in public is the most common form of social phobia, but there are countless everyday activities people may develop social phobias of, including eating and using a public restroom.
3. **Specific phobia**—the fear of a specific object or situation. This tends to be the most common type of phobia. The phobia often focuses, to an irrational degree, on specific animals, high places (acrophobia), or enclosed spaces (claustrophobia). However, there are a number of rare specific phobias people have developed.

If a phobia interferes with your daily living, talk to your health care provider about treatment options, including cognitive behavioral therapy and medications. Often the symptoms can be alleviated or eliminated altogether.

Following are some of the "wilder" specific phobias mentioned in the medical literature:

- Allodoxaphobia: an irrational fear of opinions
- Anthrophobia or anthophobia: an irrational fear of flowers
- Arachibutyrophobia: an irrational fear of peanut butter sticking to the roof of the mouth
- Aulophobia: an irrational fear of flutes

- Euphobia: an irrational fear of hearing good news
- Genuphobia: an irrational fear of knees
- Iophobia: an irrational fear of rusty things
- Pentheraphobia: an irrational fear of mother-in-law
- Phronemophobia: an irrational fear of thinking
- Pteronophobia: an irrational fear of being tickled by feathers
- Teratophobia: an irrational fear of monsters or giving birth to a monster

☞ For a list of more than 500 specific phobias, visit www.phobialist.com.

References

"Let's Talk Facts About Phobias." American Psychiatric Association. Accessed January 31, 2008. www.healthyminds.org/multimedia/phobias.pdf.
"Phobias." U.S. National Library of Medicine. Accessed January 30, 2008. www.nlm.nih.gov/medlineplus/phobias.html.
"Phobic Disorders." *Merck Manual Home Edition*. Accessed January 27, 2008. www.merck.com/mmhe/sec07/ch100/ch100e.html.

What is obsessive compulsive disorder (OCD), and what are some of the most common obsessions and compulsions that people with OCD develop?

In general, obsessions are recurring thoughts that people can't seem to escape. Compulsions, sometimes called *rituals*, are repetitive behaviors people sometimes feel they must perform in order to avoid stress or anxiety. People with OCD usually experience both conditions, often feeling compelled to perform certain compulsions in order to avoid their obsessions. This pattern can become so out of control that people with OCD may become depressed and anxious.

Many researchers believe that chemical imbalances may be responsible for obsessive compulsive disorder—especially imbalances in neurotransmitters like serotonin.

Common items that are the focus of obsessions include the following:

- Germs
- Dirt

- Order and/or exactness
- Evil thoughts
- Certain images or sounds or words
- Failure
- Bodily fluid or waste

Common compulsions include the following:

- Grooming or washing specific parts of the body
- Checking locks and/or appliances
- Repetitively touching objects
- Ordering and arranging objects
- Counting and recounting, often to a certain number
- Hoarding items such as newspapers or containers
- Seeking approval

It is estimated that as many as 3.3 million Americans experience obsessive compulsive disorder each year.

There are a couple of treatment options available to people with OCD, including cognitive behavior therapy (CBT) and certain antidepressant medications. Often a combination of the two options is the most effective way to treat OCD symptoms. It is important to understand that people with OCD are not "crazy." In fact, they are almost always aware that their obsessions and compulsions are irrational, yet they are unable to stop them.

Trichotillomania is a compulsive disorder possibly related to obsessive compulsive disorder in which a person has strong urges to pull out his or her own hair at the root.

References

"Obsessive-Compulsive Disorder." U.S. National Library of Medicine. Accessed January 16, 2008. www.nlm.nih.gov/medlineplus/obsessivecompulsivedisorder.html.

"Obsessive-Compulsive Disorder (OCD)." Mental Health America. Accessed January 12, 2008. www.mentalhealthamerica.net/go/ocd.

"Trichotillomania." Nemours Foundation. Accessed January 8, 2008. www.kidshealth.org/teen/your_mind/mental_health/trichotillomania.html.

What exactly are parasites, and what are some of the most common ones?

Parasites are organisms that survive by living on or within other living organisms, called *hosts*. Parasites are often transmitted from host to host through contaminated food or water or anything that has come in contact with the contaminated feces of a host animal. Parasites can be extremely small organisms, like protozoa, that require a microscope to be seen, or they can be fairly large multicellular organisms, like worms. **Some of the more common parasites are now associated with many forms of water-borne and food-borne diseases** and include the following:

- *Giardia duodenalis:* Also called *Giardia intestinalis,* this is a common intestinal parasite that causes diarrhea, nausea, and cramps. It is spread through contaminated food and water. This organism is one of the more common causes of watery diarrhea following a camping trip. It can be "picked up" from drinking contaminated stream or lake water that hasn't been properly sterilized.
- *Cryptosporidium parvum:* This common intestinal parasite is found in herd animals like sheep and cattle. It can pass out in the animal's stool and contaminate food and water.
- *Cyclospora cayetanensis:* Similar to other intestinal parasites, this can spread through fecal contact, or contaminate the food and water of other animals, which may then develop diarrhea, vomiting, fever, cramps, and possibly other symptoms.
- *Toxoplasma gondii:* This intestinal parasite is carried by the cat family. In people with weakened immune systems, the parasite can cause flu-like symptoms. Infants, however, may develop severe toxoplasmosis with exposure, which can lead to lifelong mental and physical problems. For this reason, pregnant mothers are often discouraged from changing cat litter or handling raw meats.

Pregnant women should not change cat litter or handle raw meats. These actions are linked to a parasite that can cause toxoplasmosis in infants, a condition that can lead to lifelong mental and physical problems.

- *Trichinella spiralis:* This is an intestinal roundworm often spread by eating raw or undercooked meats. Symptoms include headaches, diarrhea, vomiting, aching joints, itchy skin, and fever.
- *Taenia saginata/Taenia solium* (tapeworms): Tapeworms, which rely exclusively on humans for their reproductive cycle, are more prevalent in underdeveloped countries and often produce few symptoms when the infection involves adult tapeworms (taeniasis). When the infection involves the worms' eggs moving to other parts of the body, a life-threatening condition known as *cysticercosis* can occur.

Most of these parasites are identified through stool or blood tests. They can be avoided by practicing safe cooking practices, maintaining good hygiene, and drinking properly treated water.

Tapeworms can live in a human's intestinal tract for up to 30 years and can grow as long as 15 to 30 feet! Once shed from the host's body, the tapeworm eggs may continue to thrive for many months.

☞ To access an A–Z list of parasites, go to the Centers for Disease Control and Prevention's Web index of parasitic diseases at: www.cdc.gov/ncidod/dpd/parasites.

References

"A–Z Index of Parasitic Diseases." Centers for Disease Control and Prevention. U.S. Department of Health & Human Services. Accessed January 15, 2008. www.cdc.gov/ncidod/dpd/parasites.

"Diagnosis of Parasitic Diseases." Centers for Disease Control and Prevention. U.S. Department of Health & Human Services. Accessed January 9, 2008. www.cdc.gov/ncidod/dpd/public/geninfo_diagnosis_diseases.htm.

"Parasites and Foodborne Diseases." United States Department of Agriculture. Accessed January 9, 2008. www.fsis.usda.gov/Fact_Sheets/Parasites_and_Foodborne_Illness/index.asp.

"Tapeworm Infection." *Merck Manual Home Edition.* Accessed January 11, 2008. www.merck.com/mmhe/sec17/ch196/ch196p.html.

What is pica?

Pica is a type of eating disorder in which a person craves a nonfood item, usually dirt or chalk. This condition may occur in children and in pregnant women. Although many toddlers try to eat nonfood items, individuals with pica will crave and consume the nonfood items for more than a month.

Pica may be caused by abnormal nutrient levels, particularly low iron and zinc levels.

In addition to dirt and chalk, individuals with pica may also eat the following:

- Baking soda
- Burnt matches
- Buttons
- Cigarette butts and ashes
- Clay
- Coffee grounds
- Cornstarch
- Feces
- Glue
- Hair
- Ice
- Laundry starch
- Mothballs
- Paint chips
- Paper
- Plaster
- Sand
- Soap
- Stones
- Toothpaste

Pica is Latin for "magpie." A magpie is a crow-like bird known to eat almost anything.

Pica is most commonly seen in children with autism, mental retardation, and other developmental conditions. Treatment using behavioral techniques has been helpful with these children. Malnourishment and neglect may cause other children to eat nonfood items. Pregnant women with pica may have a nutrient deficiency or a family history of pica. Individuals who are dieting may eat nonfood items to help them feel full. Depending on the nonfood items consumed, pica can lead to poisoning, lead poisoning, intestinal obstruction or perforation, and parasitic infections.

References

"Pica." Nemours Foundation. Accessed December 28, 2007. http://kids health.org/parent/emotions/behavior/pica.html.

"Pregnancy and Pica: Non-Food Cravings." American Pregnancy Association. Accessed December 27, 2007. www.americanpregnancy.org/pregnancy health/unusualcravingspica.html.

Why does my urine smell funny after I eat asparagus?

Asparagus contains a sulfur compound called *methyl mercaptan*. This substance is also found in rotten eggs, onions, garlic, and the secretions of skunks. When your digestive system breaks down this substance, byproducts are released that cause the funny odor. This can happen within 15 to 30 minutes of eating asparagus.

> Methyl mercaptan, a substance found in asparagus, is also found in rotten eggs, onions, garlic, and the secretions of skunks.

Not everyone has this experience. Studies show that if you ask a large group of people whether their urine smells funny after eating asparagus, about half of them will say "yes" and the other half will have no idea what you are talking about. The reason for this has been the subject of scientific debate. Some scientists believe that about half the population does not have the ability to produce the odor. Others believe that half the population does not have the ability to *smell* the odor. Either way, it all depends on your genetic makeup.

> About half the population either does not have the ability to *produce* the odor OR does not have the ability to *smell* it.

If you can "smell the smell," though, there is no need to panic. It won't harm you. In fact, asparagus is full of powerful nutrients. It's an excellent source of folic acid (a B vitamin that helps protect against birth defects, heart disease, and cancer), potassium, vitamin A, and vitamin C. Asparagus also contains lots of healthy fiber and "phyto-nutrients" that may protect against disease.

> ☞ Asparagus contains fiber, folic acid, potassium, vitamin A, vitamin C, and other healthy nutrients. For more information about asparagus, visit www.asparagus.org.

References

Magalini, S., ed. "Urinary Excretion of Odoriferous Component of Asparagus." *Dictionary of Medical Syndromes*. Philadelphia: Lippincott-Raven, 2007.

"Questions About Asparagus." Michigan Asparagus Advisory Board. Accessed December 19, 2007. www.asparagus.org/maab/faq.html.

Somer, E. "Eau D'Asparagus." WebMD. Accessed December 17, 2007. www.webmd.com/content/article/43/1671_51089.

What is hypertrichosis?

Hypertrichosis occurs when a person has excessive hair growth. This is different from hirsutism, or excessive hair growth in women, which is related to the areas of the body affected by androgens (male hormones). In hirsutism, women may experience slight or excessive growth of hair more akin to men's, such as facial hair, chest or back hair, forearm hair, or even excessive upper-leg hair. In most of these cases, excessive androgen production leads to the excessive hair growth.

In contrast, hypertrichosis is much rarer and involves excessive growth in nonsexual hair, as in hair on the forehead, the lower leg, or the upper arm. Often this hair is fine textured and similar or identical to the hair found on a newborn infant—called *lanugo* hair. It can also be excessive growth of the vellus hair, "peach fuzz," that covers most adults' and many children's bodies.

There are a number of possible causes for hypertrichosis:

• Heredity
• Trauma to the skin, such as by an irritant
• Certain drugs, like oral minoxidil
• Disorders such as porphyria, hypothyroidism, Hurler's syndrome, and Cornelia de Lange syndrome

As for hirsutism, unless a cause for the excessive hair growth is found and dealt with, temporary hair removal strategies such as bleaching, shaving, waxing, and electrolysis may be used.

The fungicide hexachlorobenzene has also been found to cause hypertrichosis when accidentally ingested.

References

Decherney, A., and L. Nathan. "Hirsutism." *Current Diagnosis & Treatment in Obstetrics & Gynecology.* AccessMedicine. USC School of Medicine Library, Columbia, SC. Accessed January 18, 2008. Keyword: hirsutism.

Wolff, K. "Hair Growth Disorders." *Fitzpatrick's Dermatology in General Medicine.* AccessMedicine. USC School of Medicine Library, Columbia, SC. Accessed January 19, 2008. Keyword: hypertrichosis.

Wolff, K., R. Johnson, and D. Suurmond, eds. "Disorders of Hair Follicles and Related Disorders." *Fitzpatrick's Color Atlas & Synopsis of Clinical Dermatology.* AccessMedicine. USC School of Medicine Library, Columbia, SC. Accessed January 5, 2008. Keyword: hypertrichosis.

What is synesthesia, and is it real?

Synesthesia is a relatively rare condition in which a person has a sensation from an external stimulus that is not normally associated with that stimulus. For example, some people actually experience music or other sounds as colors. Other people may experience letters or numbers as specific colors. Still others have been known to actually experience tastes or shapes when they hear certain notes played on a piano, for example.

It is estimated that approximately 1 out of every 23 people may experience synesthesia in one form or another.

Although synesthesia was a relatively popular topic of research in the past, it fell out of favor for a number of years. However, some researchers, especially in areas like experimental psychology, are revisiting the phenomenon. Currently, although the exact cause of synesthesia is not known, it is believed to be neurological, likely genetic, and for the most part harmless to the person affected by the condition (the "synesthete").

Here are some other interesting facts about the condition:

- Synesthetes tend to do better on memory tests, especially when the tests focus on material that causes them to experience their form of synesthesia.
- It was first mentioned in 1880, when Francis Galton, Charles Darwin's cousin, wrote about it in the journal *Nature*.
- Certain hallucinogens, like LSD and mescaline, can mimic synesthesia.
- It tends to run in families.

- The condition tends to be more common in creative people, like artists, than in the general population.
- Some researchers believe that it may be caused by cross-wiring between parts of the brain not normally heavily connected. Others believe it may occur when different parts of the brain "cross-activate" due to chemical imbalances.
- The most common type of synesthesia involves experiencing colors in response to numbers or certain words (e.g., days of the month).

One of the more interesting cases of synesthesia is described in the 1968 book *The Mind of a Mnemonist* by A.R. Luria. It includes the case of a young man, Shereshevskii, with near limitless memory.

References

"Hearing Colors, Tasting Shapes." Scientific American. Accessed January 11, 2008. www.sciam.com/article.cfm?articleID=0003014B-9D06-1E8F-8EA5809 EC5880000.

"Searching for Shereshevskii: What is Superior About the Memory of Synaesthetes?" *Quarterly Journal of Experimental Psychology*. PsychInfo. USC School of Medicine Library, Columbia, SC. Accessed January 13, 2008.

"Synesthesia." *MedlinePlus Medical Dictionary*. U.S. National Library of Medicine. Accessed January 10, 2008. www.nlm.nih.gov/medlineplus/mplusdictionary .html.

What is androgen-insensitivity syndrome?

Androgen-insensitivity syndrome (AIS), sometimes called *testicular feminization*, occurs when a person is born genetically male (XY chromosomes) but has some or all of the features characteristic of a female. This condition is caused by an inability to respond to the male hormones called *androgens*. Sometimes, during development, mutations on the X chromosome cause male babies to become unresponsive to the androgens needed to develop male body parts and male secondary sexual characteristics. Complete AIS occurs in approximately 1 in every 20,000 births and results in a child appearing to be female but without the developed sex organs necessary to become fertile (such as a uterus). Incomplete AIS is much more varied and can lead to very different degrees of sexual ambiguity among those affected.

Following are some of the signs doctors look for in diagnosing AIS:

- Presence of a vagina but no uterus or cervix
- Normal breast development
- Testes in the abdomen, labia, or inguinal canal
- Other signs of ambiguous genitalia

Some complications that may occur with androgen-insensitivity syndrome include testicular cancer, infertility, and psychosocial issues.

Reifenstein syndrome is a type of partial androgen-insensitivity syndrome that occurs in approximately 1 out of every 99,000 people. Symptoms include infertility, hypospadias (urinary opening on the underside of the penis rather than at the tip), and decreased body hair.

Following are some tests a doctor may order to check for AIS:

- XY karyotyping to detect the presence of an X and a Y sex chromosome, which would indicate genetic maleness
- Blood test to measure luteinizing hormone (LH) level
- Blood test to measure follicle-stimulating hormone (FSH)
- Sonogram to check for the presence of testes in the abdomen
- Blood test to measure testosterone level

Overall, most complete AIS patients have a good prognosis provided that at-risk testicular tissue is removed before it can become cancerous. For incomplete AIS patients, psychological issues may require therapy and/or support of gender identity.

Intersex is the term for a group of conditions—also called *disorders of sex development* (DSDs)—in which the external genitalia and the internal genitalia show discrepancies.

References

"Androgen Insensitivity Syndrome." *Genetics Home Reference.* U.S. National Library of Medicine. Accessed January 17, 2008. http://ghr.nlm.nih.gov/condition=androgeninsensitivitysyndrome.

"Androgen Insensitivity Syndrome." *MedlinePlus Medical Encyclopedia*. U.S. National Library of Medicine. Accessed January 18, 2008. www.nlm.nih .gov/medlineplus/ency/article/001180.htm.

"Intersex." *MedlinePlus Medical Encyclopedia*. U.S. National Library of Medicine. Accessed January 20, 2008. www.nlm.nih.gov/medlineplus/ency/article/ 001669.htm.

"Reifenstein Syndrome." *MedlinePlus Medical Encyclopedia*. U.S. National Library of Medicine. Accessed January 13, 2008. www.nlm.nih.gov/medlineplus/ ency/article/001169.htm.

What is porphyria, and is it really the origin of the vampire and werewolf myths?

Rather than a single disease, porphyria is actually a group of disorders. All of these disorders share the feature of a buildup of "porphyrins," which are pigments found in plants and animals. These porphyrins assist in the production of substances like hemoglobin, which helps to carry oxygen in the blood. Depending on what type of porphyria you have, symptoms can include the following:

- Severe abdominal and/or back pain
- Chronic constipation
- Visual hallucinations
- Disorientation
- Chronic depression
- Sensitivity to the sun
- Blisters and other dermatological conditions leading to scarring
- Excessive pigmentation, especially of the face and hands
- Reddish or dark-colored urine that may darken when exposed to light

Usually the symptoms are short lived and/or reversible in what are referred to as the "acute porphyries." However, they may be permanent in the rarest of the porphyria disorders.

Some researchers believe that the "madness" of King George III of England was caused by an acute form of porphyria. This may explain why he suffered from stomach pain, limb weakness, dark urine, and mental confusion.

The idea that porphyria may be the origin of the vampire and werewolf myths began in 1985, when a biochemist for the University of British Columbia, David Dolphin, noted that some porphyria patients are extremely sensitive to sunlight, may have excessive facial hair growth, and are sometimes treated with doses of heme, a component common in blood. This theory has been largely discounted by medical experts, but it continues to be a popular discussion topic on many people's Web sites. Another factor in the "origin of the vampire myth" theory is that the prescribed treatment for certain types of porphyria is phlebotomy (bloodletting).

☞ For more information, see the American Porphyria Foundation's Web site at www.porphyriafoundation.com.

References

"About Porphyria." American Porphyria Foundation. Accessed January 5, 2008. www.porphyriafoundation.com/about_por/index.html.

"Porphyria." Griffith's 5-Minute Clinical Consult. STAT!Ref. USC School of Medicine Library, Columbia, SC. Accessed January 3, 2008. Keyword: porphyria.

"Porphyrias." *Merck Manual*, 17th ed. STAT!Ref. USC School of Medicine Library, Columbia, SC. Accessed January 6, 2008. Keyword: porphyria.

"Porphyrins-Blood." *MedlinePlus Medical Encyclopedia*. U.S. National Library of Medicine. Accessed January 23, 2008. www.nlm.nih.gov/medlineplus/ency/article/003372.htm.

"Utah Scientists Breed Sick Mice to Probe Mysterious Skin-Blistering Disorder." University of Utah News and Public Relations. Accessed January 17, 2008 www.utah.edu/unews/releases/01/jan/mice.html.

TECHNOLOGY-RELATED HEALTH QUESTIONS

Can microwave ovens be harmful to my health?

Food cooked in microwave ovens does not become radioactive. Plastic containers designed to be used in microwave ovens do not leak harmful levels of toxins into your food. Microwave ovens that are working properly do not emit high levels of dangerous radiation. It is also safe for pregnant women to use a microwave oven; it will not cause birth defects. **If the microwave oven is working properly and you are following the manufacturer's instructions, microwave ovens are very safe.**

Microwave ovens use microwaves, which are high-frequency radio waves, to cook food. The microwaves make water molecules in food vibrate. The vibrations create the heat that cooks the food. Many people confuse the type of radiation from microwaves (nonionizing) with the type of radiation from nuclear power plants (ionizing). Microwaves are considered a type of nonionizing radiation. Some other examples of nonionizing radiation are visible light and infrared radiation. Ionizing radiation, not used in microwaves, can damage human tissue and DNA. Other examples of ionizing radiation are X-rays and gamma rays.

Burns are the biggest health risk from using a microwave oven. If you are heating water in a cup, be careful when you remove the cup from the microwave. Water can become "super-heated" and erupt out of the cup. Super-heated water is hotter than boiling water but does not show signs of boiling.

Manufacturers of microwaves must meet the guidelines set by the U.S. Food and Drug Administration (FDA). The FDA sets strict emission limits for microwave ovens in order to eliminate any health risks. Microwaves may escape if the microwave door or hinge is damaged. Therefore, it is important to keep your microwave in good condition. Any materials claiming to be safe to use in the microwave, such as plastic or glass containers, are also tested by the FDA.

☞ To learn more about consumer products and exposure to radiation, visit the Food and Drug Administration's Center for Devices and Radiological Health at www.fda.gov/cdrh.

References

"Electromagnetic Fields & Public Health: Microwave Ovens." World Health Organization. Accessed December 19, 2007. www.who.int/peh-emf/publications/facts/info_microwaves/en.

"Plastics and the Microwave." U.S. Food and Drug Administration. Accessed December 19, 2007. www.cfsan.fda.gov/~dms/fdacplas.html.

"Radio Frequency Safety." Federal Communications Commission. Accessed December 15, 2007. www.fcc.gov/oet/rfsafety/rf-faqs.html.

"Use Your Microwave Safely." U.S. Food and Drug Administration. Accessed December 4, 2007. www.fda.gov/consumer/updates/microwave112107.html.

Can cell phone use hurt my health?

Many people are concerned that using cellular phones (also known as *wireless* or *mobile* telephones) can cause cancer or other health problems because they emit radiofrequency (RF) energy, which is a form of radiation. It not clear whether long-term exposure to RF radiation from cell phone use causes health problems. Because cell phone use is increasing so rapidly, it is important to learn whether RF energy affects human health.

> Because few people have used cell phones for more than ten years, it is not clear whether long-term use of cell phones causes health problems.

The problem is that cell phone technology is still fairly new and is still changing. There aren't a lot of people who have used cell phones for more than about ten years. It can take longer than this for some cancers to develop, so scientists are not sure if using cell phones for more than ten years might be a health problem.

Studies have been conducted to try to determine if cell phone use causes cancer, brain tumors, or other problems. Overall, a link between cell phone use and cancer has not been consistently demonstrated. Again, though, the data are limited because of the relatively new technology. Scientists agree that more research needs to be done before conclusions can be drawn about the risk of cancer from cell phones.

> Children's nervous systems are still developing. For this reason, they may be at the greatest risk if it turns out that cell phone use causes brain or nervous system cancers. In addition, children are likely to accumulate many years of exposure during their lives.

Following are ways to reduce your risk:

• Use cell phones only for short conversations.
• Use "landline" phones when possible.

- Switch to a cell phone with a hands-free device that will put more distance between you and the antenna (the antenna is the cell phone's main source of RF energy).

Cell phones can interfere with medical equipment such as pacemakers, implanted defibrillators, and hearing aids.

References

"Cell Phone Facts: Consumer Information on Wireless Phones." U.S. Food and Drug Administration. Accessed December 19, 2007. www.fda.gov/cell phones.

"Cellular Telephone Use and Cancer: Questions and Answers." National Cancer Institute. Accessed December 1, 2007. www.cancer.gov/cancer topics/factsheet/Risk/cellphones.

"Study: No Evidence Cell Phones Cause Cancer." American Cancer Society. Accessed December 13, 2007. www.cancer.org/docroot/NWS/content/NWS_1_1x_Study_No_Evidence_Cell_Phones_Cause_Cancer.asp.

Can computer screens damage my eyesight?

No. Working on computers will not harm your eyes. Research shows that computer monitors emit little or no harmful radiation. Often, though, when people use computers for long periods of time, they tend to blink less than usual. This can make eyes dry, which leads to the feeling of eyestrain or fatigue.

When using a computer, some people complain of a variety of eye-related symptoms such headaches, fatigue, dry eyes, eyestrain, and difficulty focusing. These symptoms are not caused by the computer screen itself. Instead, they are usually caused by conditions around the screen, such as poor lighting or improper placement of computer equipment and computer furniture.

Following are ways to avoid dry eyes or eyestrain:

- Take regular breaks.
- Look up or across the room often. Looking at objects farther away relieves the feeling of strain on your eyes.
- Keep your monitor between 18 to 24 inches from your face and at a slight downward angle.

- Have adequate lighting around your computer.
- Make sure there is no glare on your screen.
- Consider using artificial tears.

If your vision blurs or your eyes tire easily, you should have your eyes examined by an ophthalmologist.

References

"Can a Computer Screen Damage My Eyes?" Pasadena Eye Associates. Accessed December 23, 2007. www.pasadenaeye.com/faq/faq08/faq08_text.html.

"Eye Care Facts and Myths: A Closer Look." American Academy of Ophthalmology. Accessed December 22, 2007. www.medem.com/medlb/article_detaillb.cfm?article_ID=ZZZ8BUZTYIE &sub_cat=0.

Is it true that computer keyboards are contaminated by germs?

Absolutely. Studies have shown that computer keyboards are often home to various kinds of bacteria and viruses. In fact, one study found that the typical worker's desk has hundreds of times more bacteria per square inch than an office toilet seat.

The typical worker's desk has more bacteria than a toilet seat!

Bacteria are single-celled organisms that can cause strep throat, pneumonia, and other conditions. They can be treated with antibiotics. Viruses can cause colds and flu and cannot be treated with antibiotics. Both bacteria and viruses can live on keyboards and can spread from person to person.

A recent study found that hospital keyboards contained two types of bacteria that can harm patients: a staph bacterium (which can cause bloodstream infections) and diphtheroids (which can cause infections in those whose immune systems are weak). The study also demonstrated that the bacteria can be effectively removed from keyboards with alcohol, sterile water, or disinfecting wipes.

Keyboards should be cleaned often with sterile water, alcohol, or disinfecting wipes.

Other office items that harbor germs include:

* desks,
* phones, and
* computer mice.

These objects can transfer germs from person to person because people touch them so often. Coughing and sneezing can leave behind viruses that can live on a surface for up to three days. The best advice is to clean these items daily, especially during "flu season." In particular, a keyboard should be cleaned before another person uses it.

References

"Clean that Computer Keyboard." WebMD. Accessed January 3, 2008. www.webmd.com/news/20060426/clean-that-computer-keyboard.
"Is Your Desk Making You Sick?" Cable News Network (CNN). Accessed January 8, 2008. www.cnn.com/2004/HEALTH/12/13/cold.flu.desk/index.html.

ASK THE EXPERTS

Following is a list of health care professionals who can help you answer more in-depth questions related to issues discussed in this chapter. A good starting point would be your primary care physician (your family physician, internist, pediatrician, or nurse practitioner). From there, he or she might recommend that you visit with other medical specialists or health care professionals. Each one has received specialized training in his or her area of expertise. *(See the Glossary of Experts for descriptions, online directories, and credentialing information.)*

* Dermatologists
* Endocrinologists
* Family physicians
* Gastroenterologists
* Genetic counselors
* Geneticists
* Hematologists
* Internists
* Neurologists

* Nutritionists
* Obstetricians and gynecologists (OB/GYNs)
* Ophthalmologists
* Parasitologists
* Pediatricians
* Psychiatrists
* Psychologists
* Urologists

APPENDIX

Survey Tool

BACKGROUND

A link to the online survey was sent to various libraries through electronic discussion lists, or listservs. The types of libraries targeted were public, academic, school, hospital, and special libraries. There were 271 responses to the survey. The "library type" breakdown is as follows:

- Public libraries: 119
- Academic libraries: 58
- School libraries: 28
- Hospital libraries: 35
- Special libraries: 31

Responses to the survey represented nearly all 50 states. Following is the actual survey.

THE SURVEY

Health Questions Asked in Libraries

The University of South Carolina School of Medicine Library is compiling a resource highlighting the health questions most frequently asked in all library settings. We need your input! Please respond to this short survey by Monday, February 12, 2007. Thank You!

1. **What type of library do you work in?**

- Public
- Academic
- School
- Hospital
- Special

2. If you selected "Special" above, please describe:

3. What state is your library in?

4. Please list the most common health-related reference questions that you or your staff receive. (Please list as many as you can think of!)

5. What are the most BIZARRE health questions that you or your staff have been asked?

Glossary of Experts

There is more to choosing a health care provider than simply picking a name from the phone book. There are many factors to consider. What are his or her qualifications? Is the provider board certified? Is the office conveniently located? Will the office hours work with your schedule? Will the visit be covered by your insurance?

Start by asking friends, family, and coworkers for recommendations. Online message boards and support group networks are another good source for honest opinions about providers. Next, look for background information about the provider. You can contact your local medical library and ask for a biographical sketch of a physician. Also try to find out if a physician has had any disciplinary actions taken against him or her. To do this, contact your state's licensing board; if it has such information, it may be willing to share. State licensing board Web sites are listed at www.ihealthpilot.org/research/lookup.shtml (the Internet Health Pilot). You can also contact your health insurance plan provider to see if it maintains such information on participating physicians.

☞ Consumer Reports provides both free and paid services to help you check up on a doctor. Go to www.consumerreports.org/health/doctors-hospitals/choosing-the-right-doctor-getting-better-care/checking-up-on-doctor/0207_docs_check.htm.

Use the glossary we provide to determine the kind of professional you may need. We will define the types of health care providers mentioned throughout this book and provide links to online directories to help you find providers in your area. The amount of information available in these directories varies. At a minimum, they provide contact information for member physicians. Some directories may tell you where physicians attended medical school or whether they are board certified. Other directories allow physicians to include additional information, such as areas of specialization, links to their own Web sites, and even their e-mail addresses.

In addition to the resources provided in this glossary, visit the "Directories" area of MedlinePlus (www.nlm.nih.gov/medlineplus/directories .html). You may find it easier to search for a type of health care facility first and then identify individual practitioners. MedlinePlus includes links for a variety of hospitals and specialized clinics, such as sleep centers, dialysis facilities, and cancer treatment centers. You can also use the National Library of Medicine's Go Local Web site to find health care providers or facilities. Go Local is a freely available service for finding local health services. To access Go Local, visit www.nlm.nih.gov/medlineplus/golocal.

It may take some time to find the right health care provider, but doing your homework ahead of time is beneficial in the long run. Keep in mind, though, that after you identify a health care provider and schedule an appointment, you will still need to determine if the provider is someone you can talk openly with and trust. Does the health provider take time to listen and respond to your questions? Sometimes only you can decide if a health care provider meets your standards of communication and trust.

ACUPUNCTURISTS, CERTIFIED

Acupuncturists treat pain and disease by placing needles in particular places on the skin. Certified acupuncturists usually complete a master's degree program and must pass a board exam administered by the National Certification Commission for Acupuncture and Oriental Medicine (NCCAOM).

For more information, visit:
☞ NCCAOM Online Directory: www.nccaom.org/find/index.html

ALLERGISTS

Allergists, or immunologists, are board-certified doctors who specialize in determining what causes certain allergies and how to treat allergies.

Allergists often are certified by either the American Board of Internal Medicine (ABIM) or the American Board of Allergy and Immunology (ABAI).

For more information, visit:
☞ ABIM's Verify a Physician's Certification: www.abim.org
☞ American Medical Association's Find a Doctor: http://webapps.ama-assn.org/doctorfinder/disclaimer.jsp

AMERICAN SOCIETY OF ADDICTION MEDICINE-CERTIFIED MEDICAL DOCTORS

To attain the American Society of Addiction Medicine (ASAM) certificate, medical doctors must successfully complete additional training and examinations in all areas related to addiction and its treatment. These doctors often are experts in alcohol and drug addictions and treatments.

For more information, visit:
☞ American Medical Association's Find a Doctor: http://webapps.ama-assn.org/doctorfinder/disclaimer.jsp
☞ ASAM Member Directory: www.asam.org/MemberDirectorytest.cfm.

AYURVEDIC PRACTITIONERS

There is currently no national standard in the United States for training Ayurvedic practitioners, although some states have approved Ayurvedic schools. Some Ayurvedic professional organizations are working to create licensing standards. For those practitioners who study in India, training may take up to five years and can result in either a bachelor's or a doctoral degree.

BIOFEEDBACK THERAPISTS

Biofeedback therapists use electronic equipment and techniques to help you learn to control your body's responses. They are certified by the Biofeedback Certification Institute of America (BCIA).

For more information, visit:
☞ BCIA Practitioner Directory: http://bcia.affiniscape.com/index.cfm.

CARDIOLOGISTS

Cardiologists are highly trained doctors who specialize in the structure and function of the heart as well as in treating heart disorders. After becoming certified by the American Board of Internal Medicine (ABIM) as internists, they complete additional subspecialty training and certification in cardiology.

For more information, visit:
☞ ABIM's Verify a Physician's Certification: www.abim.org
☞ American Medical Association's Find a Doctor: http://webapps.ama-assn.org/doctorfinder/disclaimer.jsp

COMPLEMENTARY AND ALTERNATIVE MEDICINE PRACTITIONERS

Practitioners of complementary and alternative medicine (CAM) are often grouped under the heading "CAM practitioners." This covers a wide range of practices and therapies, including acupuncture, acupressure, massage therapy, Reiki, therapeutic touch, homeopathy, naturopathy, chiropractic, and many others. Practicing CAM often requires a license or the completion of a standard training course from an educational institution. The specific licensing requirements depend on the particular CAM as well as on the state laws where the practice takes place. When selecting a CAM practitioner, ask what training or other qualifications he or she has, including education, licenses, and certifications. If possible, contact a professional licensing organization to find out if the person meets the standards for training and licensing for that profession. **Above all, speak with your primary health care provider regarding the therapy in which you are interested. Ask if he or she has a recommendation for the type of CAM practitioner you are seeking.**

CERTIFIED CHEMICAL DEPENDENCY COUNSELORS

Certified chemical dependency counselors (CCDCs) conduct substance abuse evaluations and serve as mediators between patients and medical agencies. They may offer substance abuse–related counseling to individuals or groups and often continue to track the progress of treatment for each patient. CCDCs are usually required to have at least a bachelor's degree in a related field and complete specialized training in an approved addiction setting.

CHIROPRACTORS

See "Doctors of Chiropractic."

DENTAL HYGIENISTS

Dental hygienists are licensed specialists in preventative dental care. Although their jobs are defined by local jurisdictions, they often are able to perform cleanings and other common procedures, take X-rays, and apply sealants. Dental hygienists must become licensed in the state in which they practice.

DENTISTS

A dentist is a doctor with the degree of either Doctor of Dental Medicine (DMD) or Doctor of Dental Surgery (DDS). Although there are a large number of specialties within dental medicine, all dentists must master certain skills in order to graduate dental school. These skills allow most dentists to diagnose and treat many disorders of the mouth and nearby regions.

For more information, visit:
- ☞ Academy of General Dentistry: www.agd.org/findadentist/disclaimer.asp
- ☞ American Dental Association's Find a Dentist: www.ada.org/public/disclaimer.asp

DERMATOLOGISTS

Dermatologists are medical doctors (MDs) who specialize in diseases and conditions of the skin. To become a dermatologist, one must complete medical school, a year-long internship, and a three-year residency program for dermatology. After residency, the physician may take the board examinations necessary to be considered certified. After board certification by the American College of Dermatology, the dermatologist may even consider more schooling (such as a one- or two-year fellowship) in order to specialize in a subspecialty of dermatology.

For more information, visit:
- ☞ American Academy of Dermatology's Find a Dermatologist: www.aad.org/public/searchderm.htm
- ☞ American Medical Association's Find a Doctor: http://webapps.ama-assn.org/doctorfinder/disclaimer.jsp

DIETETIC TECHNICIANS, REGISTERED

Dietetic technicians counsel and educate patients about proper nutrition. They may additionally specialize in food service management. Unlike registered dieticians (RDs), registered dietetic technicians (DTRs) only have to obtain an associate's level degree. Like RDs, they also have to complete a dietetic program from an accredited school, pass a technical exam, and maintain a certain number of continuing education credits.

For more information, visit:
- ☞ American Dietetic Association's Find a Nutrition Professional: Registered Dietitians and Dietetic Technicians, Registered: www.eatright.org/cps/rde/xchg/ada/hs.xsl/home_4874_ENU_HTML.htm

DOCTORS OF CHIROPRACTIC

Doctors of Chiropractic, also called *chiropractors*, practice a form of health care that focuses on the relationship between the body's structure, primarily the spine, and the body's function. Chiropractors use a type of hands-on therapy called *manipulation* as their core clinical procedure. Chiropractic training is a four-year academic program that involves both classroom and clinical instruction. At least three years of college work are required for admission to a chiropractic school. Students who graduate receive the Doctor of Chiropractic (DC) degree and are eligible to take state licensure board examinations in order to practice. The Council on Chiropractic Education (certified by the U.S. Department of Education) is the accrediting body for chiropractic colleges in the United States.

For more information, visit:
☞ American Chiropractic Association's Find a Doctor of Chiropractic: www.acatoday .com/search/memsearch.cfm.

EMERGENCY PHYSICIANS

Emergency physicians work in the hospital emergency department as well as direct emergency medical technicians in the prehospital setting. These specialized doctors focus on diagnosing and treating acutely ill or injured patients who need immediate medical attention. They are certified by the American Board of Emergency Medicine. Additional training and examination are required for the emergency physician to become certified in the subspecialties of hospice and palliative medicine, medical toxicology, pediatric emergency medicine, sports medicine, and undersea and hyperbaric medicine.

For more information, visit:
☞ American Medical Association's Find a Doctor: http://webapps.ama-assn .org/doctorfinder/disclaimer.jsp

ENDOCRINOLOGISTS

Endocrinologists are medical doctors (MDs) who specialize in the endocrine system, its glands, and the hormones that these glands produce. They also are concerned with the diseases and conditions that occur when there are too many or not enough hormones present.

Depending on the subspecialization that they choose, these physicians usually complete four years of college, four years of medical school, three years of residency, and then three years of fellowship.

For more information, visit:
☞ American Association of Clinical Endocrinologists: www.aace.com/resources/memsearch.php
☞ American Medical Association's Find a Doctor: http://webapps.ama-assn.org/doctorfinder/disclaimer.jsp

FAMILY PHYSICIANS

Family physicians, sometimes called *general practitioners*, receive a diverse medical education in areas such as orthopedics, internal medicine, obstetrics, and gynecology. This training usually takes three years of residency and prepares students to take the American Board of Medicine certification exam. Upon successfully passing the exam, family physicians are allowed to see patients of all ages. Like other professionals, they are required to regularly take continuing education classes and periodically pass recertification exams.

For more information, visit:
☞ American Academy of Family Physicians: http://familydoctor.org/cgi-bin/memdir.pl
☞ American Medical Association's Find a Doctor: http://webapps.ama-assn.org/doctorfinder/disclaimer.jsp

FITNESS EXPERTS

Fitness experts, sometimes called *physical fitness trainers*, are part of a recent professional group that is slowly becoming sanctioned and governed by such bodies as the National Board of Fitness Examiners (NBFE). Fitness experts are often masters at tailoring exercise and nutrition plans to individual needs. Like other professional distinctions, to become a certified fitness expert, a person must successfully complete both training and certification exams.

GASTROENTEROLOGISTS

Gastroenterologists are medical doctors (MDs) who specialize in diseases and conditions affecting the digestive system and related organs. After completing residency following medical school, these physicians further complete a specialized fellowship in gastroenterology and are then referred to as *fellows*. They are certified by the American Board of Internal Medicine (ABIM).

For more information, visit:
☞ ABIM's Verify a Physician's Certification: www.abim.org
☞ American Medical Association's Find a Doctor: http://webapps.ama-assn.org/doctorfinder/disclaimer.jsp

GENETIC COUNSELORS

Genetic counselors are health professionals with graduate degrees and specialized training in medical genetics and counseling. They are certified by the American Board of Genetic Counseling. They provide information about genetic disorders and birth defects and support to individuals and families.

For more information, visit:
☞ American Board of Genetic Counseling: www.abgc.net
☞ National Society of Genetic Counselors, Inc. Search: www.nsgc.org/resourcelink.cfm

GENETICISTS

Geneticists are medical doctors who specialize in the study of genes and in the diagnosis and treatment of inherited problems. They are certified by the American Board of Medical Genetics.

For more information, visit:
☞ American Medical Association's Find a Doctor: http://webapps.ama-assn.org/doctorfinder/disclaimer.jsp

GERIATRICIANS

Geriatricians are board-certified medical doctors who have additional training in the prevention and treatment of diseases in the elderly. Most geriatricians have internal medicine or family medicine backgrounds. They can become certified in geriatric medicine or geriatric psychiatry.

For more information, visit:
☞ American Board of Internal Medicine's Verify a Physician's Certification: www.abim.org
☞ American Medical Association's Find a Doctor: http://webapps.ama-assn.org/doctorfinder/disclaimer.jsp

HEMATOLOGISTS

Hematologists are physicians who specialize in diseases and conditions related to blood and blood-producing organs. Like other specialized physicians, hematologists must complete four years of medical school and three years of residency; they then have to complete specialized training in hematology that lasts two or more years. They may be certified by the American Board of Internal Medicine (ABIM) or by the American Board of Pathology.

For more information, visit:
☞ ABIM's Verify a Physician's Certification: www.abim.org
☞ American Society of Hematology's Find a Hematologist: https://ash.ebiz.uapps .net/solutionsite/fah/fahhome.htm
☞ American Medical Association's Find a Doctor: http://webapps.ama-assn.org/doctorfinder/disclaimer.jsp
☞ American Society of Pediatric Hematology/Oncology's Find a Pediatric Hematologist/Oncologist: www.aspho.org/custom/directory/?pageid=235

HERBALISTS, REGISTERED

Herbalists are professionals trained to work with herbs. Their training may vary, depending on their specialty (botanical medicine, Chinese medicine, Ayurveda, etc.). The American Herbalist Guild certifies Registered Herbalists (RH).

For more information, visit:
☞ American Herbalist Guild's Find an Herbalist: www.americanherbalistsguild .com/fundamentals

HIV SPECIALISTS

HIV (human immunodeficiency virus) specialists are doctors who specialize in the care and treatment of persons infected with HIV. These specialists must meet three criteria established by The American Academy of HIV Medicine (AAHIVM): experience, education, and external validation. The doctor must maintain state licensure and have provided direct care for at least 20 HIV patients over the past two years. The doctor must have completed at least 30 credits of HIV-related continuing education every two years or must have completed an HIV-related internship or fellowship in the past two years. The doctor must also be recognized by an external credentialing entity such as the AAHIVM, which involves passing an HIV Medicine Credentialing Exam.

For more information, visit:
☞ American Medical Association's Find a Doctor: http://webapps.ama-assn.org/ doctorfinder/disclaimer.jsp

HOMEOPATHS

Homeopaths are people who specialize in homeopathy, a system of therapy based on the concept that disease can be treated with drugs (in minute doses) thought capable of producing the same symptoms in healthy people as the disease itself. Training in homeopathy is offered through diploma programs, certificate programs, short courses, and correspondence courses. Homeopathic training is part of medical education in naturopathy. Most homeopathy in the United States is practiced along with another health care practice for which the practitioner is licensed, such as conventional medicine, naturopathy, chiropractic, dentistry, acupuncture, or veterinary medicine (homeopathy can be used to treat animals).

For more information, visit:
☞ North American Society of Homeopaths' Directory of NASH Registered Homeopaths: www.homeopathy.org/directory_entrance.html

INFECTIOUS DISEASE SPECIALISTS

Infectious disease (ID) specialists are doctors of internal medicine (or, in some cases, pediatrics) who are qualified as experts in the diagnosis and treatment of infectious diseases. ID specialists complete seven or more years of medical school and postgraduate training, followed by two or three years of additional training in infectious diseases.

For more information, visit:
☞ American Board of Internal Medicine's Verify a Physician's Certification: www.abim.org
☞ American Medical Association's Find a Doctor: http://webapps.ama-assn.org/ doctorfinder/disclaimer.jsp

INTERNISTS

Internists are doctors trained in general internal medicine. They diagnose and treat many diseases of the body. Internists provide long-term comprehensive care in the hospital and office, have expertise in many areas, and often act as consultants to other specialists. They are certified by the American Board of Internal Medicine (ABIM).

For more information, visit:
☞ ABIM's Verify a Physician's Certification: www.abim.org
☞ American Medical Association's Find a Doctor: http://webapps.ama-assn.org/ doctorfinder/disclaimer.jsp

LACTATION CONSULTANTS

Lactation consultants help mothers and their babies with the breast-feeding process. They may or may not be certified, and their education levels vary. An internationally certified breastfeeding and lactation consultant (ICBLC) has passed an exam given by the International Board of Lactation Consultant Examiners and has received training to help nursing mothers and their babies.

For more information, visit:
☞ International Lactation Consultant Association's Find a Lactation Consultant: www.ilca.org/falc.html

LICENSED CLINICAL ALCOHOL AND DRUG COUNSELORS

Although not medical doctors, licensed clinical alcohol and drug counselors (**LCADCs**) are experts in addiction and its treatment. Although the requirements somewhat vary among states, most counselors are required to complete a rigorous training and examination process in order to attain the LCADC certificate.

LICENSED PRACTICAL NURSES

See "Nurses."

MASSAGE THERAPISTS

A person who provides massage therapy as a profession is often called a *massage therapist,* although there are some other health care providers (such as chiropractors) who also have massage training. To learn massage, most therapists attend a school or a training program. Many students are already licensed as another type of health care provider, such as a nurse. The United States has many massage therapy schools, most of which require 500 hours of training. In addition, the majority of states have passed laws regulating massage therapy. Some common licenses or certifications massage therapists can obtain include the following:

- LMT: licensed massage therapist
- LMP: licensed massage practitioner
- CMT: certified massage therapist

- NCTM(B): Has met the credentialing requirements of the National Certification Board for Therapeutic Massage and Bodywork for the practicing of therapeutic massage and/or bodywork

For more information, visit:
☞ American Massage Therapy Association's Find a Massage Therapist: www.amtamassage.org/findamassage/locator.aspx

NATUROPATHS

Naturopaths are people who practice naturopathy, a system of therapy based on the use of physical forces such as heat, water, light, air, and massage. Some naturopaths use no medications, either pharmaceutical or herbal. Some recommend herbal remedies only. A few who are licensed to prescribe may recommend pharmaceuticals when they feel a drug is warranted. A licensed naturopathic physician (ND) attends a four-year graduate-level naturopathic medical school and is educated in all of the same basic sciences as an MD but also studies holistic and nontoxic approaches to therapy with a strong emphasis on disease prevention and optimizing wellness.

In addition to a standard medical curriculum, the naturopathic physician is required to complete four years of training in clinical nutrition, acupuncture, homeopathic medicine, botanical medicine, psychology, and counseling (to encourage people to make lifestyle changes in support of their personal health). A naturopathic physician takes professional board exams so that he or she can be licensed by a state or jurisdiction as a primary care general practice physician.

For more information, visit:
☞ American Association of Naturopathic Physicians: www.naturopathic.org/ viewbulletin.php?id=118

NEUROLOGISTS

Neurologists are specialists concerned with the diagnosis and treatment of disorders of the nervous system (the brain, the spinal cord, and the nerves) whether caused by disease or injury. They are certified by the American Board of Psychiatry and Neurology.

For more information, visit:
☞ American Academy of Neurology's Find a Neurologist: www.thebrain matters.org/index.cfm?key=1.2.2
☞ American Medical Association's Find a Doctor: http://webapps.ama-assn.org/ doctorfinder/disclaimer.jsp

NURSE PRACTITIONERS

Nurse practitioners are licensed nurses with additional education and training. They provide similar services as doctors. They can diagnose and treat conditions, as well as prescribe medications. NPs may specialize in the following areas: acute care, adult health, family health, gerontology, neonatal health, oncology, pediatric/child health, psychiatric/mental health, and women's health.

For more information, visit:
☞ American Academy of Nurse Practitioner's Find a Nurse Practitioner: http://npfinder.com

NURSES

Nurses are health care professionals who are responsible (with others) for the safety and recovery of acutely ill or injured people, health maintenance of the healthy, and treatment of life-threatening emergencies in a wide range of health care settings. There are two types of nurses:

- Licensed practical nurses (LPNs) are nurses who have graduated from a formal practical nursing education program and are licensed by the appropriate state authority. They work under the supervision of a registered nurse (RN) or physician. LPN programs typically last one year.
- Registered nurses (RNs) are licensed nurses who work under the supervision of physicians. Becoming an RN requires a two-year associate's degree, which includes a number of specialized science courses.

NUTRITIONISTS

See "Registered Dietitians."

OBSTETRICIANS AND GYNECOLOGISTS:

OB/GYN is the abbreviation for an obstetrician/gynecologist. Such doctors both deliver babies and treat diseases of the female reproductive organs. Sometimes these doctors will be listed only as a gynecologist or an obstetrician. Gynecologists are doctors who specialize in treating disorders of the female reproductive system. Obstetricians are doctors who specialize in pregnancy, labor, and delivery. OB/GYNs, gynecologists, and obstetricians are certified by the American Board of Obstetrics and Gynecology.

For more information, visit:
☞ American College of Obstetricians and Gynecologists' Physician Directory: www.acog.org/member-lookup/disclaimer.cfm
☞ American Medical Association's Find a Doctor: http://webapps.ama-assn.org/doctorfinder/disclaimer.jsp

OCCUPATIONAL THERAPISTS

Occupational therapists help individuals who have mental and physical disabilities develop, recover, or maintain daily living and work skills. After receiving a bachelor's of science degree in occupational therapy, they must pass the National Board for Certification in Occupational Therapy (NBCOT) to become a registered occupational therapist (OTR).

ONCOLOGISTS

Oncologists are physicians who specialize in the diagnosis and treatment of cancer. They may have a background in internal medicine or surgery before pursuing this subspecialty. A clinical oncologist is usually trained in one of three primary areas of oncology:

1. Medical oncology—the treatment of cancer with medicine, including chemotherapy

2. Surgical oncology—the surgical aspects of cancer including biopsy and staging
3. Radiation oncology—the treatment of cancer with therapeutic radiation

---

For more information, visit:
☞ American Board of Internal Medicine's Verify a Physician's Certification: www.abim.org
☞ American Medical Association's Find a Doctor: http://webapps.ama-assn.org/doctorfinder/disclaimer.jsp
☞ American Society of Pediatric Hematology/Oncology's Find a Pediatric Hematologist/Oncologist: www.aspho.org/custom/directory/?pageid=235
☞ Society of Gynecologic Oncologists, Women's Cancer Network's Find a Gynecologic Oncologist: www.wcn.org/interior.cfm?diseaseid=13&featureid=4

OPHTHALMOLOGISTS

Ophthalmologists are medical doctors, sometimes referred to as "eye MDs," trained in diagnosing and treating disorders of the eyes and the areas surrounding the eyes, like the eyelids. Many ophthalmologists are able to perform surgery and may be considered specialized surgeons. They are certified by the American Board of Ophthalmology.

For more information, visit:
☞ American Academy of Ophthalmology's Find an Eye M.D.: www.aao.org/aao/eyemd_disclaimer.cfm.
☞ American Medical Association's Find a Doctor: http://webapps.ama-assn.org/doctorfinder/disclaimer.jsp

---

OPTICIANS

Opticians are professionals who provide corrective vision services and products, like contact lenses and glasses, based on the evaluations and prescriptions made by ophthalmologists and optometrists. To earn their certification, they must pass an exam through the American Board of Opticianry or the National Contact Lens Examiners.

For more information, visit:
☞ Opticianry Licensing Boards: www.abo-ncle.org/licensing.html.

OPTOMETRISTS

Optometrists are doctors of optometry (ODs) that diagnose and treat the majority of eye conditions, disorders, and injuries that occur. They are able to prescribe certain medications and sometimes perform basic surgical operations. Using a variety of tools and equipment, they are able to measure your vision and acuity in order to determine what prescription will be best for you.

For more information, visit:
☞ American Optometric Association's Dr. Locator Search: www.aoa.org/x5428.xml

PARASITOLOGISTS

Parasitologists are scientists who study parasites and their respective hosts, usually specializing in an area of parasitology, such as agricultural parasitology, medical parasitology, or immunoparasitology. Parasitology often requires advanced graduate work and the attainment of a PhD degree, especially for parasitologists interested in performing research in tenure-track university positions.

For more information, visit:
☞ American Society of Parasitologists' ASP Member Search: http://asp.unl.edu/index.php?option=com_wrapper&Itemid=8

PEDIATRICIANS

Pediatricians specialize in the health of children and adolescents. Like family physicians, pediatricians complete three years of residency after medical school; however, the focus of their residency is on preventative medicine issues related to children. They also have to pass certification and periodic recertification exams and maintain certain levels of continuing education. They are certified by the American Board of Pediatrics. They may also become specialists with pediatrics, which requires additional residency after medical school.

For more information, visit:
☞ American Academy of Pediatrics Pediatrician Referral Service: www.aap.org/referral
☞ American Medical Association's Find a Doctor: http://webapps.ama-assn.org/doctorfinder/disclaimer.jsp

PERIODONTISTS

A periodontist is a dentist who specializes in the structures that support the teeth, including the gums and the bones of the upper and lower jaws that hold the tooth sockets. They are often the professionals who dentists refer patients to when infections and diseases around the teeth occur.

For more information, visit:
☞ American Academy of Periodontology's Find a Periodontist: www.perio.org/consumer/1a.html

PHARMACISTS

Pharmacists receive a doctor of pharmacy (PharmD) degree. They are licensed individuals trained to distribute drugs prescribed by physicians and other health practitioners. They also provide information to patients about the use of medications and their side effects.

PHLEBOTOMISTS

Phlebotomists are technicians trained at community colleges, career schools, or trade schools to draw and collect blood for analysis. Their requirements vary by state.

PHYSIATRISTS

Physiatrists are doctors who specialize in physical medicine and rehabilitation. Physiatrists evaluate and treat patients with impairments, disabilities, or pain arising from various medical problems, including bone fractures. Physiatrists focus on restoring the physical, psychological, social, and vocational functioning of the individual. They are certified by the American Board of Physical Medicine and Rehabilitation.

For more information, visit:
☞ American Academy of Physical Medicine and Rehabilitation's Find a PM&R Physician: www.e-aapmr.org/imis/imisonline/findphys/find.cfm
☞ American Medical Association's Find a Doctor: http://webapps.ama-assn.org/doctorfinder/disclaimer.jsp

PHYSICAL THERAPISTS

Physical therapists are licensed professionals who help individuals of all ages with injuries or physical disabilities. They have at least a master's degree in physical therapy and must pass the National Physical Therapy Examination. They relieve pain and design treatment plans to help patients improve mobility and perform daily activities.

For more information, visit:
☞ American Physical Therapy Association's Find a Physical Therapist: www.apta.org/Content/NavigationMenu/Consumers/consumer1.htm

PSYCHIATRISTS

After medical school, psychiatrists complete four years of residency training in mental health. These board-certified professionals provide mental health services to individuals with mental disorders, including mental retardation and substance-related disorders. They are certified by the American Board of Psychiatry and Neurology.

For more information, visit:
☞ American Academy of Child and Adolescent Psychiatry: www.aacap.org/cs/ root/child_and_adolescent_psychiatrist_finder/child_and_adolescent_ psychiatrist_finder
☞ American Medical Association's Find a Doctor: http://webapps.ama-assn.org/ doctorfinder/disclaimer.jsp
☞ American Psychiatric Association's Locate a Psychiatrist: www.healthyminds .org/locateapsychiatrist.cfm

PSYCHOLOGISTS

Psychologists are mental health professionals who complete five to seven years of academic graduate study (PhD or PsyD). Most states do not allow psychologists to prescribe medications. These licensed professionals provide mental health services to individuals with mental disorders, including mental retardation and substance-related disorders.

For more information, visit:
☞ National Register of Health Service Providers in Psychology: www.nationalregister.com/osd/search.php

PULMONOLOGISTS

Pulmonologists are doctors who specialize in diseases of the lungs and airways. They treat diseases such as asthma and emphysema. They obtain a background in internal medicine, critical care medicine, or pediatrics before pursuing this subspecialty. Depending on the age group they are working with, they are certified by the American Board of Internal Medicine (ABIM) or the American Board of Pediatrics.

For more information, visit:
☞ ABIM's Verify a Physician's Certification: www.abim.org
☞ American Medical Association's Find a Doctor: http://webapps.ama-assn.org/ doctorfinder/disclaimer.jsp

RADIOLOGISTS

Radiologists are medical doctors who specialize in diagnosing and/or treating diseases using medical imaging technologies such as X-ray machines, ultrasound, computerized tomography (CT), and magnetic resonance imaging (MRI). In the United States, radiologists usually complete five years of postgraduate training after medical school. Those who complete their residency programs and pass their board exams administered by the American Board of Radiology become board-certified radiologists.

For more information, visit:
☞ American Medical Association's Find a Doctor: http://webapps.ama-assn.org/doctorfinder/disclaimer.jsp
☞ American College of Radiology's Accredited Facility Search: www.acr.org/accreditation/AccreditedFacilitySearch.aspx

REGISTERED DIETITIANS

Registered dieticians (RDs) are nutritionists who have completed certain academic requirements set up by the Commission on Dietetic Registration. Typically these requirements include at least a bachelor's degree from an accredited school and completion of a pre-professional program. RDs must also pass a technical exam and maintain a certain level of continuing education.

For more information, visit:
☞ American Dietetic Association's Find a Nutrition Professional: Find a Registered Dietitians and Dietetic Technicians, Registered: www.eatright.org/cps/rde/xchg/ada/hs.xsl/home_4874_ENU_HTML.htm

REGISTERED NURSES

See "Nurses."

RHEUMATOLOGISTS

Rheumatologists are doctors who diagnose and treat diseases of the joints, muscles, bones, and tendons, including arthritis and collagen diseases. After receiving training as an internist, they pursue a two- to four-year fellowship in rheumatology. They are certified by the American Board of Internal Medicine (ABIM).

For more information, visit:
☞ ABIM's Verify a Physician's Certification: www.abim.org
☞ American College of Rheumatology's Geographic Membership Directory: www.rheumatology.org/directory/geo.asp
☞ American Medical Association's Find a Doctor: http://webapps.ama-assn.org/doctorfinder/disclaimer.jsp

SOCIAL WORKERS

Social workers help people with many of their day-to-day social problems, including family issues, relationship problems, and drug and alcohol addictions. Many social workers specialize or focus on a particular group or population, such as those with disabilities. While a bachelor's degree in social work (BSW) is the minimum degree required, more and more social workers are attaining advanced degrees, including the master's degree in social work (MSW) and/or the doctorate in social work (DSW or PhD). The MSW degree is normally required for clinical social work (in a clinic or hospital setting). Licensure and accreditation are determined by each state and can vary.

For more information, visit:
☞ National Social Work Finder: www.helpstartshere.org/common/Search/Default.asp

UROLOGISTS

Urologists are doctors who specialize in the urinary systems in both men and women and on the reproductive system in males. They are certified by the American Board of Urology.

For more information, visit:
☞ American Medical Association's Find a Doctor: http://webapps.ama-assn.org/doctorfinder/disclaimer.jsp
☞ American Urological Association: http://urologyhealth.org/find_urologist

YOGA INSTRUCTORS

Yoga instructors teach yoga classes, which may also include meditation instruction. The Yoga Alliance certifies registered yoga teachers (RYTs) and experienced registered yoga teachers (E-RYTs).

For more information, visit:
☞ Yoga Alliance's Look up Registered Yoga Teachers (RYTs) and Experienced Registered Yoga Teachers (E-RYTs): http://yogaalliance.org/teacher_search.cfm

RESOURCES

Where to Go When You Want to Know about Health Care

PRINT RESOURCES

American College of Physicians. *Complete Home Medical Guide*. New York: DK, 2003.

An illustrated guide that serves as a reference during times of illness and as a source of advice for all family members in maintaining good health throughout life.

American Medical Association. *Family Medical Guide*, 4th ed. New York: John Wiley & Sons, 2004.

An easy-to-read, illustrated guide designed for home use.

Anatomical Chart Company. *Women's Health and Wellness: An Illustrated Guide*. Philadelphia: Lippincott Williams & Wilkins, 2002.

A guide to women's health from adolescence to menopause. Contains detailed illustrations.

Bartlett, John G., and Ann K. Finkbeiner. *The Guide to Living with HIV Infection*, 6th ed. Baltimore: The Johns Hopkins University Press, 2006.

A comprehensive guide for those living with HIV infection, developed at the Johns Hopkins AIDS Clinic. Includes medical issues, psychological and social issues, and information about HIV research.

Carlson, Jodi. *Complementary Therapies and Wellness: Practice Essentials for Holistic Health Care*. Upper Saddle River, NJ: Prentice Hall, 2003.

Provides practical information about complementary and alternative medicine. Also covers information about the many therapeutic approaches therapists use.

Children's Hospital Boston. *The Children's Hospital Guide to Your Child's Health and Development.* Boston: Children's Hospital-Boston, 2001.

A comprehensive guide designed to answer questions about child health and development from infancy through school age. Also covers pregnancy and childbirth topics.

Duyff, Roberta Larson. *American Dietetic Association Complete Food and Nutrition Guide*, 3rd ed. New York: John Wiley & Sons, 2006.

A complete guide that shows you how to maximize your health while enjoying food. Includes practical suggestions as well as scientific evidence.

Duyff, Roberta Larson. *365 Days of Healthy Eating from the American Dietetic Association.* New York: John Wiley & Sons, 2004.

An easy-to-read guide to eating healthy without sacrificing flavor and the enjoyment of foods. Offers practical and positive advice.

Ginther, Catherine, ed. *Drug Abuse Sourcebook*, 2nd ed. Health Reference Series. Detroit, MI: Omnigraphics, 2004.

An overview for consumers about illicit substances and the misuse of prescription and over-the-counter medications. Includes facts about health risks, prevention and treatment programs, a glossary of terms, and a directory of resources.

Gotto, Antonio M., ed. *The Cornell Illustrated Encyclopedia of Health.* Washington, DC: LifeLine Press, 2002.

An illustrated, easy-to-use home medical reference.

Hensrud, Donald D., ed. *Mayo Clinic Healthy Weight for EveryBody.* Rochester, MN: Mayo Clinic, 2005.

A practical overview of how to manage your weight for life. Focuses on healthy and enjoyable lifestyle changes.

Margen, Sheldon. *Wellness Foods A to Z: An Indispensable Guide for Health-Conscious Food Lovers.* New York: Rebus, 2002.

Offers clear facts about nutrition and the connection between nutrients and disease prevention. Emphasizes the importance of eating a variety of fresh foods and minimally processed foods.

Our Bodies, Ourselves: The Boston Women's Health Book Collective. New York: Touchstone, 2005.

A compilation of health research and experiences written for women. Contains first-person stories from women around the globe, bringing the health information to a more personal level.

Pelletier, Kenneth R. *The Best Alternative Medicine: What Works? What Does Not?* New York: Simon & Schuster, 2000.

> A detailed discussion of many alternative medical treatments. Includes results of domestic and international studies and explains what treatments are effective and what treatments are not.

Rybacki, James J. *Essential Guide to Prescription Drugs.* New York: HarperCollins, 2006.

> Provides a comprehensive overview of prescription drugs for consumers.

Sharkey, Brian J., and Steven E. Gaskill. *Fitness and Health*, 6th ed. Champaign, IL: Human Kinetics, 2006.

> An overview of the benefits of physical activity. Offers advice and information on how best to get physically fit and stay that way.

Somer, Elizabeth. *Nutrition for a Healthy Pregnancy*, 2nd ed. New York: Henry Holt and Company, 2002.

> A complete guide to healthy eating and proper nutrition before, during, and after pregnancy. Includes dietary guidelines for high-risk pregnancies (such as teen pregnancy), multiple births, and over-40 pregnancies.

Sutton, Amy L., ed. *Alcoholism Sourcebook*, 2nd ed. Health Reference Series. Detroit, MI: Omnigraphics, 2006.

> An overview for consumers about alcohol use, abuse, and dependence. Offers facts about the physical, mental, and social health effects of alcohol addiction. Includes a glossary of terms and a directory of resources.

WEB RESOURCES

☞ www.breastcancer.org

> Breastcancer.org. A nonprofit organization dedicated to providing the most reliable, complete, and up-to-date information about breast cancer.

☞ www.clevelandclinic.org/health/default.aspx

> The Cleveland Clinic Health Information Center, Cleveland Clinic Department of Patient Education and Health Information. Consumer health information on over 900 health topics.

☞ www.nlm.nih.gov/medlineplus/druginformation.html

> Drugs, Supplements, and Herbal Information, MedlinePlus. (Information from MedMaster, a product of the American Society of Health System

Pharmacists.) Contains detailed consumer information about prescription drugs, over-the-counter medicines, and herbal supplements. Information includes why a medicine is prescribed, how it should be used, special precautions and dietary instructions, dosage information, side effects, storage conditions, brand names, and combination products.

☞ www.eatright.org/cps/rde/xchg/ada/hs.xsl/home_4874_ENU_HTML.htm

Find a Nutrition Professional, American Dietetic Association. Enter your zip code to find a nutrition or dietetics professional near you.

☞ www.yourdiseaserisk.harvard.edu

Harvard Center for Cancer Prevention, "Your Disease Risk: The Source on Prevention." Offers interactive questionnaires to assess a person's risk of cancer, diabetes, heart disease, osteoporosis, and stroke. After completing a questionnaire, the visitor is given personalized tips on prevention.

☞ www.kidshealth.org

KidsHealth.org. Nemours Foundation. Provides doctor-approved health information about children from before birth through adolescence.

☞ www.labtestsonline.org

Lab Tests Online, American Association for Clinical Chemistry. This peer-reviewed Web site provides information to help patients understand clinical lab tests that are part of routine care.

☞ www.mayoclinic.com

MayoClinic.com. The Mayo Clinic is a medical practice dedicated to the diagnosis and treatment of virtually every type of complex illness. The Web site provides information about personal health, medical services at the Mayo Clinic, and medical research being conducted at the Mayo Clinic.

☞ http://medlineplus.gov

MedlinePlus: Trusted Health Information for You, U.S. National Library of Medicine, National Institutes of Health. A goldmine of good health information from the world's largest medical library, the National Library of Medicine.

☞ www.cancer.gov

National Cancer Institute, National Institutes of Health. Features information about cancer, including details about treatment and clinical trials.

☞ http://nccam.nih.gov

National Center for Complementary and Alternative Medicine. The Federal Government's lead agency for scientific research on complementary and alternative medicine (CAM).

☞ www.nichd.nih.gov

National Institute of Child Health & Human Development, National Institutes of Health. Provides information about all stages of human development.

☞ www.nia.nih.gov

National Institute on Aging, National Institutes of Health. Provides information about aging research.

☞ http://ods.od.nih.gov

National Institutes of Health Office of Dietary Supplements. Provides research-based information about the health effects of dietary supplements.

☞ http://kidney.niddk.nih.gov

National Kidney and Urologic Diseases Information Clearinghouse, National Institutes of Health. Contains information for families and health care professionals about diseases of the kidneys and urologic system.

☞ www.4women.gov

The National Women's Health Information Center, U.S. Department of Health & Human Services. A Web site containing information about women's health. Includes links to information sources, news clippings, a calendar of women's health events, statistics on women's health, and many other resources.

☞ http://nihseniorhealth.gov

NIH SeniorHealth.gov, National Institutes of Health. Online health information for people over the age of 60.

☞ www.nhlbi.nih.gov/health/index.htm

NHLBI Health Information, National Heart Lung and Blood Institute. Offers a wide range of resources regarding personal health, including eating plans, recipes, a menu calculator, and information about diseases.

☞ www.mypyramid.gov

Steps to a Healthier You, United States Department of Agriculture. Use the "My Pyramid Plan" to customize a food pyramid. This offers a personal eating plan with foods and amounts that are right for you.

☞ http://dasis3.samhsa.gov/Default.aspx

Substance Abuse Treatment Facility Locator, SAMHSA (Substance Abuse and Mental Health Services Administration). Search by location to find the drug and alcohol abuse treatment programs nearest you.

☞ www.fda.gov/consumer/default.htm

U.S. Food and Drug Administration, U.S. Department of Health & Human Services. "Consumer Health Information for You and Your Family." Offers information about food, drugs, medical devices, cosmetics, and other products that are regulated by the Food and Drug Administration.

☞ www.cdc.gov/vaccines

Vaccines & Immunizations, Centers for Disease Control and Prevention, U.S. Department of Health & Human Services. Offers information about all aspects of vaccines and immunizations. Includes printable immunization schedules and information about specific vaccines recommended for travelers.

☞ http://win.niddk.nih.gov/index.htm

Weight Control Information Network. Provides up-to-date, science-based information on weight control, obesity, physical activity, and related nutritional issues.

Comprehensive List of Sources Consulted

"Abcs of Preventing Heart Disease, Stroke and Heart Attack." American Heart Association. Accessed December 15, 2007. www.americanheart.org/presenter.jhtml?identifier=3035374.

"About Chiropractic and Its Use in Treating Low-Back Pain." National Center for Complementary and Alternative Medicine. Accessed January 13, 2008. http://nccam.nih.gov/health/chiropractic.

"About NORD." National Organization of Rare Disorders. Accessed January 31, 2008. www.rarediseases.org/info/about.html.

"About Porphyria." American Porphyria Foundation. Accessed January 5, 2008. www.porphyriafoundation.com/about_por/index.html.

"ACS Recommends HPV Vaccine but Cervical Cancer Screening Still Necessary." American Cancer Society. Accessed January 30, 2008. www.cancer.org/doc root/NWS/content/NWS_1_1x_ACS_Recommends_HPV_Vaccine.asp.

"Act in Time to Heart Attack Signs: Heart Attack Warning Signs." National Heart, Lung, and Blood Institute. Accessed December 10, 2007. www.nhlbi .nih.gov/actintime/haws/haws.htm.

"Acupressure, Shiatsu, Tuina." Natural Standard and Harvard Medical School. Accessed January 5, 2008. www.intelihealth.com/IH/ihtIH/WSIHW000/ 8513/34968/ 358869.html?d=dmtContent.

"Acupuncture." American Cancer Society. Accessed January 23, 2008. www.cancer.org/docroot/ETO/content/ETO_5_3X_Acupuncture.asp.

"Acupuncture: An Alternative and Complementary Medicine Resource Guide." Alternative Medicine Foundation. Accessed January 20, 2008. www.amfoundation.org/acupuncture.htm.

"Acupuncture: Sharp Answers to Pointed Questions." Mayo Clinic. Accessed January 23, 2008. http://mayoclinic.com/health/acupuncture/SA00086.

Adams, Stephen. "Breast Cancer." *5 Minute Clinical Consult Overview*. InfoRetriever. USC School of Medicine Library, Columbia, SC. Accessed December 18, 2007. Keyword: breast cancer.

Aiello, D. "The Hot and the Cold of It." Rehab Management. Accessed November 23, 2007. www.rehabpub.com/features/62004/2.asp.

"Alcohol Allergy: Is There Such a Thing?" Mayo Clinic. Accessed November 8, 2007. www.mayoclinic.com/health/alcohol-allergy/AN00818.

"Alcohol and Coronary Heart Disease." National Institute on Alcohol Abuse and Alcoholism. Accessed November 2, 2007. http://pubs.niaaa.nih.gov/publications/aa45.htm.

"Alcohol: Effects on Health." MD Consult Patient Education Handout. USC School of Medicine Library, Columbia, SC. Accessed November 13, 2007. Keyword: alcohol.

"Alcoholism." MD Consult Patient Education Handout. USC School of Medicine Library, Columbia, SC. Accessed on November 13, 2007. Keyword: alcoholism.

"Alcohol, Wine and Cardiovascular Disease." American Heart Association. Accessed November 7, 2007. www.americanheart.org/presenter.jhtml?identifier=4422.

"All About Sleep." Nemours Foundation. Accessed February 1, 2008. www.kids health.org/parent/general/sleep/sleep.html.

"Alzheimer's Disease Fact Sheet." National Institute on Aging. Accessed February 23, 2008. www.nia.nih.gov/NR/rdonlyres/7DCA00DB-1362-4755-9E87-96DF669EAE20/4285/Alzheimers_Disease_Fact_Sheet706.pdf.

American Academy of Pediatrics Work Group on Breastfeeding. "Breastfeeding and the Use of Human Milk." Pediatrics 100 (1997): 1035–1039.

American College of Physicians. "Understanding Drugs." Complete Home Medical Guide. New York: DK, 2003.

American Gastroenterological Association. "AGA Guide: Obesity." UpToDate. USC School of Medicine Library, Columbia, SC. Accessed November 9, 2007. Keyword: obesity.

American Medical Association. "Degenerative Diseases of the Brain." Family Medical Guide. Hoboken: John Wiley & Sons, 2004.

American Medical Association. "Neural Tube Defects." Family Medical Guide. Hoboken: John Wiley & Sons, 2004.

"Am I At Risk?". Ferre Institute Cardiovascular Program. Accessed November 18, 2007. www.heartgenes.org/heartdiseaserisk.html.

"Androgen Insensitivity Syndrome." Genetics Home Reference. U.S. National Library of Medicine. Accessed January 17, 2008. http://ghr.nlm.nih.gov/condition=androgeninsensitivitysyndrome.

"Androgen Insensitivity Syndrome." MedlinePlus Medical Encyclopedia. U.S. National Library of Medicine. Accessed January 18, 2008. www.nlm.nih.gov/medlineplus/ency/article/001180.htm.

"Anti-Aging Therapies: Too Good to Be True?" Mayo Clinic. Accessed November 24, 2007. www.mayoclinic.com/health/anti-aging/HQ00233.

"Antibiotics: Too Much of a Good Thing." Mayo Clinic. Accessed January 3, 2008. www.mayoclinic.com/print/antibiotics/FL00075/METHOD=print.

"Antibiotics: When They Can and Can't Help." American Academy of Family Physicians. Accessed January 5, 2008. http://familydoctor.org/680.xml.

"Antioxidant Vitamins." American Heart Association. Accessed November 5, 2007. www.americanheart.org/presenter.jhtml?identifier=4452.

"Arthritis Advice." National Institute on Aging. Accessed February 1, 2008. www.niapublications.org/agepages/arthritis.asp.

"Arthritis Basics." National Center for Chronic Disease Prevention and Health Promotion. Accessed February 1, 2008. www.cdc.gov/arthritis/arthritis/key.htm.

Asano, T., R. McLeod, and T. Asano. "Dietary Fibre for the Prevention of Colorectal Adenomas and Carcinomas (Cochrane Review)." *The Cochrane Library* Issue 1, 2007. Chichester: Wiley.

"Autism Fact Sheet." National Institute of Neurological Disorders and Stroke. Accessed February 6, 2008. www.ninds.nih.gov/disorders/autism/detail_autism.htm.

"Autism Spectrum Disorders (Pervasive Developmental Disorders)." National Institute of Mental Health. Accessed February 7, 2008. www.nimh.nih.gov/publicat/autism.cfm.

"A–Z Index of Parasitic Diseases." Centers for Disease Control and Prevention. U.S. Department of Health & Human Services. Accessed January 15, 2008. www.cdc.gov/ncidod/dpd/parasites.

"Back Pain Facts & Statistics." American Chiropractic Association. Accessed January 15, 2008. www.amerchiro.org/level2_css.cfm?T1ID=13&T2ID=68.

Barnes, P., E. Powell-Griner, K. McFann, and R. Nahin. "Complementary and Alternative Medicine Use Among Adults." *Advance Data Report No. 343.* Atlanta: Centers for Disease Control and Prevention, 2002.

Bartlett, J. and A. Finkbeiner. *The Guide to Living with HIV Infection,* 6th ed. Baltimore: The Johns Hopkins University Press, 2006.

"Basic Blood Tests." Nemours Foundation. Accessed January 16, 2008. http://kidshealth.org/parent/general/sick/labtest5.html.

Behrman, R. *Nelson Textbook of Pediatrics.* Philadelphia: Saunders, 2004.

"Be MedWise: Use Over-the-Counter Medicines Wisely." National Council on Patient Information and Education. Accessed October 30, 2007. www.be medwise.org/brochure/bemedwise_english_brochure.pdf.

"Benefits of Breastfeeding." National Women's Health Information Center. Accessed February 5, 2008. www.4woman.gov/Breastfeeding/index.cfm?page=227.

"Benefits of Breastfeeding [Issue Paper]." Raleigh, NC: United States Breast-feeding Committee, 2002.

"Benefits of Massage Therapy." MassageTherapy101. Accessed January 8, 2008. www.massagetherapy101.com/massage-therapy/benefits-of-massage-therapy.aspx.

Bennett, B. "The Low-Down on Osteoporosis: What We Know and What We Don't." *Word on Health* (2003). Accessed February 4, 2008. www.nih.gov/news/WordonHealth/dec2003/osteo.htm.

"Biofeedback." *MD Consult Patient Education Handout.* USC School of Medicine Library, Columbia, SC. Accessed December 16, 2007. Keyword: biofeedback.

"Biofeedback: Using Your Mind to Improve Your Health." Mayo Clinic. Accessed December 15, 2007. www.mayoclinic.com/health/biofeedback/SA00083.

Birks, J., and J. Evans. "Ginkgo Biloba for Cognitive Impairment and Dementia." Cochrane Database of Systematic Reviews. USC School of Medicine Library, Columbia, SC. Accessed November 23, 2007. Keyword: ginkgo biloba.

"Birth Control Pill FAQ: Benefits, Risks and Choices." Mayo Clinic. Accessed January 3, 2008. www.mayoclinic.com/health/birth-control-pill/WO00098.

"Blood Pressure." *MD Consult Patient Education Handout.* USC School of Medicine Library, Columbia, SC. Accessed December 7, 2007. Keyword: blood pressure.

"Body Mass Index." *MedlinePlus Medical Encyclopedia.* U.S. National Library of Medicine. Accessed November 10, 2007. www.nlm.nih.gov/medlineplus/ency/article/007196.htm.

"Bonding with Your Baby." Nemours Foundation. Accessed January 17, 2008. http://kidshealth.org/parent/pregnancy_newborn/communicating/bonding.html.

"Bone Loss and Osteoporosis." *Our Bodies, Ourselves: the Boston Women's Health Book Collective.* New York: Touchstone, 2005.

Boyd, K. "PointFinder: The Online Acupressure Guide." Stanford University School of Medicine. Accessed January 3, 2008. http://med.stanford.edu/personal/pointfinder/index.html.

Bray, G. "Clinical Evaluation of the Overweight Adult." UpToDate. USC School of Medicine Library, Columbia, SC. Accessed November 11, 2007. Keyword: obesity.

"BRCA-1 and BRCA-2." American Association for Clinical Chemistry. Accessed December 5, 2007. www.labtestsonline.org/understanding/analytes/brca/test.html.

"Breakfast: Why Is It So Important?" Mayo Clinic. Accessed November 19, 2007. www.mayoclinic.com/print/food-and-nutrition/AN01119.

"Buying Prescription Medicine Online: A Consumer Safety Guide." U.S. Food and Drug Administration. Accessed October 19, 2007. www.fda.gov/buyon lineguide.

"Caffeine Content of Common Beverages." Mayo Clinic. Accessed November 3, 2007. www.mayoclinic.com/health/caffeine/AN01211.

"Caffeine: How Much Is Too Much?" Mayo Clinic. Accessed November 16, 2007. www.mayoclinic.com/health/caffeine/NU00600.

"Can a Computer Screen Damage My Eyes?" Pasadena Eye Associates. Accessed December 23, 2007. www.pasadenaeye.com/faq/faq08/faq08_ text.html.

"Can Alzheimer's Disease Be Prevented?" National Institute on Aging. Accessed February 22, 2008. www.nia.nih.gov/NR/rdonlyres/63B5A29C-F943-4DB7-91B4-0296772973F3/0/CanADbePrevented.pdf.

"Cancer and CAM." National Center for Complementary and Alternative Medicine. Accessed January 7, 2008. http://nccam.nih.gov/health/camcancer.

"Cancer Trends Progress Report: 2007 Update." National Cancer Institute. Accessed February 2008. http://progressreport.cancer.gov.

Carlson, J. *Complementary Therapies and Wellness: Practice Essentials for Holistic Health Care.* Upper Saddle River, NJ: Prentice Hall, 2003.

Celestino, F. "Alzheimer Disease." *5 Minute Clinical Consult Overview.* InfoRetriever. USC School of Medicine Library, Columbia, SC. Accessed January 9, 2008. Keyword: alzheimer.

"Cell Phone Facts: Consumer Information on Wireless Phones." U.S. Food and Drug Administration. Accessed December 19, 2007. www.fda.gov/cellphones.

"Cellular Telephone Use and Cancer: Questions and Answers." National Cancer Institute. Accessed December 1, 2007. www.cancer.gov/cancertopics/factsheet/Risk/cellphones.

"Cervical Cancer Vaccine: Who Needs It, How It Works." Mayo Clinic Accessed January 16, 2008. www.mayoclinic.com/print/cervical-cancer-vaccine/WO00120.

"Change of Heart: No Link Between Low-Carb Diet and Heart Risk." Research Behind the News. *Journal of the American Dietetic Association.* USC School of Medicine Library, Columbia, SC. Accessed November 19, 2007.

"Childhood Immunizations: First Line of Defense Against Illnesses." Mayo Clinic Accessed January 9, 2008. www.mayoclinic.com/health/vaccines/CC00014.

"Childhood Vaccines: What They Are and Why Your Child Needs Them." American Academy of Family Physicians. Accessed January 10, 2008. http://familydoctor.org/online/famdocen/home/healthy/vaccines/028.html.

The Children's Hospital Guide to Your Child's Health and Development. Boston: Children's Hospital Boston, 2001.

"Chiropractic." U.S. National Library of Medicine. Accessed January 13, 2008. www.nlm.nih.gov/medlineplus/chiropractic.html.

"Cholesterol." American Association for Clinical Chemistry. Accessed December 1, 2007. www.labtestsonline.org/understanding/analytes/cholesterol/ multiprint.html.

"Cholesterol." American Heart Association. Accessed December 18, 2007. www.americanheart.org/presenter.jhtml;jsessionid=KKFQXHIJZST3QCQF CXPSDSQ?identifier=4488.

"Cholesterol Test: Sorting Out the Lipids." Mayo Clinic. Accessed November 7, 2007. www.mayoclinic.com/health/cholesterol-test/CL00033.

"Chronic Pain Medicines." American Academy of Family Physicians. Accessed November 12, 2007. http://familydoctor.org/online/famdocen/home/ common/pain treatment/122.html.

"Clean That Computer Keyboard." WebMD. Accessed January 3, 2008. www.webmd.com/news/20060426/clean-that-computer-keyboard.

"Coffee: Does It Offer Health Benefits?" Mayo Clinic. Accessed November 18, 2007. www.mayoclinic.com/health/coffee-and-health/AN01354.

"Colon and Rectal Cancers." *MD Consult Patient Education Handout.* USC School of Medicine Library, Columbia, SC. Accessed December 14, 2007. Keyword: colon cancer.

"Colon Cancer Guide." Mayo Clinic. Accessed January 2, 2008. www.mayo clinic.com/print/colon-cancer/CO99999/PAGE=all&METHOD=print.

"Colon Cleansing: Is It Helpful or Harmful?" Mayo Clinic. Accessed December 15, 2007. www.mayoclinic.com/print/colon-cleansing/AN00065/METHOD=print.

"Colorectal Cancer Screening: Questions and Answers." National Cancer Institute. Accessed January 4, 2008. www.cancer.gov/cancertopics/factsheet/ Detection/colorectal-screening.

"Colorectal Cancer: The Importance of Prevention and Early Detection." Centers for Disease Control and Prevention. U.S. Department of Health & Human Services. Accessed January 2, 2008. www.cdc.gov/cancer/colorectal/ pdf/about2004.pdf.

"Combination Pill." Mayo Clinic. Accessed January 7, 2008. www.mayo clinic.com/health/birth-control/BI99999/PAGE=BI00015.

"Common Eye Myths." Prevent Blindness America. Accessed January 29, 2008. www.preventblindness.org/eye_problems/eye_myths.html.

"Complementary and Alternative Medicine in Cancer Treatment: Questions and Answers." National Cancer Institute. Accessed January 5, 2008. www.cancer.gov/cancertopics/factsheet/therapy/CAM.

"Complementary and Alternative Methods for Cancer Management." American Cancer Society. Accessed January 7, 2008. www.cancer.org/docroot/ETO/content/ETO_5_1_Introduction.asp.

"Complete Blood Count." American Association for Clinical Chemistry. Accessed January 16, 2008. www.labtestsonline.org/understanding/analytes/cbc/multiprint.html.

"Consumer Tips." California Board of Pharmacy. Accessed October 21, 2007. www.pharmacy.ca.gov/consumers/consumer_tips.

"Coronary Artery Disease." U.S. National Library of Medicine. Accessed December 16, 2007. www.nlm.nih.gov/medlineplus/coronaryarterydisease.html.

"Coronary Heart Disease: Reducing Your Risk." American Academy of Family Physicians. Accessed December 19, 2007. http://familydoctor.org/online/famdocen/home/common/ heartdisease/risk/239.html.

"Counting Calories: Getting Back to Weight-Loss Basics." Mayo Clinic. Accessed November 17, 2007. www.mayoclinic.com/health/calories/WT00011.

Davis, J. "Lose Weight: Eat Breakfast." WebMD. Accessed November 8, 2007. www.webmd.com/diet/features/lose-weight-eat-breakfast.

Davis, M., P. Davis, and D. Ross, eds. *Expert Guide to Sports Medicine.* Philadelphia: American College of Physicians, 2005.

"Day One: After You've Tested Positive. HIV Treatment Information." Project Inform. Accessed March 24, 2008. www.projectinform.org/info/dayone/index.shtml.

Decherney, A., and L. Nathan. "Hirsutism." *Current Diagnosis & Treatment in Obstetrics & Gynecology.* AccessMedicine. USC School of Medicine Library, Columbia, SC. Accessed January 18, 2008. Keyword: hirsutism.

"Dementia." *MD Consult Patient Education Handout.* USC School of Medicine Library, Columbia, SC. Accessed January 31, 2008. Keyword: dementia.

"Dementia: Info and Advice for Caregivers." *MD Consult Patient Education Handout.* USC School of Medicine Library, Columbia, SC. Accessed February 8, 2008. Keyword: dementia.

"Dementia: What Are the Common Signs?" American Academy of Family Physicians. Accessed January 2, 2008. http://familydoctor.org/online/famdocen/home/seniors/mental-health/662.html.

Denoon, D. "Lung Cancer CT Scans No Help? CT Scans for Smokers Up Risks, Don't Cut Lung Cancer Deaths, Study Shows." WebMD. Accessed December 30, 2007. www.webmd.com/lung-cancer/news/20070306/lung-cancer-ct-scans-no-help.

"Depression: Comprehensive Version." *MD Consult Patient Education Handout.* USC School of Medicine Library, Columbia, SC. Accessed February 14, 2008. Keyword: depression.

"Detailed Guide: Colon and Rectum Cancer." American Cancer Society. Accessed January 8, 2008. www.cancer.org/docroot/CRI/CRI_2_3x.asp? rnav=cridg&dt=10.

"Detailed Guide: Colon and Rectum Cancer. Can Colorectal Cancer Be Prevented?" American Cancer Society. Accessed December 1, 2007. www.cancer.org/docroot/CRI/content/CRI_2_4_2X_Can_colon_and_rectum _cancer_be_prevented.asp.

"Detailed Guide: Lung Cancer—Non–Small Cell: How Is Non–Small Cell Lung Cancer Diagnosed?" American Cancer Society. Accessed January 3, 2008. www.cancer.org/docroot/CRI/content/CRI_2_4_3x_How_Is_Non-Small_Cell_Lung_Cancer_Diagnosed.asp?rnav=cri.

"Detailed Guide: Lung Cancer—Non–Small Cell: What Are the Risk Factors for Non–Small Lung Cancer?" American Cancer Society. Accessed December 5, 2007. www.cancer.org/docroot/CRI/content/CRI_2_4_2x_What_Are_the_Risk_Factors_for_Non-Small_Cell_Lung_Cancer.asp?rnav=cri.

"Diabetes and Pregnancy Frequently Asked Questions." Centers for Disease Control and Prevention. U.S. Department of Health & Human Services. Accessed October 14, 2007. http://cdc.gov/ncbddd/bd/diabetespregnancy faqs.htm.

"Diabetes Overview." National Diabetes Information Clearinghouse. Accessed December 14, 2007. http://diabetes.niddk.nih.gov/dm/pubs/overview.

"Diagnosis of Parasitic Diseases." Centers for Disease Control and Prevention. U.S. Department of Health & Human Services. Accessed January 9, 2008. www.cdc.gov/ncidod/dpd/public/geninfo_diagnosis_diseases.htm.

"Dietary Supplements." U.S. Food and Drug Administration. Accessed January 20, 2008. www.fda.gov/womens/getthefacts/supplements.html.

"Differential Diagnosis of Anaphylaxis and Anaphylactoid Reactions." *MD Consult Patient Education Handout.* USC School of Medicine Library, Columbia, SC. Accessed November 5, 2007. Keyword: anaphylaxis.

"Digestive Help Tips." American College of Gastroenterology. Accessed December 17, 2007. www.acg.gi.org/patients/healthtips.asp.

"Diphtheria Tetanus & Pertussis Vaccines: What You Need to Know." Centers for Disease Control and Prevention. U.S. Department of Health & Human Services. Accessed January 12, 2008. www.cdc.gov/vaccines/pubs/vis/downloads/vis-dtap.pdf.

"Diseases and Conditions: Allergy." Aetna Intelihealth. Accessed November 10, 2007. www.intelihealth.com/IH/ihtIH/WSIHW000/408/408.html.

"Do I Need a Tetanus Shot?" American College of Emergency Physicians. Accessed January 16, 2008. www.acep.org/webportal/PatientsConsumers/HealthSubjectsByTopic/Immunization/Feat.

"Do You Know the Health Risks of Being Overweight?" WIN: Weight-Control Information Network. National Institute of Diabetes and Digestive and Kidney Diseases. Accessed January 30, 2008. http://win.niddk.nih.gov/publications/health_risks.htm.

"Drug Interactions and Side Effects." American Heart Association. Accessed November 13, 2007. www.americanheart.org/presenter.jhtml?identifier= 117.

"Drug Interactions: What You Should Know." U.S. Food and Drug Administration. Accessed November 14, 2007. www.fda.gov/cder/consumerinfo/drug interactions.htm.

Duyff, R. *American Dietetic Association Complete Food and Nutrition Guide*, 3rd ed. New York: John Wiley & Sons, 2006.

"Eating Disorders: Facts for Teens." American Academy of Family Physicians. Accessed January 7, 2008. http://familydoctor.org/online/famdocen/home/children/teens/eating/277.html

"Echinacea." *Review of Natural Products*. St. Louis, MO: Facts and Comparisons, 2005.

"Echinacea Natural Remedy." *MD Consult Patient Education Handout*. USC School of Medicine Library, Columbia, SC. Accessed November 19, 2007. Keyword: echinacea.

"Electromagnetic Fields & Public Health: Microwave Ovens." World Health Organization. Accessed December 19, 2007. www.who.int/peh-emf/publications/facts/info_microwaves/en.

"Emergency Contraception.". U.S. Department of Health & Human Services. Accessed January 12, 2008. http://womenshealth.gov/faq/econtracep.htm.

"Energy Medicine: An Overview." National Center for Complementary and Alternative Medicine. Accessed January 7, 2008. http://nccam.nih.gov/health/backgrounds/energymed.htm.

"Energy Therapies: Therapeutic Touch." The University of Texas MD Anderson Cancer Center. Accessed January 10, 2008. http://www.mdanderson.org.

"Erectile Dysfunction." Mayo Clinic. Accessed February 13, 2008. www.mayo clinic.com/health/erectile-dysfunction/DS00162.

"Erectile Dysfunction." National Kidney and Urologic Diseases Information Clearinghouse. Accessed February 14, 2008. http://kidney.niddk.nih.gov/kudiseases/pubs/impotence.

"Exercise." *Well-Connected In-Depth Reports, No. 29*. New York: Nidus Information Services, 2006.

"Exercise: A Healthy Habit to Start and Keep." American Academy of Family Physicians. Accessed November 23, 2007. http://familydoctor.org/059 .xml.

"Exercise for Your Bone Health." National Institute of Arthritis and Musculo-skeletal and Skin Diseases. Accessed February 16, 2008. www.niams.nih .gov/bone/hi/bone_exercise.htm.

"Eye Care Facts and Myths: A Closer Look." American Academy of Ophthalmol-ogy. Accessed December 22, 2007. www.medem.com/medlb/article_ detaillb.cfm?article_ID=ZZZ8BUZTYIE &sub_cat=0.

"Eye Examinations." National Eye Institute. Accessed January 30, 2008. http://www.nei.nih.gov/photo/eye%5Fexam.

"Eye Exams: What to Expect." Eyecare America. The Foundation of the American Academy of Ophthalmology. Accessed January 29, 2008. www.eyecareamerica .org/eyecare/treatment/eye-exams.cfm.

"Eye Exams: What to Expect." Mayo Clinic. Accessed January 28, 2008. www.mayoclinic.com/print/eye-exams/MC00021/METHOD=print.

"FAQs About MMR Vaccines & Autism." Centers for Disease Control and Prevention. U.S. Department of Health & Human Services. Accessed February 2, 2008. www.cdc.gov/nip/vacsafe/concerns/autism/autism-mmr .htm#3.

"FDA Approves Contraceptive for Continuous Use." U.S. Food and Drug Administration. Accessed January 10, 2008. www.fda.gov/bbs/topics/ NEWS/2007/NEW01637.html.

Ferri, F. *Ferri's Clinical Advisor.* St. Louis: Mosby, 2007.

"Fit Facts: The Best Time to Exercise." American Council on Exercise. Accessed November 12, 2007. www.acefitness.org/fitfacts/fitfacts_display .aspx?itemid=53.

"Fitness Fundamentals: Guidelines for Personal Exercise Programs." The President's Council on Physical Fitness and Sports. Accessed November 13, 2007. www.fitness.gov/fitness.htm.

"Fitting in Fitness: Finding Time for Physical Activity." Mayo Clinic. Accessed November 8, 2007. http://mayoclinic.com/health/fitness/HQ01217_D.

Fodor, G., and R. Tzerovska. "Coronary Heart Disease: Is Gender Important?" *Journal of Men's Health & Gender* 1 (2004): 32–37.

"Folic Acid." Centers for Disease Control and Prevention. U.S. Department of Health & Human Services. Accessed January 4, 2008. www.cdc.gov/ ncbddd/folicacid.

"Folic Acid and Pregnancy." Nemours Foundation. Accessed January 7, 2008. http://kidshealth.org/parent/pregnancy_newborn/pregnancy/folic_acid. html.

"For People with Osteoporosis: How to Find a Doctor." National Institute of Arthritis and Musculoskeletal and Skin Diseases. Accessed February 8, 2008. www.niams.nih.gov/bone/hi/osteoporosis_find_doc.htm.

"Frequently Asked Questions About Generic Drugs." U.S. Food and Drug Administration. Accessed November 20, 2007. www.fda.gov/cder/consumerinfo/generics_q&a.htm.

"Frequently Asked Questions About Immunizations." Nemours Foundation. Accessed January 31, 2008. http://kidshealth.org/parent/general/body/fact_myth_immunizations.html.

"Frequently Asked Questions About USP Verification Program for Dietary Supplements." U.S. Pharmacopeia. Accessed January 21, 2008. www.usp.org/USPVerified/dietarySupplements/faq.html.

"Frequently Asked Questions: Cosmetics and Your Health." U.S. Department of Health & Human Services. Accessed November 9, 2007. http://womenshealth.gov/faq/cosmetics.pdf.

Gelfand, M. "Clinical Manifestations and Treatment of Listeria Monocytogenes Infection in Adults." UpToDate. USC School of Medicine Library, Columbia, SC. Accessed January 6, 2008. Keyword: listeriosis.

"General Information About Antibiotic Resistance." Centers for Disease Control and Prevention. U.S. Department of Health & Human Services. Accessed January 3, 2008. www.cdc.gov/drugresistance/community/faqs.htm.

"Generic Drugs." *Consumer Reports.* Accessed November 14, 2007. www.crbestbuydrugs.org/PDFs/GenericDrugs-FINAL.pdf.

The Genetic Landscape of Diabetes. National Institutes of Health. Accessed December 19, 2007. www.ncbi.nlm.nih.gov/books/bv.fcgi?rid=diabetes.

"Genetics of Diabetes." American Diabetes Association. Accessed December 4, 2007. www.diabetes.org/genetics.jsp.

"Genetic Testing for BRCA1 and BRCA2: It's Your Choice." National Cancer Institute. Accessed November 17, 2007. www.cancer.gov/cancertopics/factsheet/Risk/BRCA.

"Gestational Diabetes." American Diabetes Association. Accessed November 6, 2007. http://diabetes.org/gestational-diabetes.jsp.

"Gestational Diabetes." National Institutes of Child Health & Human Development. Accessed November 7, 2007. www.nichd.nih.gov/health/topics/Gestational_Diabetes.cfm.

"Get the Facts: Acupuncture." *National Center for Complementary and Alternative Medicine.* Accessed January 24, 2008. http://nccam.nih.gov/health/acupuncture.

Gilliland, B. "Arthritis, Osteo." *5 Minute Clinical Consult Overview.* InfoRetriever. USC School of Medicine Library, Columbia, SC. Accessed February 2, 2008. Keyword: osteoarthritis.

"Ginkgo." National Center for Complementary and Alternative Medicine. Accessed November 18, 2007. http://nccam.nih.gov/health/ginkgo.

"Ginkgo Biloba." *MD Consult Patient Education Handout.* USC School of Medicine Library, Columbia, SC. Accessed November 24, 2007. Keyword: ginkgo biloba.

"Ginkgo (Ginkgo Biloba L.)." Natural Standard Research Collaboration. Accessed November 23, 2007. www.nlm.nih.gov/medlineplus/druginfo/natural/patient-ginkgo.html.

Goldmann, D., and D. Horowitz. *American College of Physicians Complete Home Medical Guide.* New York: DK, 2003.

Griffith, H. *Complete Guide to Prescription & Nonprescription Drugs.* New York: Penguin Group, 2006.

"Guide for First-Time Parents." Nemours Foundation. Accessed January 18, 2008. http://kidshealth.org/parent/pregnancy_newborn/pregnancy/guide_parents.html.

"Harmful Interactions: Mixing Alcohol with Medicines." National Institute on Alcohol Abuse and Alcoholism. Accessed October 27, 2007. http://pubs.niaaa.nih.gov/publications/Medicine/medicine.htm.

"Health Care Topics: Antibiotic Resistance." American College of Physicians. Accessed January 5, 2008. www.doctorsforadults.com/topics/dfa_anti.htm.

"Healthy Breakfast: The Best Way to Begin Your Day." Mayo Clinic. Accessed November 23, 2007. www.mayoclinic.com/health/food-and-nutrition/NU00197.

"Hearing Colors, Tasting Shapes." *Scientific American.* Accessed January 11, 2008. www.sciam.com/article.cfm?articleID=0003014B-9D06-1E8F-8EA5809EC5880000.

"Heart Attack, Stroke and Cardiac Arrest Warning Signs." American Heart Association. Accessed November 22, 2007. www.americanheart.org/presenter.jhtml?identifier=3053.

"Heart Disease Fact Sheet." Harvard Center for Cancer Prevention. Harvard School of Public Health. Accessed November 2, 2007. www.yourdiseaserisk.harvard.edu/hccpquiz.pl?lang=english&func=show&quiz=heart&page=fact_sheet.

"Heart Healthy Diet: What Are the Components of a Heart Healthy Diet?" *MD Consult Patient Education Handout.* USC School of Medicine Library, Columbia, SC. Accessed November 14, 2007. Keyword: healthy diet.

Hendrick, V. "Premenstrual Syndrome." U.S. Department of Health & Human Services. Accessed January 19, 2008. http://womenshealth.gov/faq/pms.htm.

Henschke, C., and P. McCarthy. *Lung Cancer: Myths, Facts, Choices—and Hope.* New York: W.W. Norton, 2002.

Hensrud, D., ed. *Mayo Clinic Healthy Weight for EveryBody.* Rochester, MN: Mayo Clinic, 2005.

"Herbal Products and Supplements: What You Should Know." American Academy of Family Physicians. Accessed January 20, 2008. http://family doctor.org/online/famdocen/home/otc-center/otc-medicines/860 .html.

"Heredity as a Risk Factor." American Heart Association. Accessed November 5, 2007. www.americanheart.org/presenter.jhtml?identifier=4610.

"High Blood Cholesterol: What You Need to Know." National Heart, Lung, and Blood Institute. Accessed December 13, 2007. www.nhlbi.nih.gov/ health/public/heart/chol/wyntk.htm.

"High Blood Pressure." U.S. Food and Drug Administration Office of Women's Health. Accessed November 17, 2007. www.fda.gov/womens/get thefacts/hbp.html.

"High Blood Pressure: Getting the Most Out of Home Monitoring." Mayo Clinic. Accessed December 6, 2007. www.mayoclinic.com/print/high-blood-pressure/HI00016/METHOD=print.

"High Blood Pressure (Hypertension)." Mayo Clinic. Accessed December 1, 2007. www.mayoclinic.com/print/high-blood-pressure/DS00100/DSECTION =all&METHOD=print.

"HIV/AIDS: Risk Factors and Prevention of Transmission." *MD Consult Patient Education Handout.* USC School of Medicine Library, Columbia, SC. Accessed November 9, 2007. Keyword: HIV.

"HIV and AIDS: How to Reduce Your Risk." American Academy of Family Physicians. Accessed November 6, 2007. http://familydoctor.org/online/ famdocen/home/common/sexinfections/hiv/005.html.

"HIV Infection and AIDS." *MD Consult Patient Education Handout.* USC School of Medicine Library, Columbia, SC. Accessed November 10, 2007. Keyword: HIV.

Hopkin, K. "Egg Beaters: Flu Vaccine Makers Look Beyond the Chicken Egg." *In Focus* (2004). Accessed January 16, 2008. www.sciam.com/article.cfm? articleID=0005CA0F-B46F-101E-B40D83414B7F0000.

"Hormones and Menopause: Tips from the National Institute." National Institute on Aging. Accessed January 4, 2008. www.niapublications.org/tip sheets/hormones.asp.

"Hot vs. Cold Treatment." The Gym Sports Resource Center. Accessed November 2, 2007. www.usgyms.net/hot_vs_cold.htm.

"How HIV Is Spread." San Francisco AIDS Foundation. Accessed November 16, 2007. www.sfaf.org/aids101/transmission.html.

"How Often Should Teeth by X-Rayed?" *Simple Steps to Better Dental Health.* Columbia University College of Dental Medicine. Accessed January 29, 2008. www.simplestepsdental.com.

"How Safe Is the Blood Supply in the United States?" Centers for Disease Control and Prevention. U.S. Department of Health & Human Services. Accessed November 2, 2007. www.cdc.gov/hiv/resources/qa/qa15.htm.

"How to Give Medicine to Children." U.S. Food and Drug Administration. Accessed November 1, 2007. www.fda.gov/FDAC/features/196_kid .html.

"How to Give Medicine to Children: Do You Know How to Give Medicine to Children?" U.S. Food and Drug Administration. Accessed November 1, 2007. www.fda.gov/opacom/lowlit/medchld.html.

"How Vaccines Work." Mayo Clinic. Accessed January 5, 2008. www.mayo clinic.com/health/vaccines/ID00023.

"HPV Vaccine Questions & Answers." Centers for Disease Control and Prevention. U.S. Department of Health & Human Services. Accessed January 13, 2008. www.cdc.gov/std/hpv/STDFact-HPV-vaccine.htm.

"Human Papillomavirus (HPV).". American Academy of Family Physicians. Accessed January 28, 2008. http://familydoctor.org/online/famdocen/ home/common/sexinfections/sti/389.html.

"Hyperemesis Gravidarum." American Pregnancy Association. Accessed January 15, 2008. www.americanpregnancy.org/pregnancycomplications/hyper emesisgravidarum.html.

"Ice Packs Vs. Warm Compresses for Pain." Oregon Health & Science University. Accessed November 1, 2007. www.ohsu.edu/health/health-topics/topic .cfm?id=10318&parent=11981.

"Infant Massage." *MD Consult Patient Education Handout.* USC School of Medicine Library, Columbia, SC. Accessed January 19, 2008. Keyword: infant massage.

"Infant Massage: Communicating Parents' Love Through Touch." Infant Massage USA. Accessed January 17, 2008. www.infantmassageusa.org/imusa/ aboutimusa.shtml.

"Influenza Virus Vaccine." Center for Biologics Evaluation and Research. U.S. Food and Drug Administration. Accessed January 17, 2008. www.fda.gov/ cber/flu/flu.htm.

"Information About Your Medicine." *MD Consult Patient Education Handout.* USC School of Medicine Library, Columbia, SC. Accessed November 7, 2007. Keyword: medicines.

"International Travel: Tips for Staying Healthy." American Academy of Family Physicians. Accessed January 10, 2008. http://familydoctor.org/online/ famdocen/home/healthy/travel/311.html.

"Intersex." *MedlinePlus Medical Encyclopedia.* U.S. National Library of Medicine. Accessed January 20, 2008. www.nlm.nih.gov/medlineplus/ency/article/ 001669.htm.

"Introduction to Naturopathy." National Center for Complementary and Alternative Medicine. Accessed January 10, 2008. http://nccam.nih.gov/health/naturopathy.

"Introduction to Reiki." National Center for Complementary and Alternative Medicine. Accessed January 13, 2008. http://nccam.nih.gov/health/reiki.

"Is a Low-Carbohydrate Diet Right for Me?" *AAFP News & Publications.* American Academy of Family Physicians. Accessed November 12, 2007. www.aafp .org/afp/20060601/1951ph.html.

"Is Your Desk Making You Sick?" Cable News Network (CNN). Accessed January 8, 2008. www.cnn.com/2004/HEALTH/12/13/cold.flu.desk/index.html.

Katon, W. "Anxiety." *5 Minute Clinical Consult Overview.* InfoRetriever. USC School of Medicine Library, Columbia, SC. Accessed January 6, 2008. Keyword: anxiety.

"Key Facts About Influenza (Flu) Vaccine." Centers for Disease Control and Prevention. U.S. Department of Health & Human Services. Accessed January 18, 2008. www.cdc.gov/flu/protect/keyfacts.htm.

"Key Facts About Influenza and the Influenza Vaccine." Centers for Disease Control and Prevention. U.S. Department of Health & Human Services. Accessed January 9, 2008. www.cdc.gov/flu/keyfacts.htm.

"Kids Aren't Just Small Adults: Medicines, Children and the Care Every Child Deserves." Center for Drug Evaluation and Research. U.S. Food and Drug Administration. Accessed November 4, 2007. www.fda.gov/cder/consumer info/kids.htm.

"Learning About Breast Cancer." National Human Genome Research Institute. Accessed December 5, 2007. www.genome.gov/page.cfm?pageID=10000507.

"Learn to Recognize a Stroke." American Stroke Association. Accessed December 6, 2007. www.strokeassociation.org/presenter.jhtml?identifier=1020.

"Let's Talk Facts About Phobias." American Psychiatric Association. Accessed January 31, 2008. www.healthyminds.org/multimedia/phobias.pdf.

Linde, K., B. Barrett, K. Wolkart, R. Bauer, and D. Melchart. "Echinacea for Preventing and Treating the Common Cold." Cochrane Database of Systematic Reviews. USC School of Medicine Library, Columbia, SC. Accessed November 15, 2007. Path: echinacea; common cold.

"Listeria Monocytogenes Risk Assessment Questions and Answers." FDA Center for Food Safety and Applied Nutrition. Accessed January 8, 2008. www.cfsan.fda.gov/~dms/lmr2qa.html.

"Low-Carb Diet Better for Lipids Than Low-Fat, High-Carb Diet." *This Week in Medicine.* USC School of Medicine Library, Columbia, SC. Accessed November 24, 2007.

"Lung Cancer (PDQ): Prevention." National Cancer Institute. Accessed December 17, 2007. www.cancer.gov/cancertopics/pdq/prevention/lung/patient.

"Lycopene: An Antioxidant for Good Health." American Dietetic Association. Accessed November 19, 2007. www.eatright.org/cps/rde/xchg/SID-5303FFEA- A120B9BE/ada/hs.xsl/nutrition_5328_ENU_HTML.htm.

Magalini, S., ed. "Urinary Excretion of Odoriferous Component of Asparagus." *Dictionary of Medical Syndromes*. Philadelphia: Lippincott-Raven, 2007.

"Magnet Therapy." Aetna InteliHealth. Accessed January 12, 2008. www.inteli health.com.

"Mammogram." *MD Consult Patient Education Handout*. USC School of Medicine Library, Columbia, SC. Accessed December 8, 2007. Keyword: mammogram.

"Mammograms." U.S. Department of Health & Human Services. Accessed December 8, 2007. http://womenshealth.gov/faq/mammography.htm.

Mannschreck, D. "Depression." *5 Minute Clinical Consult Overview*. InfoRetriever. USC School of Medicine Library, Columbia, SC. Accessed January 7, 2008. Keyword: depression.

Margen, S. *Wellness Foods A to Z: An Indispensable Guide for Health-Conscious Food Lovers*. New York: Rebus, 2002.

"Massage and Stress." MassageTherapy101. Accessed January 7, 2008. www.massagetherapy101.com/massage-therapy/massage-therapy-and-stress-reduction.aspx.

"Massage Therapy as CAM." National Center for Complementary and Alternative Medicine. Accessed January 10, 2008. http://nccam.nih.gov/health/massage.

McPhee, S., M. Papadakis, and L. Tierney, eds. *Current Medical Diagnosis & Treatment*. Los Altos, CA: Lange Medical Publications, 2007.

"Medical Tests for Prostate Problems." National Kidney and Urologic Diseases Information Clearinghouse. Accessed February 8, 2008. http://kidney .niddk.nih.gov/kudiseases/pubs/medtestprostate/index.htm.

"Medication Exposures During Pregnancy and Breastfeeding: Frequently Asked Questions." Centers for Disease Control and Prevention. U.S. Department of Health & Human Services. Accessed October 18, 2007. www.cdc.gov/ncbddd/meds/faqs.htm.

"Medicine and Pregnancy." U.S. Food & Drug Administration Office of Women's Health. Accessed October 19, 2007. www.fda.gov/womens/getthe facts/pregnancy.html.

"Medicine and Your Child: How to Give Your Child Medicine." American Academy of Family Physicians. Accessed November 3, 2007. http://family doctor.org/online/famdocen/home/children/parents/ safety/097.html.

"Medicines in My Home." U.S. Food and Drug Administration. Accessed November 15, 2007. www.fda.gov/medsinmyhome.

"Medicines: Use Them Safely." National Institute on Aging. Accessed October 22, 2007. www.niapublications.org/agepages/medicine.asp.

"Meditation." National Center for Complementary and Alternative Medicine. Accessed January 17, 2008. http://nccam.nih.gov/health/meditation.

"Meditation: Take a Stress-Reduction Break Wherever You Are." Mayo Clinic. Accessed January 17, 2008. www.mayoclinic.com/print/meditation/HQ01070/METHOD=print.

"Menopausal Hormone Therapy." *MD Consult Patient Education Handout*. USC School of Medicine Library, Columbia, SC. Accessed January 2, 2008. Keyword: hormone therapy.

"Menopause." *Well-Connected In-Depth Reports, No. 40.* New York: Nidus Information Services, 2006.

"Menopause and Menopause Treatment." U.S. Department of Health & Human Services. Accessed January 7, 2008. http://womenshealth.gov/faq/menopaus.htm.

"Mental Health." Society for Women's Health Research. Accessed January 5, 2008. http://swhr.convio.net/site/PageServer?pagename=hs_consumerfacts_mental.

"Mental Health." Society for Women's Health Research. Accessed February 21, 2008. www.womenshealthresearch.org/site/PageServer?pagename=hs_consumerfacts_mental.

Moore, C. "Should Everyone over Age 75 Take a Multivitamin?" Cleveland Clinic. Accessed November 7, 2007. www.clevelandclinic.org/health/health-info/docs/3500/3523.asp?index=11776.

"Morning Sickness." American Academy of Family Physicians. Accessed January 17, 2008. http://familydoctor.org/online/famdocen/home/women/pregnancy/basics/154.html.

Mosher, W. "Use of Contraception and Use of Family Planning Services in the United States: 1982–2002." *Advance Data from Vital and Health Statistics, No. 350.* Centers for Disease Control and Prevention. Accessed June 2007. www.cdc.gov/nchs/data/ad/ad350.pdf.

Mullen, D. "Strength Training for Weight Loss Success." Spine Universe. Accessed November 13, 2007. www.spineuniverse.com/displayarticle.php/article887.html.

"Multiple Medicines." *Consumer Reports*. Accessed November 12, 2007. www.crbestbuydrugs.org/PDFs/MultipleMedicines-FINAL.pdf.

National Organization of Rare Disorders. *NORD Guide to Rare Disorders*. Philadelphia: Lippincott Williams & Wilkins, 2003.

"Nausea and Acupressure." *MedlinePlus Medical Encyclopedia*. U.S. National Library of Medicine. Accessed January 5, 2008. www.nlm.nih.gov/medlineplus/ency/article/002117.htm.

"Non–Small Cell Lung Cancer." *MD Consult Patient Education Handout*. USC School of Medicine Library, Columbia, SC. Accessed December 17, 2007. Keyword: lung cancer.

"Obsessive-Compulsive Disorder." U.S. National Library of Medicine. Accessed January 16, 2008. www.nlm.nih.gov/medlineplus/obsessivecompulsive disorder.html.

"Obsessive-Compulsive Disorder (OCD)." Mental Health America. Accessed January 12, 2008. www.mentalhealthamerica.net/go/ocd.

"Occupational and Physical Therapy for Arthritis." Cleveland Clinic. Accessed February 7, 2008. http://my.clevelandclinic.org/disorders/arthritis/hic_occupational_and_physical_therapy_for_arthritis.aspx.

Ogunmodede, F. "Listeriosis Prevention Knowledge Among Pregnant Women in the USA." *Infectious Diseases in Obstetrics and Gynecology* 13 (2005): 11–15.

"Oral Health for Adults." National Center for Chronic Disease Prevention and Health Promotion. Accessed January 28, 2008. www.cdc.gov/OralHealth/factsheets/adult.htm.

"Osteoporosis Overview." National Institute of Arthritis and Musculoskeletal and Skin Diseases. Accessed February 16, 2008. www.niams.nih.gov/bone/hi/overview.htm.

"Osteoporosis Prevention." National Osteoporosis Foundation. Accessed February 7, 2008. www.nof.org/prevention/index.htm.

"OTC Drugs: Getting the Most from Your Medicine." American Academy of Family Physicians. Accessed October 18, 2007. http://familydoctor.org/online/famdocen/home/otc-center/basics/851.html.

OTC Drugs: Reducing the Risk of Adverse Effects." American Academy of Family Physicians. Accessed November 6, 2007. http://familydoctor.org/online/famdocen/home/otc-center/basics/852.printerview.html.

"OTC Drugs: Special Groups at Risk of Adverse Effects." American Academy of Family Physicians. Accessed October 15, 2007. http://familydoctor.org/online/famdocen/home/otc-center/basics/853.html.

"Over-the-Counter Medications and Breastfeeding." Cleveland Clinic. Accessed October 18, 2007. www.clevelandclinic.org/health/health-info/docs/3800/3882.asp?index=12353.

"Over-the-Counter Medicines." U.S. National Library of Medicine. Accessed October 30, 2007. www.nlm.nih.gov/medlineplus/overthecountermedicines.html.

"Overweight and Obesity: Health Consequences." Office of the Surgeon General. U.S. Department of Health & Human Services. Accessed January 28, 2008. www.surgeongeneral.gov/topics/obesity/calltoaction/fact_consequences.htm.

"Pain Medicines." Cleveland Clinic. Accessed November 6, 2007. www.cleveland clinic.org/health/health-info/docs/3600/3663.asp?index=12058.

"Pain Relievers." *MedlinePlus Health Topics.* U.S. National Library of Medicine. Accessed November 13, 2007. www.nlm.nih.gov/medlineplus/painrelievers .html.

"Pain Relievers: Understanding Your OTC Options." American Academy of Family Physicians. Accessed November 15, 2007. http://familydoctor.org/ online/famdocen/home/otc-center/otc-medicines/862.html.

"Pap Test (Cervical Smear)." *MD Consult Patient Education Handout.* USC School of Medicine Library, Columbia, SC. Accessed January 12, 2008. Keyword: pap test.

"Pap Tests and Cervical Health: A Healthy Habit for You." National Cancer Institute. Accessed January 25, 2008. www.cancer.gov/cancerinfo/pap-tests-cervical-health.

"Parasites and Foodborne Diseases." United States Department of Agriculture. Accessed January 9, 2008. www.fsis.usda.gov/Fact_Sheets/Parasites_and_ Foodborne_Illness/index.asp.

Pelletier, K. *The Best Alternative Medicine: What Works? What Does Not?* New York: Simon & Schuster, 2000.

"Pelvic Exam." *MD Consult Patient Education Handout.* USC School of Medicine Library, Columbia, SC. Accessed January 20, 2008. Keyword: pelvic exam.

"Phobias." U.S. National Library of Medicine. Accessed January 30, 2008. www.nlm.nih.gov/medlineplus/phobias.html.

"Phobic Disorders." *Merck Manual Home Edition.* Accessed January 27, 2008. www.merck.com/mmhe/sec07/ch100/ch100e.html.

"Pica." Nemours Foundation. Accessed December 28, 2007. http://kids health.org/parent/emotions/behavior/pica.html.

Pirisi, A. "Meaning of Morning Sickness Still Unsettled." *Lancet* 357 (2001): 1272.

"Plastics and the Microwave." U.S. Food and Drug Administration. Accessed December 19, 2007. www.cfsan.fda.gov/~dms/fdacplas.html.

"PMS: What You Can Do to Ease Your Symptoms." American Academy of Family Physicians. Accessed January 23, 2008. http://familydoctor.org/ online/famdocen/home/women/reproductive/ menstrual/141.html.

"Pneumococcal Conjugate Vaccine: What You Need to Know." Centers for Disease Control and Prevention. U.S. Department of Health & Human Services. Accessed January 5, 2008. www.cdc.gov/vaccines/pubs/vis/downloads/ vis-PneumoConjugate.pdf.

"Pneumococcal Pneumonia Shot." *MD Consult Patient Education Handout.* USC School of Medicine Library, Columbia, SC. Accessed January 5, 2008. Keyword: pneumonia.

"Pneumococcal Polysaccharide Vaccine: What You Need to Know." Centers for Disease Control and Prevention. U.S. Department of Health and Human Services. Accessed January 4, 2008. www.cdc.gov/vaccines/pubs/vis/downloads/vis-ppv.pdf.

"Pneumonia." *MD Consult Patient Education Handout.* USC School of Medicine Library, Columbia, SC. Accessed January 8, 2008. Keyword: pneumonia.

"Polarity." Aetna InteliHealth. Accessed January 13, 2008. www.intelihealth.com.

"Porphyria." *Griffith's 5-Minute Clinical Consult.* STAT!Ref. USC School of Medicine Library, Columbia, SC. Accessed January 3, 2008. Keyword: porphyria.

"Porphyrias." *Merck Manual,* 17th ed. STAT!Ref. USC School of Medicine Library, Columbia, SC. Accessed January 6, 2008. Keyword: porphyria.

"Porphyrins-Blood." *MedlinePlus Medical Encyclopedia.* U.S. National Library of Medicine. Accessed January 23, 2008. www.nlm.nih.gov/medlineplus/ency/article/003372.htm.

"Post-Traumatic Stress Disorder, a Real Illness." National Institute of Mental Health. Accessed January 10, 2008. www.nimh.nih.gov/publicat/NIMH ptsd.cfm.

"Pregnancy and Pica: Non-Food Cravings." American Pregnancy Association. Accessed December 27, 2007. www.americanpregnancy.org/pregnancy health/unusualcravingspica.html.

"Premenstrual Syndrome." *Well-Connected In-Depth Reports, No. 79.* New York: Nidus Information Services, 2006.

"Premenstrual Syndrome (PMS) and Premenstrual Dysphoric Disorder (PMDD)." *MD Consult Patient Education Handout.* USC School of Medicine Library, Columbia, SC. Accessed January 19, 2008. Keyword: premenstrual syndrome.

"Prescription Drug Abuse." *MD Consult Patient Education Handout.* USC School of Medicine Library, Columbia, SC. Accessed November 7, 2007. Keyword: prescription drug abuse.

"Prescription Drug Abuse Chart." National Institute on Drug Abuse. Accessed November 9, 2007. www.nida.nih.gov/DrugPages/PrescripDrugsChart .html.

"Prevention: Calcium & Vitamin D." National Osteoporosis Foundation. Accessed February 15, 2008. www.nof.org/prevention/calcium.htm.

"Preventive Services: Diabetes Screening, Supplies, and Self-Management." U.S. Department of Health & Human Services. Medicare. Accessed December 13, 2007. www.medicare.gov/health/diabetes.asp.

"The Problem of Antibiotic Resistance." National Institute of Allergy and Infectious Diseases. Accessed January 5, 2008. www.niaid.nih.gov/fact sheets/antimicro.htm.

"Prospective Cohort Study of Coffee Consumption and Coronary Heart Disease in Men and Women." *Hurst's The Heart.* AccessMedicine. USC School of Medicine Library, Columbia, SC. Accessed November 8, 2007. Path: coffee; heart disease.

"Prostate Health: What Every Man Needs to Know." *FDA Consumer Magazine.* U.S. Food and Drug Administration. Accessed February 10, 2008. www.fda.gov/fdac/features/2006/306_prostate.html.

"The Prostate-Specific Antigen (PSA) Test: Questions and Answers." National Cancer Institute. Accessed on February 7, 2008. www.cancer.gov/cancer topics/factsheet/Detection/PSA.

"Protect Your Baby and Yourself From Listeriosis." USDA Food Safety and Inspection Service. Accessed on January 7, 2008. www.fsis.usda.gov/Fact_ Sheets/Protect_Your_Baby/index.asp.

"Questions About Asparagus." Michigan Asparagus Advisory Board. Accessed December 19, 2007. www.asparagus.org/maab/faq.html.

"Questions and Answers About Homeopathy." National Center for Complementary and Alternative Medicine. Accessed January 9, 2008. http:// nccam.nih.gov/health/homeopathy.

"Questions and Answers About Using Magnets to Treat Pain." National Center for Complementary and Alternative Medicine. Accessed January 11, 2008. http://nccam.nih.gov/health/magnet/magnet.htm.

"Radio Frequency Safety." Federal Communications Commission. Accessed December 15, 2007. www.fcc.gov/oet/rfsafety/rf-faqs.html.

Rakel, D. *Integrative Medicine.* Philadelphia: Saunders, 2007.

"Reifenstein Syndrome." *MedlinePlus Medical Encyclopedia.* U.S. National Library of Medicine. Accessed January 13, 2008. www.nlm.nih.gov/med lineplus/ency/article/001169.htm.

"Reiki." Aetna InteliHealth. Accessed on January 14, 2008. www.intelihealth .com/IH/ihtIH/WSIHW000/8513/34968/360056.html?d=dmtContent.

"Research on Breastfeeding." National Institutes of Child Health & Human Development. Accessed February 2, 2008. www.nichd.nih.gov/womens health/research/pregbirth/breastfeed.cfm.

Rybacki, J. *Essential Guide to Prescription Drugs.* New York: HarperCollins, 2006.

"Safe Sleep for Your Baby: Ten Ways to Reduce the Risk of Sudden Infant Death Syndrome (SIDS)." National Institutes of Child Health & Human Development. Accessed February 2, 2008. www.nichd.nih.gov/publications/ pubs/safe_sleep_gen.cfm#risk.

Salzman, B., and R. Wender. "Male Sex: A Major Health Disparity." *Primary Care: Clinics in Office Practice* 33 (2006): 1–16.

Saper, R. "Clinical Use of Echinacea." UpToDate. USC School of Medicine Library, Columbia, SC. Accessed November 19, 2007. Keyword: echinacea.

"Screening." National Cancer Institute. Accessed December 13, 2007. www.cancer.gov/cancertopics/wyntk/colon-and-rectal/page5.

"Screening Mammograms." *Our Bodies, Ourselves: the Boston Women's Health Book Collective.* New York: Touchstone, 2005.

"Screening Mammograms: Questions and Answers." *National Cancer Institute Fact Sheet.* National Cancer Institute. Accessed December 23, 2007. www.cancer .gov/cancertopics/factsheet/Detection/screening-mammograms.

"Searching for Shereshevskii: What Is Superior About the Memory of Synaesthetes?" *Quarterly Journal of Experimental Psychology.* PsychInfo. USC School of Medicine Library, Columbia, SC. Accessed January 13, 2008.

"Seven Steps to Safety." Drug Digest.Org. Accessed November 14, 2007. www.drugdigest.org/DD/Home/Safety/0,21909,,00.html.

"Sex Differences in Mental Health." Society for Women's Health Research. Accessed January 11, 2008. http://swhr.convio.net/site/PageServer?page name=hs_facts_mental.

"Sexually Transmitted Disease Prevention." *MD Consult Patient Education Handout.* USC School of Medicine Library, Columbia, SC. Accessed January 6, 2008. Keyword: STD.

"Sexually Transmitted Diseases (STDs)." National Institute of Child Health & Human Development. Accessed January 15, 2008. www.nichd.nih.gov/ health/topics/sexually_transmitted_diseases.cfm.

"Sexually Transmitted Infections." *Our Bodies, Ourselves: the Boston Women's Health Book Collective.* New York: Touchstone, 2005.

Sharkey, B. and S. Gaskill. *Fitness and Health,* 6th ed. Champaign, IL: Human Kinetics, 2006.

"Shots for Travel." *MD Consult Patient Education Handout.* USC School of Medicine Library, Columbia, SC. Accessed January 16, 2008. Keyword: travel immunization.

"Sleep and Children: What's Normal?" *MD Consult Patient Education Handout.* USC School of Medicine Library, Columbia, SC. Accessed February 2, 2008. Keyword: sleep.

"Sleep and Preschoolers." Nemours Foundation. Accessed February 8, 2008. www.kidshealth.org/parent/growth/sleep/sleep_preschool.html.

Smith, S. "Experts Disagree on Ideal Time of Day to Exercise." Cable News Network (CNN) Accessed November 15, 2007. www.cnn.com/2003/ HEALTH/diet.fitness/05/27/exercise.time/index.html.

Somer, E. "Eau D'Asparagus." WebMD. Accessed December 17, 2007. www.webmd.com/content/article/43/1671_51089.

Somer, E. *Nutrition for a Healthy Pregnancy: The Complete Guide to Eating Before, During, and After Your Pregnancy.* New York: Henry Holt and Company, 2002.

Somerville, R., ed. *The Medical Advisor: The Complete Guide to Alternative & Conventional Treatments,* 2nd ed. Alexandria, VA: Time Life, 2000.

"Spiral CT Scans for Lung Cancer Screening: Fact Sheet." National Cancer Institute. Accessed January 3, 2008. www.cancer.gov/cancertopics/fact sheet/lung-spiral-CTscan.

"STIs: Common Symptoms & Tips on Prevention." American Academy of Family Physicians. Accessed January 13, 2008. http://familydoctor.org/ online/famdocen/home/common/sexinfections/ sti/165.html.

"Strength Training: Get Stronger, Leaner and Healthier." Mayo Clinic. Accessed November 4, 2007. www.mayoclinic.com/health/strength-training/ HQ01710.

"Stress: Comprehensive Version." *MD Consult Patient Education Handout.* USC School of Medicine Library, Columbia, SC. Accessed January 8, 2008. Keyword: stress.

"Study: No Evidence Cell Phones Cause Cancer." American Cancer Society. Accessed December 13, 2007. www.cancer.org/docroot/NWS/content/ NWS_1_1x_Study_No_Evidence_Cell_Phones_Cause_Cancer.asp.

"Substance Abuse Treatment for Children and Adolescents: Questions to Ask." American Academy of Child & Adolescent Psychiatry. Accessed November 17, 2007. www.aacap.org/page.ww?section=Facts+for+Families &name=Substance+Abuse+Treatment+For+Children+And+Adolescents %3A+Questions+To+Ask.

"Synesthesia." *MedlinePlus Medical Dictionary.* U.S. National Library of Medicine. Accessed January 10, 2008. www.nlm.nih.gov/medlineplus/mplusdictionary.html.

"Taking Medicines." National Institute on Aging. Accessed November 4, 2007. http://nihseniorhealth.gov/takingmedicines/toc.html.

"Tapeworm Infection." *Merck Manual Home Edition.* Accessed January 11, 2008. www.merck.com/mmhe/sec17/ch196/ch196p.html.

"Ten Ways to Be MedWise." National Council on Patient Information and Education. Accessed October 12, 2007. www.bemedwise.org/ten_ways/ ten_ways.htm.

"Tetanus, Diphtheria Pertussis (Tdap) Vaccine: What You Need to Know." Centers for Disease Control and Prevention. U.S. Department of Health & Human Services. Accessed January 14, 2008. www.cdc.gov/vaccines/pubs/ vis/downloads/vis-tdap.pdf.

"Therapeutic Touch." American Cancer Society. Accessed January 8, 2008. www.cancer.org/docroot/ETO/content/ETO_5_3X_Therapeutic_Touch .asp?sitearea=ETO.

"Think It Through: A Guide to Managing the Benefits and Risks of Medicines." Center for Drug Evaluation and Research. U.S. Food and Drug Administration. Accessed October 11, 2007. www.fda.gov/cder/consumerinfo/ think.htm.

"13 Questions to Ask When Choosing an Addiction Treatment Program." Partnership for a Drug-Free America. Accessed November 20, 2007. www.drug free.org/Intervention/Treatment/13_Questions_to_Ask.

"Tips on Blood Testing." American Association for Clinical Chemistry. Accessed January 12, 2008. www.labtestsonline.org/understanding/test tips/bloodtips-2.html.

"Tips to Help You Get Active." *WIN: Weight-Control Information Network.* National Institute of Diabetes and Digestive and Kidney Diseases. Accessed November 10, 2007. http://win.niddk.nih.gov/publications/tips.htm.

"Total Cholesterol Test." *MD Consult Patient Education Handout.* USC School of Medicine Library, Columbia, SC. Accessed December 7, 2007 Keyword: cholesterol.

Traisman, E., ed. *Guide to Your Children's Health.* New York: American Medical Association, 1999.

"Treatment: Pain." *Merck Manual Home Edition.* Accessed November 4, 2007. www.merck.com/mmhe/sec06/ch078/ch078d.html.

"Trichotillomania." Nemours Foundation. Accessed January 8, 2008. www.kids health.org/teen/your_mind/mental_health/trichotillomania.html.

"Understanding Alzheimer's Disease." National Institute on Aging. Accessed February 20, 2008. www.nia.nih.gov/NR/rdonlyres/F463CE6C-B0A7-47F4-882A-8EA143020193/0/understandingalzheimers.pdf.

"Understanding Stroke." Cleveland Clinic. Accessed October 31, 2007. www.clevelandclinic.org/health/health-info/docs/0900/0992 .asp?index=5601.

"USDA National Nutrient Database for Standard Reference, Release 18." United States Department of Agriculture. Accessed November 13, 2007. www.ars.usda.gov/Services/docs.htm?docid=9673.

"Use Caution Buying Medical Products Online." U.S. Food & Drug Administration. Accessed October 18, 2007. www.fda.gov/fdac/2005/105_buy .html.

"Use Your Microwave Safely." U.S. Food and Drug Administration. Accessed December 4, 2007. www.fda.gov/consumer/updates/microwave112107 .html.

"Utah Scientists Breed Sick Mice to Probe Mysterious Skin-Blistering Disorder." University of Utah News and Public Relations. Accessed January 17, 2008. www.utah.edu/unews/releases/01/jan/mice.html.

Van Voirhees, B. "Getting a Prescription Filled." U.S. National Library of Medicine. Accessed November 2, 2007. www.nlm.nih.gov/medlineplus/ency/article/001956.htm.

Verberk, W., A. Kroon, and P. DeLeeuw. "Home Blood Pressure Measurement: A Systematic Review." *Journal of the American College of Cardiology* 46 (2005): 743–751.

"Weight Loss Diets." *MD Consult Patient Education Handout.* USC School of Medicine Library, Columbia, SC. Accessed November 25, 2007. Keyword: diets.

"Weight-Training and Weight-Lifting Safety." American Academy of Family Physicians. Accessed November 18, 2007. http://familydoctor.org/198.xml.

"What Diabetes Is." National Diabetes Information Clearinghouse. Accessed December 12, 2007. http://diabetes.niddk.nih.gov/dm/pubs/type1and2/what.htm.

"What Does a Safe Sleep Environment Look Like?" National Institutes of Child Health & Human Development. Accessed February 10, 2008. www.nichd.nih.gov/publications/pubs/upload/BTS_safe_environment.pdf.

"What I Need to Know About Prostate Problems." National Kidney and Urologic Diseases Information Clearinghouse. Accessed February 9, 2008. http://kidney.niddk.nih.gov/kudiseases/pubs/prostate_ez/index.htm.

"What Is Autism?" Autism Society of America. Accessed February 10, 2008. www.autism-society.org.

"What Is Ayurveda?" Ayurveda Holistic Community. Accessed January 12, 2008. www.ayurvedahc.com/articlelive/authors/1/Swami-Sadashiva-Tirtha.

"What Is Ayurvedic Medicine?" National Center for Complementary and Alternative Medicine. Accessed January 6, 2008. http://nccam.nih.gov/health/ayurveda.

"What Is Chiropractic?" American Chiropractic Association. Accessed January 15, 2008. www.amerchiro.org/level2_css.cfm?T1ID=13&T2ID=61.

"What Is SIDS?" National SIDS/Infant Death Resource Center. Accessed February 13, 2008. www.sidscenter.org/WhatIsSIDS.pdf.

"What You Need to Know About Stroke." National Institute of Neurological Disorders and Stroke. Accessed October 29, 2007. www.ninds.nih.gov/disorders/ stroke/stroke_needtoknow.htm.

"What You Need to Know About Vaccinations and Travel: A Checklist." Centers for Disease Control and Prevention. U.S. Department of Health & Human Services. Accessed September 9, 2008. http://wwwn.cdc.gov/travel/content Vaccinations.aspx.

"What's in a Bottle? An Introduction to Dietary Supplements." National Center for Complementary and Alternative Medicine. Accessed January 18, 2008. http://nccam.nih.gov/health/bottle.

"Why Breakfast?" *Nibbles for Health 6: Nutrition Newsletters for Parents of Young Children.* USDA, Food and Nutrition Service. Accessed November 11, 2007. www.fns.usda.gov/tn/Resources/Nibbles/why_breakfast.pdf.

Wilson, J., and D. Hill. "Nausea and Vomiting of Pregnancy." *American Family Physician* 68 (2003): 121–128.

"Wine, Beer and Alcohol Allergy." *Allergy New Zealand.* Accessed November 9, 2007. www.allergy.org.nz/allergies/aZAllergies/beerWine.php.

Winkler, D. "Gender-Specific Symptoms of Depression and Anger Attacks." *Journal of Men's Health & Gender* 3 (2006): 19–24.

Wolff, K. "Hair Growth Disorders." *Fitzpatrick's Dermatology in General Medicine.* AccessMedicine. USC School of Medicine Library, Columbia, SC. Accessed January 19, 2008. Keyword: hypertrichosis.

Wolff, K., R. Johnson, and D. Suurmond, eds. "Disorders of Hair Follicles and Related Disorders." *Fitzpatrick's Color Atlas & Synopsis of Clinical Dermatology.* AccessMedicine. USC School of Medicine Library, Columbia, SC. Accessed January 5, 2008. Keyword: hypertrichosis.

Wong, C. "Natural Remedies for Morning Sickness." About.Com: Alternative Medicine. Accessed January 8, 2008. http://altmedicine.about.com/od/healthconditionsdisease/a/morningsickness.htm.

"Yoga." American Cancer Society. Accessed December 19, 2007. www.cancer .org/docroot/ETO/content/ETO_5_3X_Yoga.asp?sitearea=ETO.

"Yoga: Minimize Stress, Maximize Flexibility and Even More." Mayo Clinic. Accessed December 20, 2007. www.mayoclinic.com/print/yoga/CM00004/METHOD=print.

"Your Dental Visit: What to Expect." *Simple Steps to Better Dental Health.* Columbia University College of Dental Medicine. Accessed January 29, 2008. www.simplestepsdental.com.

"Your First Pelvic Exam: a Guide for Teens." Center for Young Women's Health. Children's Hospital Boston. Accessed January 4, 2008. www.youngwomens health.org/pelvicinfo.html.

"Your Guide to Lowering High Blood Pressure." National Heart, Blood, and Lung Institute. Accessed December 20, 2007. www.nhlbi.nih.gov/hbp/index.html.

Index

About the Authors

Laura Townsend Kane, MLIS, is the Assistant Director for Information Services at the School of Medicine Library, University of South Carolina. She is the author of *Straight from the Stacks: A Firsthand Guide to Careers in Library and Information Science* (ALA Editions, 2003) and "Access Versus Ownership" in the Encyclopedia of Library and Information Science (Dekker, 2003). She is a Distinguished Member of the Medical Library Association's Academy of Health Information Professionals. She lives in Columbia, South Carolina, with her husband and two children.

Rozalynd P. McConnaughy, MLIS, is the Assistant Director for Education and Outreach at the University of South Carolina School of Medicine Library. She has published a number of articles in peer-reviewed journals and appears regularly on the local radio show, "Health, Wealth, and Happiness." She lives in Columbia, South Carolina, with her husband.

Steven Patrick Wilson, MLIS, MA in English Literature, is a medical librarian at the University of South Carolina School of Medicine Library and Coordinator of the Center for Disability Resources Library collection, which is one of the largest developmental disability collections in the southeast. He lives in Columbia, South Carolina, with his wife, Sarah, and their menagerie of pets.

David L. Townsend, MD, is an Internal Medicine physician practicing in North Carolina. He graduated summa cum laude with a double-major in biology and psychology from the University of Georgia, and then attended medical school at the Medical College of Georgia, where he graduated with top honors. He completed his residency in Internal

Medicine at Wake Forest University Baptist Medical Center in North Carolina and was selected to serve as Assistant Chief of Medicine at that institution. He currently resides in Winston-Salem, North Carolina, with his wife and two children.